TRANSCA

ROY K. KIYOOKA

EDITED BY SMARO KAMBOURELI
AFTERWORD BY GLEN LOWRY

Copyright © Estate of Roy Kiyooka 2005
Afterword copyright © NeWest Publishers Ltd. 2005

All rights reserved. The use of any part of this publication reproduced, transmitted in any form or by any means, electronic, mechanical, recording or otherwise, or stored in a retrieval system, without the prior consent of the publisher is an infringement of the copyright law. In the case of photocopying or other reprographic copying of the material, a licence must be obtained from the Canadian Reprography Collective before proceeding.

National Library of Canada Cataloguing in Publication
Kiyooka, Roy
Transcanada letters / Roy Kiyooka.

ISBN 1-896300-68-5

1. Kiyooka, Roy. I. Title.

PS8521.I9T72 2004   C811'.54   C2004-900764-5

Editor for the Press: Smaro Kamboureli
Cover image: Roy Kiyooka, Mirak, 1964, acrylic on canvas, Vancouver Art Gallery, Gift of Ian Davidson VAG 64.34 (Photo: Trevor Mills).
Interior images: pages vi and 133, courtesy of the Kiyooka family.
Photo sequence on pages 137 to 154: Roy Kiyooka, Long Beach to Peggy's Cove, 1971, silver print, Vancouver Art Gallery, Vancouver Art Gallery Acquistion Fund VAG 96.22 a-f (Photo: Teresa Healy).
Cover and interior design: Ruth Linka

Canada Council for the Arts   Conseil des Arts du Canada   Canadian Heritage   Patrimoine canadien   edmonton arts council

NeWest Press acknowledges the support of the Canada Council for the Arts and the Alberta Foundation for the Arts for our publishing program. We also acknowledge the financial support of the Government of Canada through the Book Publishing Industry Development Program (BPIDP) for our publishing activities. NeWest Press also acknowledges the assistance of the National Association of Japanese Canadians Endowment Fund with this project.

Every effort has been made to obtain permission for quoted material and photographs. If there is an omission or error the author and publisher would be grateful to be so informed.

NeWest Press
201-8540-109 Street
Edmonton, Alberta
T6G 1E6
t: (780) 432-9427
f: (780) 433-3179
www.newestpress.com

1   2   3   4   5   09   08   07   06   05

PRINTED AND BOUND IN CANADA

"The business of art is to live in the complete actual present, that is the complete actual present, and to completely express that complete actual present."

—Gertrude Stein

*in so far as
these Letters/ Etcetera have
a DEDICATION they are
dedicated w/ much affection to
Monica Mariko Jan Kiyo Kit
and Daphne. they're for
my mother father brothers sisters
and all my correspondents.
begun as a book for the G.S.W.S.
in Halifax N.S. Sept. 71
with the title From Under
The Granville Street Bridge---
Sunday after the War---Outwards
it is the book of a painter
poet husband father brother friend
and lover 'who' found a few of
the missing pieces of a life
and put them together.*

"It is a map of the soul's groupography"

        (J.J. /F. W.

"Ecclipsed eye that eye incapable of quite
assembling the true meaning of the universe but
striving to do so with heirogyphicks quite
          dismembered"

Henry Vaughn)

Portrait of my Mother and Grandfather

an Intermin Report for The Canada Council

a Tokioborn painter sd theres was no reason for him to go
off to Europe or America as most of the art in the world passt
thru Nippon sooner or later defines the plenitude of A R T
you can see here. they've got no sense of us Canucks as artists –
or Im not sniffing the right wind for directives. anyhow here
is a few whiffs for whatever its worth outside of these tight lil'
islands. any similarity between the living and the dead artist
is more than a mere coincidence: heres the gist of it

inc.   a petrified egyptian sovereign and a young girl's bust
          in translucent pink porphyry

inc.   banal buffet's blocklong retro and maillol's medi-
          godesses in ueno park

inc.   klee-eyed grafics call'd the happy people and
          not so ancient greekeries in marble mausoleums w/ doric columns

inc.   rodin's gate of hell   the burghers of calais   and
          sung dynasty porcelains in a back street antique store

inc.   the 1000s version of the 32 views of mt. fuji
          and a faded pillow book of sexual delectations

inc.   jasper johns   george mathieu   zou wou ki   sam francis
          the spaniards picasso   miro   tapies and fieto   to name a few

inc.   appalling trickles by dharma bums and slashing sumis
          kline would have shunned

inc.   18th century psuedo Sesshu's   and
          a heavenly host of bodhisattvas thread'd in gold

inc.   robust nudes in crude colours   and
          starcht geishas in fastidious fold-outs

inc.   morita's agile calligraphy   and
          the deft salutations on chiyomizu ware pottery

inc.   4 ft. high pre-columbian funereal figures
          brought here via germany, u.s.a., mexico.   contemporaneous
          with native haniwa the comparisons reveal meaning

inc.   plaster casts of plaster casts of plaster casts of small
          medium large and economy size venus de milos

inc.   meiji restoration style pre-raphaelism and
       the twist'd figures haunted by a nightmare bomb. hiroshima
       and nagasaki spewed up a group named the wasteland

inc.   saito's woodcut postcards of everything inimitably Japanese
       big brother tourists buy like hotcakes

inc.   at least 3 post meiji paris train'd old mod masters
       inflecting the native landscape with medi-impressionist eyes

inc.   mannesier's post cubist ikons and the whole of
       the ecole d' paris post war revisionisms   perhaps the dominant
       therefore abominable influence here

inc.   the gutai group in osaka beam'd to europa via
       michael tapies. rent paper neo dada nihilisms and happenings

inc.   a life sized glazed cupid taking an immortal piss
       into the carp filled pond in a coffee shop on kawaramachi

inc.   takahashi's woodcut evocations of the seasons   lift'd
       frm sheets of plywood chosen for its grain

inc.   2000 yrs of domestic and agrarian tools at the T.M.of M.A.
       the highlight of the summer season

inc.   the processional along the tokkaido road on the walls of
       a georgian granite bank   a blowup of a woodcut render'd in oils

inc.   allen ginsberg's ten dollar sumi of a bleacht skull with
       grass shooting up thru the eye sockets   done by an
       anonymous painter in his 80th year

inc.   utamaro's woodcut of kintaro with his wet nurse
       her hair a torrent of hairbreadth lines

inc.   the whole spectra of modernisms   the copies of copies
       from art international all served up with japanese accents

inc.   this thot of questionable origins: that the meiji restoration
       is the precise intersection of the glory thats past with
       its gory mementoes and the first flowering of the beatific future
       perhaps no less gory – Now gathering awful momentums

inc.   takahashi a recent buddhist convert and yrs truly
       taking all of it in with lots of hot sake, weary feet + grin

inc.   all artists named and un-named bound together in
       the celestial light of a cold planet

       possibilities
HERE
         (or, Anywhere
no larger than Everyman's Vision –
      has it ever been more
      than this ?

ALL THINGS SWIRL

making for whats possible

               HERE/NOW

Dear Victor

        apropos   Nevertheless These Eyes
                                – – – – – – – – – – – –
                                  heres one of the 100s of letters
                                  S.S. wrote to his wife Hilda   even after
                                  her death . it might help to under-
                                  stand the 'enfoldings'. it   otherwise
                                  delineates what I wld do – – – if I did
                                  biographies .

"I want my writings and your writings.
 My drawings good and bad and your drawings. If
you do not want me to do the nude of you
you could do it yourself. And if D.C. wanted
to be in the book she might be with our combined
permission but only such drawings of hers
we approved. My drawings of her would be in it.
What a wonderful hodge-podge the book would
be – – – showing both our journeys."

                    "The women say what I like about
                    each other. Each woman is my love-letter
                    to the other. Down the familiar street
                    I pass through the unknown land of women"

                    .

                    The wind ruffles their skirts. Their
                    songs are not diminished by a mountain.
                    These words lie under a cloud of tears
                    fallen   from the Beloved's eyes

                    S.S./R.K

4/ 66
montreal, quebec

miscellaneous

i am moved by the fervor with whc Montreal painters/ poets/
sculptors/ & Others confront public apathy.

whatever else makes Montreal inimitable i know (nonetheless
that the truly inimitable is made-in-solitude .

what i want as a painter is not very different frm what
Others want - in the same world .

what we come to in our solitude is the recovery of our
singleness defined, by s i l e n c e .

to recover our solitude the immeasurable silence that lies
at the heart of things is to define the future of Art .

any definition of a masterwork (whatever moves you) must
answer to The Silence it commands .

listening to W. R. sound off i thot tough could also be
a kind of virtu without whc Art got s-o-f-t

no homos pleez!) as if Soft Art: the artless objects of Clas
Oldenburg were impossible. or Pissaro's gentleness .

the BOMB continues to grab the headlines. so also the Space
Cadets, Vietnam & Gerda Munsinger . . . no one pays for silence .

who has not attended their own vermissage & not been sick to
the pit of their stomach .

Modern Art circa 1966 is only a conundrum for folks who
have eaten the cake insist its only apple pie .

George Braque sd 'I dont do what i want i do what i can.'
Communication begins with Buber's 'I' and 'Thou'

the rest of it is a massive lie . none of us 'exists' out-
side of Traditions not even yr avant garde .

to fit it together tongue and groove is the Historian's Job .
to make it is the painter's   but the painter as his own historian
is a faustian compact with madison avenue .

Wallace Stevens sd 'that poetry(painting) must resist the
intelligence   almost successfully.'   ya!

Oct. 5th '66
Montreal PQ

Dear Michael

– – – –WOW! like you sat down and wrote a preface to
a DREAM BOOK of ICONS yet to be made   (let alone
publisht– – –i mean i wld gladly be reproduced in it
for yr Preface's sake   but its far too many words
for an invitation to my show: my *painting's silences*.
should we not use words w/   utmost discretion   viz
painting/s lest they get in the way. words as step
ping-stones– –a hop skip and a jump over/into   the
painting . . . (the stones forgotten . etc.

A Testament :

. . . its at least possible   that
simple obsessions have complex significances
and that   complex signs need simple
statements . viz   simple-geometry is for simple simons .
pie-men can have their cake and eat it   too.
these paintings attest to my desire to 'embrace an
absolute geometric circle– – –the naked loss
stays with you   like a picture echoing'+

these paintings pursue complex signs thru
simple statements: they are   in that sense
a testament to   my obsessions .

      use it if you want to .

+ thanks to J. Spicer)

7

10/ 19/'66
Montreal Quebec

Dear Margaret

– – – –You sd you were terrified but
would come to Sir George to read your poetry.
Its as good as any reason I know   tho
we simply want to hear you including whatever
terror your poems hold .

Assuming you will be teaching til 4PM
we will book yr flight out of Toronto for 6PM whc
will bring you to us abt 7.30PM. That will
give you abt an hour and a half   to prepare for
the reading etc. Stan Hoffman will be
attending to your reservations and welfare .

Again) Thank you for accepting

5/ 1/'67

550.000 Folks at EXPO today!
Yesssireee

Dear Earle

re your phone call
you read here Friday February 23rd
at 9PM .

(Imported) German beer $3.80
a bottle   at EXPO

terms $100. honorarium
plus air-fare Toronto/   return and
a nite at the Ritz   meals
and all the booze you can stomach .
.
after this prolonged exposure
to Canadian-Identities therell be
no place to hide 'cept in
under the bed   or the annual Fed. Fiscal
report .

8

   aint Academia a drag
   now May/Time adrenalin flows?

      1/ 16/.67
      Montreal Quebec
Dear Iain Baxter at
  Simon Fraser U. Burnaby BC

  Enclosed dossier shld inform you that
  I am still interested in teaching at S.F.U.
  and intend to return to the
  West Coast, eventually . I enclose a drawing of
  yours truly by my youngest daughter– – –
  notice the deftness w/ which she has drawn
  glasses and eyes, etc. it is meant to dis-
  place the customary passport photo
  which institutions want for whatever reason.
  And if you need more specific details
  WRITE me at Sir George .
      Pleeze return my dossier
  intact as its all I have between me and anonymity .
  H A!

      2/ 8/'67
      Montreal Quebec
Dear Paul Blackburn

  Rumour has it that
  your gonna stay w/ my family which
  includes 3 lively girls .
  You do have a choice you know and
  can stay at The Ritz Carlton .
  I simply made the offer thinking you just
  might want to pocket the
  difference. And you dont have to
  make up yr mind til you
  arrive as reservations will be held
  til the last moment at
  both establishments .

  Speaking for the committee We
  look forward to your reading to all of us

5/ 17/'67
Montreal Quebec

Dear John

– – – –No not dead, yet but dying, ya. You
too, perhaps ? We will pay yr air-fare to and
from 'Anywhere' Canada but not frm Mexico
Paris France or even California. Your honorarium
of $100. the same as Birneys Atwoods or a
Alden Nowlan . The date (again) is Fri. Feb. 9th.

Have you held D.L.'s latest w/ my cover and
illustrations ? Theyre my first XEROX manifest-
ations like I ran the images thru as many as
6 or 7 times added letra-screen hatchings and ran
'em thru again and again til the values cohered .
Nevertheless These Eyes via Coach House shld be out
late summer . Otherwise days follow daze . . . . .
every one of 'em a pisser .

June 19th '67
3.30PM/ Monreale

Dear Margaret

    They had been playing after school with
their pet gerbil named Cripple. They had given
him that name because of the way he scurried
around on his three good legs. The withered 4th
one simply hung. And it was his name his
true name tho as casually given as their own.
There they stood at the backdoor in tight-lippt
fearfulness the tears barely held back. When
I asked what had happened Jan handed the glass jar
half-filled with grass to Beth and gave her a
shove in front of me. Choking back her tears Beth
sd . . . .I didn't mean to . . . he fell from my hand
and I I steppt on him. Beth cried. All the others
cried. They passed the small dead thing from
hand to hand asking if it might not be 'alive'-
its eyes were half-opened. Then, they made him
a shoe-box coffin lined w/ cloth and green grass
and scotch-taped him in it and buried him in
the flower bed under the front window. NOW they
are all out playing in the back alley a small death
singing, singing in their delicate bones

        and/ I am 'dumbfounded'

                    Montreal Quebec
                    June 21 '67

Dear T e t s u o

   .... I have been thinking abt your suggestion that
   I write a piece for Morita's magazine on
   'Art at Expo'. Despite the number of times I have
   been there to look at what I could see of it
   along with 200.000 others) ... I am at a loss to say
   what it in aggregate is all abt . I mean most of
   the so called Art is inextricable frm the masses of
   the mazes of peoples and buildings . 'like' its
   a confabulation of kulturs a veritable melting pot
   a ubiquitous tableau of the arts. I mean the art
   the painting and graphicks is everywhere. and theres
   no occasion when you can see it without looking in
   and thru a bunch of people the jostle the fatigue of
   multitudes . thus, VISION or simply 'sight' is im-
   paired . nonetheless theres enough Art to make one's
   head reel– –if it can be got at . The CRITICAL prob
   lem is then 'f o c u s'– – –how to be able to simply
   see a small Redon in the midst of a crowd .... with
   out yelling FIRE! to make a small space if not the
   concomitant quiet, etc. It is desperate and I for one
   abhor such complicities– – –all for BIG BIZ's sake .
   And despite LSD P.O.P. and the DaDa revival not to
   mention the large as earth breadth of the conceptual-
   ists   How one comes to a THING a painting a poem
   or a woman is always singular and hopefully a dialogue
   .... unless its a dance on the piazza . I talk abt
   the particulars   thus the impossibility of a critical
   assessment of 'Art at Expo'   believe me who also
   had the experience of Tokio's 5 O Clock EXITS .

       "a bird in hand is worth two in the bush"
       sez it, plainly .

                       p/s perhaps by Summer's end
                       when the crowds thin ....
                       how much time have I got to
                       do the job
                              etcetera .

late Autumn on 57th Street, N.Y.
Montreal . '67

for Max and Charlotte Bates   at

the other edge of the continent–

the layers of tin hovels hidden away frm
the blue surge surf / sea-side promenades   tell me

how cheaply i purchast a silver medallion at
the San Paolo Bienniale .

theres no much difference between Art News or
Le Devoir when it comes to silly art reviews . you pays

yr dues and git yr name list'd among
A/rtists A/nonymous, John Diefenbakers   or a Dow-Jones .

and a man named Manfred I've never met   writes
again for my autograph . i scrawl it on the back of a postcard

of the empire state building with my ball point pen
and send it off to him . "anonymity is death"

"destroy those who make us invisible"
"black (cunt) s beautiful"   and "fuck you, too"

selections from the definitive collection of Graffiti– –
on the last train to Brooklyn .

a timely New Yorker sez medical-science hasn't found
the definitive pill to kill off P/ ublic R/ elations yet .

"have you tried our crest'd toilet papers . . ."

.

i danced at the Dome :
Claude sd he had a gun pull'd on him there .

Emil the manager of the George Washington Hotel sent
congratulations . his japanese wife

Barnett Newman, Pat Martin Bates, Edwin Dickinson
and Tim Deverell all showed up .

too bad we couldn't get drunk together
at Max's Kansas City .

ah   my Ellipses   i hope yr having swell dreams under

13

Oldenburg's vinyl and kapok machinations .

Grippi and Waddell Gallery
West 57th Street .

.

frm   the avenue of the nations :

he saw himself thru the blackout with
the candles from his birthday cake

spent ten yrs in a cold water flat five stories up
on Madison Avenue: his cupboards filled

with a decade's work . –How cld i complain abt
the cold/ early/ morning/ racket/ s?

.

yr name O Liberty! writ in blank ledgers fill
a million warehouses

even in Aklavik/Alaska . she sd
"Central Park s a terrifying place after dark "

rubble   rumble, everywhere– – –
rust corrodes yr stainless towers

yr Cries Echo– – –
thru concrete underground

corridors   into the putrid sea
where Dawn waits

patiently–
for the 'A' Train .

.

i want my own children
their friends and other children to

be the measure of my acts .
as for Those who wld have us use

their yard-sticks– – –
go measure the light suffusing this room

and leave us to devise our own
measurements.

.

he tells me he's astonisht– –!
seeing   her light yellow pubic fluff

'cause further down   her
long black-hairy legs, bristled .

the Biggest Show in Town :

M. Ernst's
Remains
Archetypically
Surreal
His titles
Cryptic

Recent work/s
Show a Gloved Hand
Fastidiously
Lifting scraps frm
Libidinous
Id's

The
Veritable
Bottom
Of the Un-
Conscious
Garbage
Can

Long Live
Surrealism's Brute
Fantasias
Andre Breton
Hans Arp   &
Sigmund Freud.

+

i want the restoration of Magick
magical incantations any number can hum

i want my baselines
the rituals i plumb from

if only a black/   white/   yellow/   red or/   green Godess wld
abide in me and show me the secret colour of Mud

colours
dont lie . . .

+

Rene Levesque– – –
i love you a bushel and a peck and
a hug around the neck   But i
wont stand behind you when you raise
Separatism's flag– –remembering
how the rising sun nearly bled to death
when the great bald eagle swoopt
down on it. if, however, you want me to
stand at the curbside waving as She
rides on by i'll come running
running to your side .

+

some days Monreale's snow looks as if
some God had wiped his arse on armfulls of it

+

sun/light   over
my left shoulder spills

a precise triangle
on the polisht wood floor

.

to live in
the presence of

these words
this breath enables . . .

+

fuck Marcel Duchamp's Descartean Ploys   I'll take
W.C. Field's crooked billiard cue, any day

+

Libidinous Dreams shall destroy
All yr IBM   D-A-T-A

Theres gonna be a Reign-of-Shit over
Everything til Kingdom Cometh

I remember Virgin Country
No surrealist nude ever steppt onto

Visions of hell-flowers   clutcht
In the hands of a Beatrice Claudia or Monique

High embankments of primary colours
The Red Yellow and Blue 'stains' of Paradise

+

to eat/ sleep/ love/ work/ and sing
what else is there

Orpheus? i believe in my feelings when
i feel like 'a song'

+

            V e r m i c e l l i
            M a x
            - - - - - - - - - - - - - - - -
            H o w s   y r
            D a f f o d i l s
            C h a r l o t t e ?

Montreal '68

Dear Monica

>viz Stanley Spencer
>His Visionary Nibble He Sd

>"I move towards Art as
>a means of joining myself to
>its rich and lovely
>atmosphere"

>>whc has of course been
>>my drift too.

It was in 47/48 as an art student in Calgary
I first came across his work in the Penguin Modern
Painters Series. Since then I have had to re-
discover him most recently in a biography written
by Maurice Collis   (publisht by Harvill in 62.

Spencer painted abt 450 canvases. He did 1000s of
drawings and miscellaneous sketches   and wrote
incessantly leaving over 2 million words behind.

What grabbed me was Spencer's intensely naive
erotic-vision A Vision woven into the very substance
of his paintings drawings and writing. Even his
so-called 'pot boilers' are tainted with it. About
all the women who enter'd into and passt thru
his life M.C. suggests   "They people his art from 1927
til his death and are the recurring subject of all
his writings." All of which spoke to me of How I also
also wld celebrate the women in my life. Further
You and the Others merge with Stan's women   into the
Beloved in all her guises. My poems in N.T.E.
are an attempt to speak abt these these mysteries.
Thats what I have come to understand abt these
otherwise hopeless little poems.

– – – –all this because I do want want very much for
you to understand what I am abt. And whatever
it is that I continue to do I want to be able to say
it better much better than I have accomplisht.

>hang in there you also have
>your necessities

           Oxford St. Momtreal
                '68 .

dear Carole

> . . . your birth-letter continues haunting me   it
> proposes this question : how do I stand to the woman
> i love who goes thru birth's ardours? I wld add- - -
> for the sake of the Earth we as co-equals love .
>
> Bri & I that awful stoned night   joking over your
> grave concerns– our altogether too too clever conceits
> barely disguised our stupid complacencies. i re-call
> our irritations viz the constant interruptions of
> the chess game we were playing. as if to say "thats
> your problem baby–we have other things on mind,
> ok." im haunted by that evening the subsequent guilt
> (heartlessness)–i hope this letter says more than.
>
> How a woman feels in the very act-of-birth   how she
> feels deep within herself–i can only surmise.
> I cant have her feelings. i have only my own which owe
> some part of their existence to her. further back–
> i am my own mother's offspring. somewhere, back of both
> his/her feelings we are all loopt together to
> form one huge W H O O P !
>
> Carole i sperm'd three children but did not attend
> the birth of even one of them and i did not have any
> feelings of guilt abt it. - –from the very moment of
> their births I have in my way attempted to celebrate–
> their sheer presence on this our miraculous earth.
>
> We can/ do 'respond' as Walt wld have it   to one/an/
> other when entuned to each other's wave-length.
> otherwise the circuits broken and each is left with
> their ofttimes sodden tune. Love, according to
> this idea proposes we keep *all our circuits open*.
> in between its mostly lack-lustre   or doleful words.
>
> Im not at all involved in the argument viz   whether
> woman giving birth to a child is 'more' creative than
> man shaping matter with his mind and hands. its a
> dullard's contention–leading nowhere but to heartless
> abstractions. Carole WE ALL BLOW LIFE INTO EXIST-
> ENCE beyond our least despairs. I who add that to abide

in that fecundity is all in all.

yrs ago i came upon this ". . . then think it not heavy
to dwell with thy Mother in her wide house   thou who
laist in the straight chamber of her womb . . ." I thot to
use it as preface to a poem abt my own mother but did
not as it sd more than my own poem managed. mother will
have to wait for her poem.

I know of women who have prayed that their child
might be born whole. and I know painters & poets who
care that their fecundity will have a wholeness.
Carole i have this thot: that both men and women have
complementary fecundities born frm their consecration to
one another and the earth.

To conclude ". . . in Life/ there are more than the 12
labours/ and the life you live is only one/ who sees
the world as a hospital/ must live in it as an invalid/
and his infirmity/ will have been willed . . ." sez
Goethe   quoted by Nelo Risi, origin 2nd series no. 13:
which can stand as a partial answer to our jaundiced
response that evening.

forgive us: Our Quest (equally) is to discard
every infirmity .

                love to both of you

Montreal, Quebec
'68.

Dear T o d

    this is going to be a letter that addresses itself
to your L e t t e r s t o S t e l l a . of Her---
as of Keats'beloved Fanny there is much to talk abt.
All of us have our Stella our Fanny or a Mabel:
shaped from all of the women in our lives 'real' or
'fictive', no matter. Nevertheless These Eyes is
my earnest attempt to articulate such thots as i have
had about Her and i see that my failure is due to
the loss of her substantive presence in the world of
the poems. i mention this only to show that i also
have the cursed habit of generalizing from the par-
ticulars of sound and image   that is as i see it the
whole business of poetry. its in and thru such recog-
nitions that i want to say that your Stella has
no real presence in all the letters —she is there ok
but as a ghost to hang your dogmatics upon. you sd
you intend to include lighter matters—to mitigate yr
awful solemnity—with which i thoroughly agree.
it was a Stearn Thomas Eliot who sd that Keat's Letters
were great because he folded the insights (he had abt
his life and poetry) among the ongoing trifles. which
is quite properly where both belong. i mean   if you
dont lay them side by side in a letter where else to
bed them together? is it too much to suggest that
EVERYTHING WE PUT OUR HANDS TO SHOWS
FORTH THE SELF .

    in Toronto Gwendolyn MacEwen told me over a drink she
had recently spent time in Edmonton with Eli Mandel who
told her how after years of thinking abt poetics   he
had workt out a deceptively simple system of measuring
the value of a poem. he warned her tho that his system
had to be used with a fine discretion. it consisted of
substituting the noun 'moose' for every noun as it oc-
curred in a line of poetry. apparently Eli had not made
his mind up as to whether his system could be applied
to prose. anyhow, according to Eli's theory   if the noun
moose sounded more effective than the poet's original
noun that line of verse could be sd to be defective.

whereupon Gwendolyn recited various examples —that left
us holding our guts. thank god 'laughter' is a verb.

on Bloor St. i told her i was born in Moose Jaw Saskat-
chewan! AHa! Trifles or a Rifle to put to the Lady's
head—for the sake of T h e D a n c e . p/s Her
real being (mysterious & simple) is huger than my mere
talk . . . Tod, let it all hang out   or put it all in.
I mean Stella wants more than your thots

October 21st '68
Monreale, PQ

Dear Prof. Theall :

concerning artscanada

being painter/   sculptor/   sometime poet &
a full-time teacher for almost 20 yrs – – –
i want to say that artscanada formerly C/A is
more important than i wld have cared to
admit to . i am bored 'turned off' as the hip
young ones here at sir george wld say   w/
the innocuous pronouncements (dead as a dodo
that fills to nausea our dailies/weeklies/
monthlies/ quarterlies/& annuals. i mean 'where'
can one find relevant canadian art criticism
if its not going to be in artscanada? its
our one and only sounding board for relevant
commentaries and appraisal   hence, its
indispensableness .
          further– –i wld insist
artscanada's policy as evident in recent issues
is a positive direction in these days of sheer
profusion, change and animosities. i think its of
some importance that artscanada enables us to
'see' that whats happening here in CANADA has its
anticipations and parallels with like phenomena
in other places viz the U.S.A. if not the U.S.S.R.
the 'eternal delight' of Blakean ENERGIES is
central to the arts and does come in frm every
direction, imaginable . artscanada focuses such
radiations—it is one of *our antennas* .

– –F O C U S

      Oxford St. Montreal
      '68 .

dear C a r o l e

 . . . . your books a post gutenberg-galaxy of D E L I G H T
i will savour over and over into my old age
30 yrs hence: like Bosch's prodigious figure I'll unbutton
my tatterd waistcoat–pluck its yellow foxed pages out–
to pinch/ scan/ tickle/ thumb/ caress/ & plumb page after
page of goodness knows what treasures. then, I'll tuck
it back in amongst the myriad lost treasures and button–
myself up again (for the last time? but not before i
find a long lost pain that lasted 5 months or will it
have shrunk into an infinitesimal point–along with
lesser pains, little anguishes, tiny fears, traumas, tics,
long lost head-aches, petrified toe nails, dandruff
and pubic hairs. not to mention a wrinkly appendectomy
scar from my ninth year. WOW! whata delicious orgy of
multitudinous phenomena to be had for the least un-button
ing! Zippers only zip up and down I'll take buttons any
time. who invented the button and did the same guy invent
the button's hole? i read somewhere that along with the
chastity belt and powder pistol the button & its hole are
among the most important of the secondary inventions.
or was it a hash'ddream of a patent's office file clerk–
checking out the hierarchy of inventions. beside me my
faithful corset with rubber lining plus steel staves lies
folded. i just took the damned thing off. i eye it coolly–
as my bent back never could. one day I'll add it to my
cornucopia of wondrous things to be buttoned up for good.
your book is a lovely thing a love-letter to a bird of a
similar feather. and with what discretion Bri is there.
as if you needed to be discreet abt him who is that very
discretion we both respect. Carole your assorted images
lead to whatever paradise we are given 'given' each his
or her own measure.

shopping the other day Monica almost left a finger in
our car door. she later sd ". . . i started to walk away not
knowing my finger was caught in there." she was wearing
gloves at the time which helped cushion the pain. and
the children percolate they do seem to dig everything–

even their attenuated little boredoms. they squander fist-
fulls of energy on whatever is to hand—each fulsome
moment. and it all goes on and on now into early
March:

      WATCH OUT ! for the hare bell and crocuses . . . .

Sir George Williams U

Fine Arts Dept. F E S T I V A L '6 8

    OK call this a pep-talk   a tonic
    with directives– – –

Beyond this rehearsal
your all on yr own: A W E !   the Response/abilities !

    We wont/   cant 'succeed' unless
    all of us embrace even even failure tho
    theres nothing to prove by it. So–
    E N J O Y yrself yr exuberances will find
    equivalents but only in/ and thru
    what each one of us has got to accomplish.
    Blake sez "Energy is the only life
    Energy is the life divine."
                          ABIDE! ABIDE!

T H E A T R E (equal) RITUALISTIC ENACTMENTS

        IS CELEBRATION OF THE 4 ELEMENTS PLUS US AS A
        5TH COORDINATE.

                      REGARD/   EVERYTHING YOU DO AS
    INHERENTLY 'DRAMATIC' The Way you Bend Lift Walk
    Stand Skip Flip Jump SHOUT as integral with
    all thats going on. Each moment of our plays as
    an occurrence in full view of Everybody.
    We BEGIN   CARRY THRU and END– –via EMPATHY   Be
    A-W-A-R-E of each other thru-out   that is
    each one's discreet act shld call out to another's.
    REMEMBER   all-of-our-acts an enactment of
    and inside of the ACTUAL. The simple notion is
    THERE IS NO-WHERE TO BE BUT PRESENT.

    "ASTONISH ME" He sd   turning a cartwheel.

    The Mezzanine Our/Their Stage
    as a field-of-actions/   interactions. In so far
    as We need demarcations let 'em be
    chalkt-lines– –depending on the actual encroachments.
    'you' as participant and 'you' as audience
    to be thot of as interchangeable. Ideally– – –
    We want to INCORPORATE them. Entire.

    And incorporate all the audi/visual technos too.

1/ signature/s

in order of appearance:

4 to put up the banners
2 erect dancer's shell and fill w/ foam particles
2 bring out easles paints canvases etc.
1 as dancer carried in (asleep) on a stretcher
4 with motorcycles
2 in audience who come forth to paint
1 light/sound man
4 in audience w/ flashlights
.

form a corridor w/ banners.
set up dancer's shell mid-corridor
leave end open for entrances
and exits. set up easels at end of corridor.
bring on the equipment for painting.
fill dancer's shell w/ foam.
bring her in on a stretcher then lay her in foam.
no lights yet just the mez lights.
the motorcycles come up freight elevator
drive thru crowd to their places
idle their engines w/ light off. the music starts.
motorcycle lights directed on each canvas
as 2 come out of crowd to begin
painting. one to each canvas.
isolated in her dark shell–
the dancer slowly rises out of foam bed
moves toward first one then the other
canvas – –thruout dark corridor.
the 2 painters return into the crowd as others
step forth to continue the work.
the dancer moves out in front of each canvas
she mimes the movement of paint as
the painters change and others carry on til
each canvas is completely covered.
the music progressively amplified the cyclists
rev their engines   then its all lights out
all engines silenced as the flash-
lights in the crowd scan first the ceiling
then each canvas with circular

movements of light. meanwhile the cyclists
drive off   the dancer returns to her shell
 in its total darkness . all light on–
the paintings are carried to selected place
near escalators for viewing

2/   t h r o b

in order of appearance:

4 protectionists their equipment
3 set up plastic cube around each projectionist
4 with ladders to be wired-up
1 as white-smockt technician w/ magical kit
4 brightly clad dancers
1 light/sound man coordinator of heart/beats

protectionists wheel on their machines to
designated places. wait for cues.
each group of 3 set-up plastic cubes around them
and their machines. after which they all
become audience. the ladders   placed as designated
the carriers stand lean sit straddle them as
the technician comes on and opening his kit begins
to wire each of them up. the heart-beat tape
slowly quietly begins throbbing. now
the dancers come on they dance abt each
projectionist in his cube. the protectionists play
colourfill'd light images on them on the
4 wired-up ones as the heart beat tape throbs louder
and louder. now the dancers gyrate abt each of
the wired-up ones– – –the ladders a locus
of male/female intertwinings. when the heart-beat
the throbs reach optimum decibels– – –
everything stops the projections all stop the
dancers freeze the hearts stop   and
our technician comes on to slowly un-wire the
wired-up ones. finis

3/   p o l y- u r- t h e n e

in order of appearance:

4 projectionists their equipment
4 couples erect the 4 cubes, inhabit them
4 others 1 to each cube bring on
   the furniture and sets it within each cube
4 dancers
1 light/sound man
1 man for the air compressor
.

protectionists take their place/s.
2 by 2 bring out and erect their plastic cube/s
leaving 4th panel ajar for furniture etc.
place furniture in each cube.
lay the weather balloon on the table hookt-up to
the compressor. attach strobe light as
designated. each couple enters their shell the 4th
panel shut encloses them. they sit down
opposite each other and make small-talk as
protectionists play a riot of colours on
and all abt them. meanwhile the compressor begins
to blow up each of the 4 balloons which
slowly enlarge upon the table between each couple.
the strobe turned onto it. the sound
track plus the chugg chugg chugg of the compressor
accompanies the dancers who move in and abt
each of the shells-as tho curious, wanting in.
images are projected onto them too.
now the weather balloon shld assume the entire
shell and slowly rise up as one of the couple
slits a hole in one panel and shves it out-into
the crowd who chase after it. each couple
has now climbed up out of the shell and joins even
the dancers in the chase of the balloons
w/ the projections following its bounding move
ments .
            stop it all when the balloons POP–

Later Draft/s of the Stanley Spencer pomes

for John and Rosemary Miller : 12/ 12/'68

– –tell 'em Stan   How you
finger'd her 'heavy burden of hair'–
and (in your drawing) became God
the father and God the son with happy
children dancing round. you always
needed **a happy association** to
make them come alive. 'the gesture'
you sd, had to be just right.

/

1st self-portrait:

Lattice/s of
light

a young face knows
already

/

The Wool Shop

w/ an eye for precise detail– –
but whats the guy tossing a skein of wool in the air for?
and have you ever seen a woman her sweater and hair
woven frm the same ball of yellow wool?
nobody ever takes inventory in the cock-eyed wool shop:
its all an invention even the woman braiding
her hair in the back room while tweedy husband tilts beer
playing darts at the local pub .

/

The Last Supper

its the row/s of out-sized feet
sticking out from the stiff folds that
lead us to the broken bread. its

how he painted each brick its own red
that puts the bread into our eyes
and mouths . its the last supper he had

/

Parents Resurrecting

old Victorians
upholster'd Edwardians w/ sideburns
Anglican Bishops
pin-striped Clerics w/ furl'd umbrellas
retired Naval Officers
English Professors
Colonial Gentlemen and their
Gentile Women
Nabobs   Bums   and bona fide
Eccentrics

B E W A R E O F W O M E N A L L W O M E N !

especially Those who keep all
'Ten Commandments'–
have a fat hand in yr pocket and love
coarse-woven worsted.
be wary of them!
Theyll get down on their knees for
your least indulgences

/

2nd self-portrait

a Don Juan in grey underwear
sniffing the heels of

the woman who call'd him
a prick and a genius– –

making out with many / one
in sight .

/

Separating Fighting Swans

beak to beak–
they go at it as
the Christian
Science/ Monitor
slips from
her idle hands . . . .

/

The Coming of the Wise Men

according to Spencer– –
The Wisemen came garb'd in white
robes sashed with rope:
theres seven of them count them
five with heaven-knows-why
outstretcht arms crowding a sixth
red bowl to fat lips. the
seventh and first blesses a child
in red polka dot dress. while
mother Mary hugs a fat pillow to
herself He kicks up an
inside fuss
     dont confuse the holly
     tuckt behind the pictures on
     the pin-striped wall
     with plastic mistletoe. Pleez!

/

The Visitation

an everyday affair in Cookham
where Mary and Ann clasp hands over

the threshold. beyond the front porch–
corrugated iron roof/s tell of 'how'

an ordinary afternoon's tea is fraught
with sun-lit consequence/s

/

Saint Francis and the Birds

shows a fat man in his dressing gown
heading for the out-door larder
with all the barnyard birds flapping at
his heels. he is the humble saint
alias his own father 'rememberd' when
the village thief made off with his
one and only pair of trousers

/

Christ in the Wilderness

forty small panels one for each day
He spent among the rocks– –

painted on a small table beside the window
in the wilderness of his living room .

forty panels showing how he spent each day
praying in Gethsemone's Garden .

/

3rd self-portrait

wire spectacles– –
unkept hair

no light or shade
no profile

or three quarter view
just the lean–

keen eye looking straight
out, at you

/

un-finisht letter to Hilda

D u c k y : I've kept all your letters,
their glad tidings encircle me
like the mist in Widbrook Meadow. if you
happen to believe in dust-bins   my
charred remains will tell you where i am.
where i will have gone is just an-
other letter. Ducky, despair is a smile
on an angel's face . . . O Sweete Themmes
runne softly til I end my song

Stanley Spencer's Temple of Love

O A p h r o d i t e

     consists of

  a parish church w/ 2 private houses a–
butting the church walls .

  tiny chapels 8 ft. square   dot the
church grounds .

             all bedroom doors open
into the church . along the church aisle 12
small chapels   each chapel a cubicle   w/
paintings of married couples– –for, he sez
contemplating marital bliss .

    within the chancel
    angels introduce animals to their mates .

    within the 2 house and passage ways
    into the church
             Emblems of Love   viz
    clothes/ scents/ hats/ jewelery/ hair brushes
    etcetera .

    along (unspecified) alley way
    large paintings of men and women in various
    stages of undress . leading into
    (unspecified) rooms filled w/ nudes making love
    and/ or simply lying about (in cheek to jowl
    paintings .

– –The whole schema
more or less detailed as to
the numbers of rooms
walls passage ways etcetera
their measurements given

                    (for Ernie Lindner who
                    among Canadian Painters wld
                    re-habilitate
                            Love's Temple

12. 22nd. '68
Monreale Quebec

Dear Peg and Jim

    let me a prairie boy tell you abt snow   even this
grey Monreale snow   or shall I tell you abt how
our lottery has drawn a blanko and to make up for
the lost millions our property taxes will go up
an average 23% I-N-F-L-A-T-I-O-N is when you cant
save a fucken centavo even if your income exceeds
10thou   to hell with the snow even what a prairie
lad knows abt it 'cause I want to tell you HOW
the Blacks at Sir George have finger'd their Bio/
Prof viz 'racism' Now we're having a closed-circuit
re-play-showing the academic tribunal how
they are trying to prove the charge-of-racism, etc.
and every last one of us is involved: THERES SO
MUCH FLACK FLYING THRU THE AIR THERES NO POINT IN
EVEN DUCKING ! I was going to tell you all abt snow
but have ended up telling you abt the Black/s what
a prairie born Jap-boy knows abt racisms and other
tenuous demarcations based on the ubiquitous rites-
of-colour   lets all fuck one another lets make a
rainbow-hue'd child   lets let the devil take the arse
hole   in the letter I shld have written before this
one I was going to tell you abt my Toronto Show how
it failed financially to spite all the banalities
in the local newspapers   and I have applied for a
yrs leave without pay and I wld if I cld pray that
the C.C. our Medici might bless me   We've had a huge
snowstorm whc left most of us stranded   I spent 2
hours shovelling my van out frm under only to find
that some sonofabitch smasht in my right headlight
whc cost $20. to replace   2 days later I left my van
in a downtown parking lot to go shopping and came
back to find that both of my headlights had been bust'd
that cost $50. plus installation charges– –see what
I mean abt snow its tyrannies! and further back–
in the letter before this one   was going to tell
you abt how I spent part of each winter during the war
on the killing floor at Swift Canadian in Edmonton–

during each 8 hr shift approx 200 head of cattle a
1000 hogs and 100 sheep got processed   I stood on
a 2 ft high greasy steel platform with a metal sheath
full of sharp knives around my waist   my job consist'd
in scraping the fat the extraneous matter frm both
the inside and outside of the quarter'd beef then grade
them before they went into the freezer   I remember
the twitchy nerve-ends the pulsations long after each
carcass had been divest'd of everything but MEAT   I
was going to tell you abt snow what a prairie boy knows
abt it and have ended up telling you abt death whc
he nonetheless knows nothing abt   and most of the young
ones I'm teaching these days know nothing abt Pearl
Harbor or Buchenwald   imagine the pleasure of Michael
O's 20 Cents Review of my reading and show in London
Ontario its reprinted in Oct. issue of artscanada
I've begun revisions of Nevertheless These Eyes   I hang
in on the sounds shift a word or comma turn a stanza
on its head to see if it rings better I am throwing out
some of the pomes and including others since written
all for what if not the sake of a dense claritus–which
cld nonetheless be bullshit   'cause I am also working
thru my own obtuseness my confusions   its also how I make
paintings and sculptures so why why shld the fitting to-
gether of words be different?   its snowing again my white
van is heapt with it, again   let 'it' then tell you all
abt itself how the very night hides under its silences–
its awesome white silences

Spring '69?
Montreal Quebec

1/   To a Young Painter who wld be a Teacher

    . . . .despite all I have got from other men I have not
been given to teach more than I actually know.
And it is out of the sense of 'the paucity of' my own actual
knowing that I've often had a terrifying sense of
incompetence. Nonetheless I wld insist its out of your
day to day obsessions as a painter that is/must be
the substantial ground for your teachings. I assume you
are possessed by an omnivorous curiosity without whc
you had better go and find another vocation. I mean that
both painting and teaching will demand all of your
empathic agilities– –nothing less than 'wholeheartedness.'
For myself the heart/ pith of callit a pedagogy an eco/
system, mythology or history begins in **the absolute
mystery of the world viz untrammeled surface of a newly
stretchd canvas** and goes from there. No matter if
we be teachers or students WE all start here and go on to
where the painting or whatever takes us. It is then
that your attentiveness to whats happening under hand
viz yr own/their paintings is important–for only in
that watchfulness from moment to moment will you be witness
to callit the process of 'actualization'. its there
right there **in front of you** that the whole business of
teaching occurs it is the painting that will inform
you abt itself, thus, them. There will be the occasions
for mouthing off and there'll be the occasions when its
better far better to be silent–let as it were **the work
speak for itself.** And if I wld insist on anything
its that you be responsibly-present to yr own utterances,
viz the clarity of your mouthings. Dont try to get away w/
un-examined propositions they backfire and lead to
yr own and their further confusions. I believe there is
a 1-to-1 relationship between confused mouthings and
the efficiency of our act/s, etc.
Martin Buber named it "I" and "Thou". So it ought to be
even in a crowded classroom : I teacher to I painting
to I student at I time each time we are given the time to
attend to **the particulars.** As teacher/ student We show

ourselves in a variety of ways– –there are 'signs'/
'signals'

        Whitman's R E S P O N D E Z ! - - - sez it.

2/

Some Thoughts: Away from the thoughts that attend
upon the making of a painting: some thoughts concerning
AESTHETICS or What qualifies a work of Art? Why?
Where? When? and How? – –so-called B e a u t y can and
does occur (in even the shards of type-written words .
Under my hands under my very eyes – –in the act of shaping
words, clay, colour or any other substance there is no
thought abt Beauty . There's only the act of taking up
'words' as they occur and in and thru their occurrences tell
how wood has innate substance not to mention a
shapeliness, pungency and heft. And yet the *urge* nonetheless
to hew/ chisel/ hack/ saw/ or whittle a form into
its very substance– –whc may show forth another
shapeliness, inherent, in wood and the mind's combined
substance . . . must have something to do with so-called
Aesthetics . There are the myriad sounds we wld shape
in a language whc has the soundings-of-things and their
acts inherent in them. 'How' these sounds fall onto
and in our ears (in all their seeming randomness)–to be
taken up, yield an image, a sharp incision in
the sounds, the substances shaped and in the world.
Nonetheless, beyond all our schemes the 'phenomenology of
the natural world' proposes a shapeliness beyond even
the wildest dreams . Its with some such sense of callit AWE
that I propose you go on making things. Whats
Beautiful? Whats its form its substances? Its plenitudes?
Its ASTONISHMENTS? Mind is matter or else a tattered
coat on a stick, a windswept scarecrow . . . . the unsounded word
whispers to
        Yeah keep in there with the I am Curious bit
        and lean on me– –if yu have to .

3/

What is named Art is always an act of 'recognition'– –
it has many faces yet seems always to be the same
stone face. From the Venus of Willemdorf to Gaston Lachaise
or its the model for both these faces–the woman who
lives next door pulling weeds from her garden in an act
of her own recognitions. How a hand/eye holding a brush
chisel of scalpel makes an incision upon the bare canvas
or block of stone even into a body, bears **the signs** (seeds)
of our recognitions. And it will be despite our
faulterings a communication, is that at least, to all intents
and purposes. And it follows that it is out of our re-
cognitions We have a stance to so-called History.HISTORY
IS (YOUR)(MIND)(THEIR) RECOGNITIONS. Otherwise as a
sheer compendium of happenstances its unfathomable as
ocean's depth what is it that turns you on and How
it relates to a host of other things is an **act of obedience** both
our recognitions and history proposes. For instance– – –
I've carried a series of repros of Botticelli's Primavera
with me for a number of yrs and tho I have never seen
the original work   I think I can say its nonetheless mine
by virtu of living   (dwelling)within its illuminations.
What is named Art : is **our recognitions our certitudes**
our Histories .

>Gaston Lachaise– –
>you who sang her praises in bronze
>called her 'the mountain'
>
>tell those who harm her How
>you made bronze sing her orifices.
>How the shine in her hair left
>
>its traces on her sculpted form.
>and Gaston, add this, her tears will wash
>the dirt from any man's eyes
>
>frm Nevertheless, These Eyes

>sez it one way
>there are other ways of saying it

including yours. she has
afterall a multitude of faces: each
face an act of recognition.

KEEP IN TOUCH (also sez it .

4/

"To my ideal history of art all sorts of servants would
bring tribute, all sorts of workmen would be summoned to help.
The delver in archives surely would be among them. So would
the student of the materials and techniques; but neither singly
nor collectively would they constitute a history of art.

"Taken together, the history of the arts should be the history
of the humanization of the completely bipedized anthropoid. In
so far as the representational arts like painting, sculpture,
and literature are concerned, their business is to teach man how
to hold himself, how to look, what gestures to make, what attitudes to
take, and so on; all of which react violently on his psychosis
and tend to make of him the civilized being we hope he may
at some far distant date become. it is the business of the same
arts to teach him not only all that, but also what kind of a
world he should live in.

"We must not mistake the history of techniques, or the
history of artists, for the history of art. I dream of a history
of art in which the name of an artist would never be mentioned.
I regard all questions of technique as ancillary to the aesthetic
experience. Human energy is limited, or at least mine is; but
if I had greatly more, there is nothing about all the ancillary
aids to the understanding of a work of art that I should not
try to master."

Bernhard Berenson's foreword:
The Materials and Techniques of Medieval Painting
by Daniel V. Thompson

4. 8th. '69
Montreal PQ

Dear Monica

... this is the 3rd letter I've started and
goddammit Im going to get this one off to you. I've
had my last classes therell be the end of year
meetings the markings and other matters to tidy up.
Then, because We wont be coming back theres all
my belongings (in the office) that have to be packt.
Etcetera. The York U. fiberglas mural nearly complete–
Chris and I intend to hire a truck and take it to Toronto
Sunday the 20th. –If you get back in time you shld be
able to see it before we pack it.

Carole the baby sitter and a former student has taken
pictures of the children rehearsing their fashion
show. Yesterday she gave me the prints to take home and
show them. I had a long hard look at each print and
thot my gawd how they have grown even more beautiful–as
they become more and more singular: I have always
wanted to let them 'be' and tho I have been irresponsible
towards them that thot remains constant. I want to
let them be more than anything else. and the same goes for
you my dear wife. even you shld 'be'.

Abt. The House: I need a more precise figure of
how much it's going to cost, within a thousand dollars say.
and I want a written agreement from Harry that he will
hold to that price before we go ahead. It wld be useful to
know how long it will take to build as we cant afford to
build and pay rent at the same time. (Ideally) we
want to move from here in the late summer straight into
the new house. (p/s its gonna cost a thousand plus to get
our goods and chattel back to the westcoast.) As for
the strip of land the Copithornes want figure out how much
it costed as per square foot then measure of their piece
and charge them the same plus the costs of surveying.
I suppose all this will have to go thru the city hall for
it to be legitimate–will you look after it?

As for the Expo '70 commission and the Winnipeg Ballet
commission I've not had a contract frm either so
its all still up in the air. Theres been no time to worry
abt it anyhow with so much to do.

Anne one of our other baby sitters has a luvly head.
She tells me abt her acid-trips. She is a friend of
the children and very very gentle. I wld say she was one of
the tribe Marcuse talks abt in the Georgia Straight
vol. 3/ no. 51 (March 28/April 3rd '69 issue). If you have
time read it   it will enable you to
grasp my stance.
Now I am beginning to see more clearly the
issues involved in the Sir George Williams U. racial/
computer: BUST and I am glad that I stood against
those whose anger turned into ugliness. Racial prejudice
is the stirrings of hypocrites whatever their colour.
I am really clear at this moment this turning point in
our lives. How many many times have 'i/'we' turned
to go off in other directions? How many circuits have we
closed and how many open ones have we left? This is
getting altogether too abstract– –more concretely
when you get home. And yes do fly bugger the expenses
WE ARE ALL WAITING FOR YOU COME WHAT MAY.

Love to Carole and Brian
tell em we will see them come May

Summer '69
Kyoto City, Japan

Dear Daphne

    almost) every afternoon abt 3PM
Origin's child C.C. slopes into the Java Shop
on Shijo above Higashi. Almost every
afternoon abt 3PM you or whomever may be just
passing thru can find him there. He will
most likely have his nose in a book but in-
variably looks up when some one enters   and if
its someone he recognizes like you or me his
full face lights up. and before you know it
theres lively conversation. Whenever I'm in
the vicinity I always drop in to have a tea
with him. We seem to have things to say to each
other—without tripping over egos or formal-
ities. Surrounded by the imperatives of a too
too dense humanitus We sprawl across N.A. in
our topicalities. And all thru the late afternoon
local shop-girls dresst fit to kill drop in
for a turkish coffee while the television tells
of the latest sumo match—C.C. follows as avidly
as G.B. follows baseball back home. Now
the little red blue white and green neons come on
and we get up to go home. C.C. is standing at
the curb waving for a cab as I head for Higashi
turn east to my home away frm home. Almost
everyafternoon abt 6PM C.C. takes a cab Utano
his tiny wife and home.

                He gave me a copy of 0 3/16 w/
                yr poems. Let me say that
                yr light on yr toes that yr prose
                dances, obliquely .

                – —will buzz you when I get back

Backcountry Trip

—out of Green Rock Mountain's maw
6 long blocks of squat open-front shops
all hawking polisht-carvings   hewn–
frm its emerald-flanks .

"we got no time for stone cathedrals . . ."

                 HURRY! HURRY!

        O Carnivores of Time–
        your bus leaves in 15 minutes . . .
        & Autumns a scarletshine
        in yr mind's blue-flare lit caves

                  Uda–onsen

Dear M.

      The View frm our inn in Uda-onsen is
      thick grey drab: grey corrugated tin roofs w/
      thickets of t.v. antennas   sumi'd against
      grey pall sky . . . other grey etceteras .
      theres hundreds of places like this thru out
      Nihon I'll never visit-tho i know well
      how soothing mineral waters can be .
      at night little Uda leaves off her grey drab
      puts lip stick & red rouge on as pale
      blue violet white little neons drive abysmal
      shadows down a hundred narrow alleys .
       our next stop will be Ogori where we intend
      to rent a U-Drive to take us along the
      Inland Sea   to Hiroshima

after hot bath
out on to wet cobblestone
back streets–
Syuzo strides along arms tuckt
in flutter-sleeves

i wobble on high getas
. . . steamy
mineral water
boiling up
thru earth crust
porosities . . .

        WHEW!

        out, at last . . . on to

N E O N G L O W P L E A S U R E S B I G B I Z S T R E E T S
* *
        its
        flee pit bars   strip clit
        tease   tiny tea pews   las vegas
        patchinko palaces   queens
        blue porno pop yr cob movie houses
        duck-in noodles &
        YES!
        pussy galore!

"she gave you the sign why didnt you go w/ her-
i thot she was pretty"

". . . i dislike paying for what i can have for the asking
back home ok?"

                Night Wind up
                our arse—almost
                brothers click-
                in' wet cobbles back
                to the inn

. . . .Father and I sit side by side   swaying thru
long night fetid-dream tunnel . The garbage heapt under
our feet tumbl'd knee-deep into the aisle . Father
has his own face . Mine, the dream sd lies buried in

his shoulder   a rock or craggy precipice . Then, Im running
running hard thru hissing steam my foot steps echo under
black night canopy–Father! Father! Wait! Wait!
for me Father! The DREAM sd he waited patiently for me
poised on the topmost EXIT stair . He sd "Son this is where
I have to get off you better hurry back to the train."
Then he turned his back on me and step by steep darkening step
his small bent back became the dark pit EXIT . Back on
The Train i stare at his empty white plastic cup stark against
night window. . . . my swaying body un-comforted .

. . . .

          "Good bye Uda –
          keep yr efficacious mineral-rites
          I'll hang on to Time

                    – –T h a n k y o u !
Ogo-ri

     O-go-ri

Ogo-ri

         Ogoreee–

–in the early bird morning

9 / 10 / 69

Dear Charlotte,

. . . . my sculpture is a flag wavering in my mind's eye.
its a Magritte flag fluttering at half-mast on a windless day.

we keep working away on it tho
and if Im lucky & I am one of those who continue to believe in
such quaint possibilities it will get made by Dec. 1st
as planned. (meanwhile
I keep going to and fro from Expo '70 Osaka
as tho I had a 9 to 5'r and a newspaper & umbrella under my arm.

you wld be interested in a double bill here
in Kyoto, across the street from each other
         :   a big G A U G U I N S H O W
         :   & T H E B O B U K I G R O U P (calligraphy 10 ft. tall!

(P.G. wld turn over in his you know what
if he cld see the yellow hordes queued up . . .walking
a prescribed route (re: chronology) with
ear phones on telling the story of his romantic trip.
ya, all this and more out-of-step with
his oftimes savage wit.
for yrs truly growing-up with
The Impressionists and The Group of Seven, it was
a sentimental journey etc.

as for the CALL(ita)GRAPH ers
the esoteric ones who base image on chinese ideograms
(roots go deeper than brush marks tell . . .)
they fill room after room with
                   HUGEBLACKMARKINGS – – – – – – –.
:talk abt yr wall/flower! yr wall/paper!

(its the moment supple move-
ment of agile wrist and eye –grabbin' up
big chunks of white space . . . with
a salute/   a salutation/ & a song– – – – –WHAM–O!
I take it then that
the action is
where any-of-us (at any moment
happens to be .
       where are you? . what have you to report?

       yrs unruly,

10/ 13th/ '69
Kyoto City/ Japan

Dear Mariko

    Your letter is the first real one Pa has received from one of his daughters. Oh there have been other delightful scrawls drawings and pictographs but yours is the first one I have been able to read without interpretations. Keep them coming and tell your sisters to write too.

    Your grandpa and i went via airplane to Kochi. We spent a long afternoon with grandpa's younger sister and her son and wife and their two children. The girl's name is Kana she has pen pals all over Japan and other places in the world. She askt me to tell you she wld be interested in corresponding. Her address is Miss Kana Odani/ 10-16 Seiyo-cho/ Kochi City/ Japan. Which reminds me that I had a Hawaiian girl for a pen pal when I was in grade seven or eight. She was probably my first heart tremble even tho I only loved a glossy colour photo of her in a long grass skirt with a lei of flowers abt her neck. We wrote to each other regularly for abt 2 years . . . but I've completely forgotten even her name. its all a long timorous time ago its gone for good. Anyhow all this seems to say that writing letters can be a way of getting news of/frm the world.

    did you get the bolt of cloth I've sent?

10/ 15th/ '69
Kyoto City, Japan

dear Gladys

.... accustom'd as i am to central heating– –
its a real drag to be numb with cold. not that its
really that cold but that we have no heat. like
inside or outside the same temperature. or aggravated
as when winter sun glows but dont penetrate in.
Im sittin' here with a thick wool blanket across my lap.
my stocking'd feet sit upon a petrol foot-warmer.
Im wearing a thick wool jacket on top of more than
the usual underclothes. plus a heavy overcoat on
top of all this. and its just mid-October like Indian Summer
back home, etc. or we're all sitting around the low
kitchen table our legs tuckt under the quilted apron whc
hangs to the floor. under the table
theres a small electrical heating element. its
i suppose a miniature central heating system (with a
small perimeter of warmth)–bolster'd with cups of hot sake
electronic energies off the colour'd teley.
then as often as not i'll have a late-night bath the kind
where you soap first then rinse off before getting in
to the hot hot water–to soak up the heat. and any number
can use the same water with no accumulation of grey
scum 2/3rds of the way up the tub. Phil Whalen told me
he fucken near froze to death last winter (his lst winter
here. he sd he didnt get sick didnt even get a cold– –
just felt as tho he might freeze to death, daily.
and when theres a storm outside your window think how
nice it is to be able to go abt bare-arsed
if you shld want to. and to hell with the romantical
theories of how great literature gets written in
draughty stone castles. gee Glad-eyes aint central heating
one of the so called marvels of these stoned ages!

... thru successive re-visions
yours truly continues to be
as they say most unruly .

10/ 15/ '69
Kyoto Japan

dear Phil

          heres the letter i composed   as
          you hove into view– –

I came to Daigo-ji cause Cid gave me an invite to
a viewing of their treasures. i waited for you . . . .
when you didnt show up i lookt again at the card
and it sd (they showed their treasures) yesterday.
I then took a cab all the way over to Daitoku-ji
where their treasures wld be on view today. its
where i shld have met you . . . lets try again say one
yr. from Now. Ok?
it was a pizza-pleasure havin' american style
chinese food   served up by a friendly jap who lived
in canada & talkt abt tor onto. lets do that a-
gain also .

          p/s wont be able to go to the Noh
          with you come sunday 'cause Pa & i are
          invited to an 'enaka matsuri'. how-
          ever   if theres some other occasion for
          us to get together   phone 561-0144.
          c/o Yoshimura's .

							446-hachi ken machi
							furukawa cho/ sanjo kudaru
							higashiyama ku/ kyoto

							10/ 18th/ '69

dear C l a u d i a

	....H a i r ! yeah hair W O W! : well why not-
	even hair. here everyone's got black hair or orange
	hair as when a neighbourhood bar girl sees them
	white wimmen on colour television with flaming orange
	colour'd hair then taints her own. occasionally a
	head taller you'll see yellow/ gold/ even red hair and
	a pair of lovely slender legs–the kind that
	stride thru my unbidden dreams. ladies here with fat legs
	are called 'daikon aishi' which comes out as 'radish
	legs' in english. imagine speaking abt a woman's legs that
	way . as for Hair whether its curly/ kinky/ wavy/
	knott'd/ frizzled/ or lank–Hair, whatever colour or length
	turns me on. (. . . wish i could get my hands on some!
	i once upon a time wrote abt a woman with abundant yellow
	hair–who could smother any man with it–five yrs be-
	fore we met, etc. Sandro Botticelli's women all have hair
	like you do. as say Utamaro's women got hair like the
	trad women of Kyoto still do. and further, the finest Japanese
	Dolls have jet black hair shorn from the greatgreat grand
	children of Uta's women. or else its real shiny strands
	of plastic filaments. on teley one night i got fascinated
	by a female pop singer (crooning unrequited love). her
	real black hair hung down to her waist between shoulder-
	blades. whereas the wig she also wore framed her face. i
	got caught up in how the t.v. lights grabbed each filament
	of hair surrounding her face whereas her real hair did
	not gleam so. like it had a soft sheen as real hair does.
	or again really well-painted hair of whatever colour has:
	like you cld tell if the painter were accomplisht by the
	soft sheen he caught it up in as against the black velvet
	high-light'd ripples of yr amateurs, etc. and tits–
	dont count for as much as hair does. renoir could ignore
	her nipples but not her hair–as she emerges from the
	sun-lit bower, light dappled. then thars the Yank who paints

the all-american nudey as tho she had red plastic suction
cups or artificial buttercups, for tits. tits as art-i-facts
cld be a serious contribution to Connoisseurship if only
some university grad got busy on it. as for media-photos–
even them grand colour'd blow-ups of 'em–the illusion
of infantile gratification is not a gratifying delusion. the
same with paintings of 'em. both lie flat on the page.
yeah why dont you make a movie all abt Hair? start with yr
own tresses) Primavera ! 'like' i say hair is brazen.

                    19/ 10/ '69
                    c/o Yoshimura's at
                    446-hachi ken machi
                    furukawa-cho   sanjo kudaru
                    higashiyama-ku
                                    kyoto city

for Coolhand Luke &
    Others in fine arts at
    Sir George Williams
    University   Montreal,Quebec

'here' as over 'there' or almost 'anywhere' theres television–
you get the so-call'd 'real world' comin' at u via techni-
color'd visors: Locus is 2 eyes in front of a teley screen
'anywhere'. but   what gets shown (again, everywhere) is
the *unredemptive world* comin' on like SIN was goin' out of
style. all the so-called documentaries (purporting to give
us a slice-of-life) do that but seldom more–
i mean dont we all want (simply/complexly)   more than
mere that? I take it to be the artist's biz to splice to-
gether the whole fucken picture   inc *the shit* . . . Honey.

you'd find lots interesting here where human density
makes for more spread tho not necessarily breadth. theres
more children visible and more old folks visible   (as they
are more in evidence everywhere here). theres dozens of
abbot & costello stand-up comics tongue-twisting the
jap language–pokin' fun at their sacred-cows. again
those arty-farty jap movies we see in canadada is daily fare
here   as are the jap ma perkins   their sudsy tears.
& the long hair'd cats wailin' pelvis/pudenda rock-songs glee
fully. we dont have equivalents of their media-ads 'cause
theyre non-christian eat fish dig stone gardens.

BUT: Here too TIME EQUALS MONEY. like how the Media
soft peddles the 'big lie' –what-you-should-buy-that-you-dont-
need-but-will-pay-thru-the-nose-for-time-after-time-at-15%-
compounded. Shit! aint it sech awful bullshit? –its
gotta be prime-time at any time during 24 hours when your
caught up in the rush of it   utterly. p/s its 2am –see
what i mean!
            48 hrs after–saw the Oct. 15 events in USA.

Here: world news is mostly Asiatic News. you can listen to how the prevailing winds are comin' up from the phillipines. Monreale is a mere dot on the map of the world. if Mc-Luhan ever gits translated into japanese he'll sound like concrete poetry ideogramm'd in romanji .
      keep the homefires burning

10/ 26/ '69
Kyoto City Japan

Dear Phyllis

. . . . yeah i is also dis-located sometimes.
like, who isn't? otherwise i seems to be where
i am   doing my thing   whatever that thing
happens to be. and YES i do know   (intimately
that awful feeling of 'is it any fucken good?'
viz a poem/   painting/   or any thing. i is saying
all this knowing it aint much consolation to
an other *mired in* the depths of her doubtings.

and its true i am ambi-dextrous but your left-
hand bit reminds me its also my left hand that keeps
fingering the past. does that imply that my right
hand thumbs the future?

(thinking i might have the time to work on 'em
i brought along so-called 'works-in-progress' but
haven't really re-enter'd them. i mean i seem to
be bored quite thoroughly bored with them and i think
i know why– –its like re-gurgitating what had
once upon a time, obtained. or, its the impossibility
of meddling with the past which wont yield. then
again–if i bring 'em over into the present G.S. sense
of "the complete actual present" it all might make
good sense?

                been going abt taking lots of photos.
                i just keep looking under-foot or
                to left and right, back and front with
                in say a 10 meter circumference:
                FOCUS viz yr camera/   eye must then be '
                'locus' or even Olson's 'polis'

                no matter– –the evidence of whats there
                (underfoot) accumulates.

                .

                . . . right after She wrappt the fish up
                in last week's news, sd "thank you– –"
                she turned on her child and sez   " PISS
                piss your always pissing yr buggy

Furukawa-cho Market Marginalia)
and I've met so-called Foreigners here who haven't had
a good fuck for years. Tho yrs truly aint exactly one he
will soon have to get out of here   or start using Max
Factor Makeup and go a-haunting homosexual bars– – – –HA!

book-of-pomes in the mail to lift you up and out of the
dumpings

in the face of
'your words' – – these: a response
-̲-̲-̲-̲-̲-̲-̲-̲-̲-̲-̲-̲-̲-̲-̲-̲

to Gail Dexter (center spread
of the 5¢ review – – here, in Kyoto

*

Here –
There, where you (also) face
the same world

'left' is
as 'Right' is, a stand-
ard stance:

        concretized
        feel-
            ings,
        contra-
        dictions, a

        racket

            un-
          relevant
            un-
          lovely
            un-
          reason-

                able-alibi's

        for making
        a mountain out of
        Mao Tse,

        and, A dam (Nation
        out of liberalibations,
        my country – –

'tis of thee'
the maple leaf forever!

*

Yeats' real-
ity included A Vision,
and the Irish
senate

'mysticism'
if you will) &
'politics'
as it happens) could

happen to you.
its 'where'
you place the world,
and your 'face'
in it

*

'relevance'
is
    no more – –
    no less – –

than ALL

    your contraries,
    etc.

        love(ly) ambi-
   dextrous
        Gail .

12/ 10/ '69
c/o Yoshimuras – –
446- Hachi ken machi,
Furukawacho, Sanjo kudaru,
Higashiyama ku,
Kyoto City, Japan.

(LETTER FROM KYOTO)
for
    (dear) Phyllis Webb:

        after taking leave of Phil Whalen outside of Daitoku-ji
I took a cab to Shinkyogoku to see a flick called THE SWEET PUSSY, yet!
In Japanese my kinda Japanese it comes out 'ami neko' with none of
the pubic insinuations English gives .

Cats inc: *Loverbuoy* alias Loversnuts, Smoothie, Dumdum, Nonentity etc.

    Peral White the heroine. (you know why gentlemen prefer brunettes
with small arses after seeing her.

    Brunhilde, Peral's bigtit sis. (someone even DeSade woulda
taken the cat-o'-nine-tails too.

    The White Cat, Bruny's cat. (the kind that look at you as if
tail all tail was a drag.

    & *The Porno Ghosts* (legions of 'em leering & clankin' their chains
behind each o lecherous scheme– –knowing that porno-equals-shit-
equals-money, even here in Kyoto where the old men still walk
the banks of the Kamo on hot sumnier nights in their underwear.   ya.)

& here, d(EAR Phyllis is a reader's digress of
the whole tempestuous plot :

        Loversnuts makes poor lil' Peral fuck everything
in sight to keep him in pin-stripe suits, booze, & vaseline.

        or, He does that, he fucks everything he kin lay
his hands on but only if Peral is there to watch 'em do it.

(theres a scene where he has her bound and gagged while making it
with a wench with small tits.   & so on– –ad nauseum.)

depending on who ya empathize with you cld almost believe that
Dumdum is (oh) so wicked he oughta have the thumbscrews on his balls
while chinese water drips slow-ly drop by drop on his forehead.

I'll have to tell ya abt shopping for porno-prints
in Kyoto. How one thing led to another leading to the possession of
6 lovely Utamaro woodcuts–showing how elegant the act of
making it can be.

> whats left in mind's eye is an image. its a choice of
> images (imaginings) – – 'porno' is (at least) as much in
> the beholder's eye, etc.

    Loverbuoy had a girl a gem of a girl name of Peral White who
tells the oh so tragic truelife tale of her sordid life thru a diary she kept.
Bigsis Brunhilde buys the diary from Peral's landlady for a fat price
after the awful accident when Peral thru herself under the wheels of a car:
like wht else could a virtuous girl do-hearing all that panting come from
his bedroom. Anyhow Bruny reads and re-reads lil' sis's diary and each time
Peral was humiliated   the angrier she got. She determined to revenge her sister's
death.
    Cunningly she arranges a meeting with our hero. He's not impressed
with Bruny's flagrant display of her (ugh) anatomy. He thinks that a fuck is a fuck tho
and she could be worse. Then, we see him across the street from her 2nd story
apartment window. He's wearing his fawn-colored trench coat and a snap brim hat.
A cigarette dangles from his insolent lips.
    The apartment is cushy there's lots of fur around. Theres even a fie-fi-fo-fum
hi-fi teleplunken playing viennese schmaltz. And the white cat, you know
the kind I mean   with that look of perfect contempt for anything less than caviar.
    Loversnuts is no sooner up the stairs and into her apt. before he's pulling off
his tie with one hand and with the other grabbing ahold of her tit . . . when
she says to him (in broken eengleesh, "wait, why dont you go mix yrself a drink
while I get myself ready . . . for you know what."
He goes over to the bar, mixes a stiff one, downs it in a gulp, then mixes another
and downs that one . . . just as Bruny returns smiling lasciviously thru her sheer-black
peek-a-boo negligee. Loverbuoy is swarming all over her and is about to pull down
her drawers . . . when he flakes out on the satin bedspread. Doped.
Hours later non-hero finds himself chained hands and feet to a thick pipe in
a small dark room. He doesn't know the room is sound-proof and has a false wall that
slides back on a one way window opening on Brunhilde's bedroom.
    Im gettin' tired & bored of . . . so lets skip some of the ho-hum-tedium scenery.
Here's resume of what bigsisbrunhilde did to avenge poor lil' Peral White :
    She induces Dumdums equally stupid best male friend up for a drink and just as
he is about to give her the gears he passes out. Doped. (nonhero sees all
of this thru the one way window).
    She then has herself fucked by the clunk(wouldya believe it–his name is Joe!

who delivers the groceries. Joe naturally doesn't smoke or drink so he really
came on fast and (as they say) blew his tool. (shackled, our boy grimaces and lets out
despairing moans).

    Loversnuts other girl-fiend comes by looking for him. They talk about him
as tho he was dead . . . have a drink then another and before you know it
both of 'em are down to their black bikinis and its tit for tat (while Loverbuoy
wears his most tormented look). The women agree it was fun and promise
each other to do it again tomorrow night.
    Then thars a sequence with the two women and a pair of nondescript males.
Bruny's shown playing footsie on the bed with one of the guy's noses. Mate, meanwhile
is sucking the other guy off and playing with a dildo . . . & they don't letcha see
howit all turned out !
      Then yr with the camera down on the floor beside nonhero looking towards the door.
Bruny comes in wheeling a small surgical table with assorted knives and sundry things
on it. Your led to believe that she cuts off his 'you-know-what'. Then ya see him
staggerin' down grey symmetrical tree-lined street and he's frothing at the mouth and
his grey mucus orbs are spinning in their sockets and the camera pans clear pans blurr
pans his wobbly feet the wet grey cobblestones and stately trees and your led to
believe he outa his noodle and ya he falls falls down again and again and finally
he's down dead. ya wet, and dead. ya, dead.

to uh conclude :

Titles, & dialogue (sech as they were) given in (Japanese)-English.
The several faces were Italian/ German/ Slav. Their voices
    dubbed-in by several other mouths lisping English with foreign accents.
If ya had a close-up the 'voice/voices' seemed to come from
    the next room & long shots revealed shouting in your ears.
The moving image(s seemed shot thru a brownie box camera. On location,
    somewhere in and around the Black Sea or it coulda been
    Russian side of the Baltic?
The sound-squack coulda been a Strauss waltz playing backwards on tape,
    it was that (sic).

    &, Imagine the grimaces/moaning/panting/ slovering/ pussy-foot-ing-it
    a round & a round
        in the name of *what dont ya call it anyhow!*

        T H E E N D .

. . . . honest, cross my heart & spit over my left shoulder etc. –
every word of it is true. I aint made any-of-it, UP
&
  HOW ARE YOU ?

    Love,

vancouver bc
3rd wk of Jan '70

dear Jos & Marken

<u>moshi (Hi) moshi (Hi)</u>

. . . WHERE begin to unravel all the so-called
S p a c e / T i m e cover'd since
we were all together in Montreal spring '69 ?

when i was a juvenile delinquent type golf-fiend
(Gene Sarzen my hero) i once uncoil'd all the rubber-
string bit by broken bit frm an old 'pro-flite' golf
ball til it lay in a confused heap at me feet many times
larger than the original ball. the core of it was
the size of a (dib) (agate) or marble – – its some
thing like that .

at least) : got myself, like any
lousy tourist does in Nippon a real good camera a 35mm
C A N O N with a z-o--om l-e-n-s. took 36 expos a day
for several months. 100's of pics. upshot: hrs spent
editing for a wee book of pomes & pics to be called– –
S t o n e d G l o v e s ya.

my Expo '70 tricolor'd pyramids is an accomplisht fact:
They'll be able to fold it up like the proverbial A
rab's tent and no-one will ever know how it shone
apparell'd in its own colours by day and
aglow of fluorescents (within) by night.

. . . more to tell you i am back in
soggy van (for good?

love

       3/ 12/ '70
       vancouver bc

dear P H I L

 Thank You for
 placing me atop *The Bear's Head*-
 mighty fine view of Whalen County from
 that prominence that firm ground

   Joanne Ebbe & Geo Stanley Here
   in Vancouver) to read poetry.
   Gary comin' up in a week for more
   of the same. (im readin' too.

   & flubbin' abt gettin' located. havent
   done a fucken thing 'cept run abt – –
   sayin' 'HEY! IM BACK! ' 'WHY DONCHA GIT ME A JOB!
   HUH!'

     (Shit!) Phil
     Kyoto continues to con me tho
     Im back where cherry blossoms (also
     bloom come Spring

        take care

Dear R o n

    yr little piece on Ernie Lindner
    in the current artscanada   remind'd me how
    the last time we met you were in a
    hospital bed and . . . . We almost got through
    to one another we almost sd how we both
    dreaded the proprieties the ease of which pre-
    vented how we truly felt, etc. Now, Liz
    sez you have made a real change in your life–
    and I want to say its been coming. I mean
    if We dont DO WHAT WE INTEND TO DO
    (soon, rather than later)   there is that that
    awful despair to live up to. Love to both
    your Dorothys– –. tell the one who wrote abt
    Bladen and Murray I think her arguments
    why R.M. is less than a R.B. not useful to one
    or the other tho I do agree that R.B. is one
    of the best sculptors around. At least– –
    both are where the rest of us 'should' also
    also BE .
            (GEEZ! aint our old friend
              E. Lindentree come into his own ?

           I mean how my middle-age body
           Ahhhhs at his deciduous young women

           its My Gawd the plangencies of
           An old man's E r o t i c- F i s s i o n !

           H a l o 'd be him.)

dear D a n i e l l e

> heres **the preface** (pre-amble
> or whatever you call it
> for S t o n e d g l o v e s .
>
> dont of course know 'if'
> its what is needed but its what
> I found possible. if you can
> use it do so. if not i shall re-
> write it to suit. Ok?
>
> . . . .
>
> **value of photos:**
> all with length of 30"/ 40"
> @ $100.oo each.
> all others (the larger ones
> @ $200.oo each. as a
> modest estimate for yr insurance
> etc .
>
> .
>
> . . . . tell J. Boggs yr boss I
> really do need the money, pronto.
> i want to fund other projects.
>
> as far as i am concern'd 'no-body'
> seems to buy my art—so where
> am i going to get the bread frm?
>
> .
>
> extensions/ for you :
>
> Ou?
>
> Ce qui n'est pas dans la pierre,
> Ce qui n'est pas dans le mur de pierre et de terre,
> Meme pas dans les arbres,
> Ce qui tremble toujours un peu,
>
> Alors, c'est dans nous .
>
> .
>
> . . . .imagine me S t o n e d g l o v e s
> goin' off to Paris . none of 'em
> ever thot to achieve such an eminence. . . .
>
> regards,

                              5/ 17th/ '70
                              Vancouver B.C.

dear A n n
        (UBC Fine Arts Gallery)

        Danielle C. writes to say UBC has bookt
        S t o n e d G l o v e s frm Nov. 15th thru Dec. 15th.
        which is a pleasure as i do like the thot that
        they might originate from the city i am closest to tho
        the gloves hail from Osaka & Expo '70 .
        .
        shall i come by to help put them up? then
        i could give a reading of the poems whc accompanies 'em
        at the opening or later–for a small fee .
        i wld try using the walls and floor to lean some of
        the long serial photos against. also flat on the floor if
        feasible. even hung from the ceiling. whatever makes
        for the tightest and most audacious hanging.
        .
        . . . just abt completed my end of the show. if you or
        Alvin want to see 'em come on by 1923-Granville   before
        month's end. just bring your notebook and smile .
        .
        . . . whatever else they are i cant imagine.
        i see them as a graph of a eye/mind in movement–
        grabbin' up life-signs as I've come upon 'em.
        they are in that sense 'relevance' stumbled upon .

        regardez

Dear Victor

    heres S t o n e d g l o v e s.
    except for the xerox copies i sent to John
    George and yrself and the possible re-
    visions you all come up with which i may want to
    incorporate, its complete. whatever you all
    suggest wont affect the poems that much - - - or
    we might have to throw the whole works out!

    anyhow its HURRAH out 'there'
    and thank god I've no more sap left for it .

        the 51 fotos have
        all been selected and placed in
        hopefully   a relevant
        sequence viz the (complementary)
        poems .

    and if and when SG does come out
    do you think it will be recognized as
    a five finger'd litany to . . . . BREATH ?

            as soon as
            my vexations ease up I
            intend to go East
            if we dont hear frm you we'll
            see you soon

T h e s e / for S a r a h:
‒ ‒ ‒ ‒ ‒ ‒ ‒ ‒ ‒ ‒ ‒ ‒

Slim sd you wrote and told him how
a childhood girl-friend in the USA had written
to say She got a giant plastic SLUG for
I think she sd that you had sd, her birthday yet.

He was last seen lighting up a joint for one of his
girl friends down on Kits Beach. She, it seems
had curly blonde hair to match her blonde burly posture.
Moments later Slim turned into a flaming match– –
while she became a purple screem.

And the last time I saw Slim He showed me his
latest acquisition– –a round/brown scufft-up velvet case
with, he insisted, a   (tarnisht)   gold hasp, Lytton
Strachey might once have owned. Slim opened it
what do you think it is? I thot its a tiny piece of
petrified turd. He sd, turd indeed!– –its a whole
Egyptian slug. He added that Egyptians thot
petrified slugs were the best aphrodisiacs.

.

Victor   whatever happens)   I want 50 copies for
my assorted friends.

                    See you when you head West– – – –

Summer '70
Vancouver BC

Dear Victor

George B. returned SG w/ some subtle changes whc
I want to incorporate– –IS THERE TIME TO?
are deletions more bothersome than further additions
re typos?
Let me know whats possible? Pronto!

– –one day I shall have to write abt my gloves
their history all the way back to the very lst pair
our primate forebear pieced together   for his
equally soft palms, vulnerable fingers . . . . *but* not
before my hands have learnt a measure, worthy of our
agilities. Not a day before that.

.

(. . . is a schizoid someone moving thru time/space at
a snail's pace while his mind flashes I-M-A-G-E-S– – –
faster than a digital computer?) *viz* Stan before he
left for Toronto, said he's freakt and preferred
to "see me over the phone."

yr friendly
neighbourhood glove

Dear Victor

       ((((HMMMMMM! . . . . jus scored sum   DONT
          know how good it is . . . . butt its SHITTY
          ANYHOW . . . W-O-W !))))

--- if you is too far into SG to want to or
can attend to these additions/re-visions foregoe
'em   tho they're G.B/s later than yesterday
succinct suggestion and therefore to be taken
as it were *seriously*. geez he sure knows   his
syntax despite the vexations he stands to.

anyhow '4 Variations' to go where 'get down on yr
knees' is.
        Otherwise I'm well placed eh?
        with no more harangues abt any of it.

– – – –if there aint gonna be 'proofs' you're my official
proof-reader   OK ?

.

Danielle (lovely dame) thinks the SG(loves
elegiac– –but I am thru with them. Already I am on
another O MUthur Fucken Trip another H-I-G-H
which our ole friend Art is all about   aint it?

Dear Victor

    re-visions

    after (palimpsest
    ‒ ‒ ‒ ‒ ‒ ‒ ‒ ‒ ‒

        – –if you put your ear to
        his cuppt hand

                you will hear his pain
            re-echo thru the pome

        like a naked hand reaching out
        for its shadow

    after (if this finger was
    ‒ ‒ ‒ ‒ ‒ ‒ ‒ ‒ ‒ ‒ ‒ ‒

        – –if you haven't stumbled on
        old gloves
                you'll never know

        how They fell into the dirt

            palms up

even)
my hand knows nothing
abt *the dirt*

    glove   lies
    gently
            under

Dear Victor

    Liz float'd into town w/ side-kick Emily– –
    Gerry phoned he sd "We've got to do something quick
    like sending both back to Toronto . . . I cant
    dont want to cope with 'em." So– – went over to
    Ian Ridgeways to greet them. We got into the van
    drove over to the CNR and got both of 'em traintickets
    then drove over to the Aki for a forlorn meal be-
    fore I left all of 'em off at Stanley Park where They
    sd they wld rest till train-time. And all this time
    Emily hung on by her teeth, fiercely. lst, you and Sarah
    plus the baby then Liz her pal Emily followed by a
    freakt Bevington . . . almost ENUFFF to blow the cool off
    a middle-age rage: DONT WE ALL CEASELESSLY RUB OFF
    ON ONE/ ANOTHER, BROTHER! THREE LUSTY CHEERS!
    FOR THE COACH HOUSE GANG– –MIND-FUCKERS ALL OF THEM!

        Michael De C. tells how
        he and Lorraine went to a micro-biotic session
        in Americun North-West where two Nips– –
        leading the group of abt 100 folks just smiled
        all day long . ". . . christ every time I lookt
        they had that silly crack where a mouth shld be"
        & ". . . it really bugged me."

        .

        (. . . perhaps We have afterall come to
        the end of what began with the Greeks–that
        extended era of 'hierarchies' from now
        on therell only be innumerable I's 'equal' in
        everything under the sun . . . .)

PHOTOGRAPHY: as
when the eye (shutter) opens
and closes on each frame of a succession
of images/ imaginings

Photo/Graphs as

>ledgers .
>legerdemain .
>after-image .
>compost heap .
>image bank .
>*Memories*

Goin to Hornby Is. tomorrow AM w/
my 35MM CANON   asst. lenses 50 rolls of 36 expo
black and white (tri-x) film   plus a
cheap POLAROID w/ 15 packs of film   plus my
tripod my tape recorder my tent bedding the I Ching
and Technicians of the Sacred. I've got a cap
of acid for each day to burn the scum of
my reptilian eyes: all for Sea/ Sky/ Shore/ Stone/s
and the B.C. A l m a n a c

>stocky Tom McInnes
>black-smith and iron monger for
>Riverside Iron Works   had
>all 4 walls even the ceilings of his
>tiny house covered w/ paintings.
>he came to my evening classes for 2 yrs
>cld quote his Shakespeare at the
>drop of a hypothesis and cum blizzard or
>sub zero weather never misst a class.
>He painted a Springtime meadow w/
>an oval pond smack in the middle the blue sky
>and white clouds tippt in it.
>and thats when I began to teach
>circa early 50s.

>.

>aint We all
>Technicians of the Sacred ?

>aint that the job to be done ?

                    frm the Point
                    Hornby Is. B/C
                    June end '70

Dear Victor and Sarah

    6AM Windward on the Point
acid-visions of sand/ stone/ water corrugations

        L o v e ' s   B o d y   O   N o r m a n
        O   B r o w n   8 0 %   W a t e r

        s a n d / s t o n e / w a t e r
        P O R O S I T I E S– –meta body . E p i-
        d e r m i s under microscope these/
        my million/interlaced pores : W i n d o w s

    all glass tensed in glass and steel curtain
    walls   impenetrable . . . . Kafka's great
    China Wall compact'd with human bodies   an
    aggregate of dense litanies

        Ginsberg's
                    yes, yes,
                            thats what
                I wanted,
                        always wanted,
                I always wanted,
                        to return
                to the body
                        where I was born

            imprint'd
            t r a n s l u c e n c i e s
            g l o b e s   o f   l i g h t
                    M e a t 's
                C-o-n-g-e-r-i-e-s . . . .

77

7/ 20/'70
Vancouver BC

Dear Doris/ Jack

    Now that we are all back from our
assorted travels I have the thought that it all
has something to do with a quest for our
'Sources': Roots or Ground, no matter, there is
the urgencies of travel, the places We need
and the depth of self the place may reveal to our
selves. During the 4 yrs spent in Quebec I
thought many times of how easy it wld be to grab
a plane and fly to Europe for even a week-end.
I never did and now that I'm back on the westcoast
again) I am beginning to wonder if I ever will.
Whereas, the Orient (sources?) seems to be
a necessity therefore inevitable. The more so since
I find it hard to have purchase of the sod I
find myself an heir to. Thus, I see my own travel-
ling as an actual need to plumb my own back-
ground. Or its that we are all 'nomadic' and possess
nothing nothing but our own bodies and that for
only a short while. Ah for jean Dubuffet's
it must be Gallic-Grace when he sez "I have been on
a thirty years holiday."

.

apropos A Decades Work;
or its in memory of a ten year itch– –

We ought to try and get a hold of all
my scatter'd works from '60 to '70 particularly
the so called 'best works'. That way We
can select the best of them and send the rest back
without apologies). This wholesale gathering
wld be the real beginnings of an even
limited retrospective. Further I think I shld
have a hand in the actual selections– –
whc I hope you are counting on?

I dont like phone calls or across the desk
conversations much so I will write to you regularly
concerning my part in the '60s/'70s Show.

7/ 24/ '70
Vancouver BC

dear George and Angela

S t o n e d g l o v e s (Now) in Victor's hands.
it includes all the varied suggestions
you victor and john made that i could use without re
writing the whole damned thing. yr take on
the poems with insistence on the exact soundings
added some polish tho its too late in the day
to worry abt the start of the sequence whc
yr right in sayin its too damned rigid plodding or
some stiff thing.

        Angela– –come what may
        "Today is the first day of
        the rest of your life"

        sez church hoarding
        corner of burrard + georgia

– –so far we've had a luvly summer with
everyone out in the sun or under the forest trees.
s-t-o-n-e-d they test 'where' theyre at and
'what' it feels like there and what to do abt it if
doing be necessary. old compulsions remainder'd–
momentarily mitigated by acid visions of Blakean/Dream
S p l e n d o u r s .

Ah Monreale (encapsulated) microspeck
lost in cellular brain synapses. someday–I'll
lean on a pearly button and therell be
an instant codification of E-V-R-Y-T-H-1-N-G that
happened there– –F L A S H: only then there
might be a wee pome no longer than a gasp a reed
wind butterfly pome .

.

p/s working on SEA: SHORE: STONE
a photo-sequence of The Point, Hornby Island
whc is gonna be one of many books to be
called T h e   B. C.   A l m a n a c .

re: *numberd duck*   unless i have a re-newal of
that vision so i can make it better you cant have it
tho i've got a single good page abt Angela's High
whc you could have. the rest of it (ugh) is a dismal
aesopian fable.

"Every artist was first an amateur" sd Emerson
via backside of Eddy Match Box. Ok but how deal with
the fact that one can at forty still be that . . . ?

why dont you do somethin abt gettin Al and Marguerite Neil
plus Gregg Simpson out there—to turn you on. they gave an
extra-ordinary concert at V.A.G. and shld be heard at S.G.W.U.
where Eng/Lit Guardians keep pluckin' metaphors frm British
Rubbles with fastidious fingers—as if in that numb act theyve
found some lofty thing. George none of us shld turn down a
beatific trip for whatever reason unless its to attend to our
own beatitudes. like dont you also want the extra-ordinary
to become the altogether ordinary daily pleasure?

> H U R R A H
>   f o r
> B O U R A S S A !
>   a n d
>   R E N E
> L E V E S Q U E !

An improvisation for Angela of whom its been sd
the stream-of-consciousness is just a diadem in her belly button

> w o r d s / w a n d s
>   w o r d s / w a n d s / w o r t h
> e a r t h / h e a t / m e a t
>   w o r d s / h e a t / m e e t — —
> m r. w i l l i a m / c a r l o s / w i l l i a m s
>   etc.

> meanwhile
> at the China Creek Cycle Track
> the pedal pushers are hummin' around
> and around the oval

> Opal Alberta was never like this
> back in '42 . . .

7/ 24th/ '70
Vancouver BC

Dear Chris & Vivian

>   unbelievable The Weather here—its
>   a incredibly subtle light show the way hot sun moves
>   slowly thru the heavens to the purple end of
>   the colour spectrum and hangs in there past 10pm and
>   all the stars turn on.
>
>   —it aint hard on days like this to think of
>   the pacific rim as some sort of paradise where us
>   artists dont have to talk softly and carry a
>   big stick as Ad Reinhardt suggests he shld in N.Y.
>
>   .
>
>   . . .E v e r y t h i n g s up in the air and
>   none of it comin' down   for grabs. or
>   you cant step into the same stream twice sez it but
>   i keep adding pages to my storied Life which
>   if not a fiction is the equal of mother fuckin fact.
>
>   theyve laid synthetic turf on the football field
>   here and some of them big guys are complaining theyre
>   havin a hellofatime the way they and the ball
>   skitters all over the uniformly dumb grass.
>   anyday now we'll be able to buy yards of it to lay out
>   on our front lawns til fall when we can roll it up
>   and store away in the basement til the following Spring
>   and itll never wear out or need to be waterd.
>   any day then we'll all be down on our fours to forage
>   for whats left of god's real grass . . . .
>
>   .
>
>   S t o n e d G l o v e s : photos/ poems
>   shld be out late August

7/ 29th/ '70

Vancouver BC

Dear David Silcox

... have i already had (spent?) my 3rd or is it
4th installment? it seems so long ago ... I've lost
the records for the grant along with all my other
so called important papers . no matter–if its the 3rd
then send on the 4th & last. if i have had it–
this letter serves as a final report on my asst.
doings .

since the big computer bust at Sir George W's :

I've completed a 16 ft. high 4 part
vinyl skin/ steel and fluorescent light/Sculpture
for Canada's Pavilion at Expo '70. plus a
6 ft. high replica of the above with appropriate
modifications due to scale.

.

40 piece photo/graph exhibition called
S t o n e d G l o v e s to be circulated by
the National Gallery, Ottawa. plus a
book of photos/ poems with the same title issued
by Coach House Press as catalogue/complement
to the show.

.

(also) 1oo pages of Japan Journal together with
miscell. scribblings.

in the works) 5 part series of fiberglas reliefs
to be made in a limited edition.

photo project tentatively titled
S e a / S h o r e / S t o n e s for N.F.B.'s
B.C. Almanac Show.

.

... if you have the time ask Danielle C. to
show you S t o n e d G l o v e s. they have already
made a host of people take a hard look at even
their own hands. and, if you hear of a university or
an artschool wanting an artist-in-residence or a
competent teacher I am up for grabs. ... have to sub-
sidize my art and family, somehow. as whats his name
sd, "there aint no money in Art, just Art."

82

frm T h e G r a n g e
under the Granville Street Bridge
Vancouver B.C. July 1970

H I N G E :
the new city associates

A Design / Project Group
using the latest communication tools
& documentation resources of
a city   to re-generate

      The City's I M A G E / S

          Glen Toppings
          John Keith-King
          Dallas Selman
          Ricardo Gomez
          Sherry Grauer
          Gary Lee Nova
          Roy K. Kiyooka
          Others

  – –come see us under the bridge
     anytime

31/ 7/ '70
Vancouver bc

dear Victor

    frm: book III

        commentaries/ wu wang/ innocence/
    T H E I M A G E

      under heaven thunder rolls:
      all things attain the natural state of innocence.
      thus the kings of old
      rich in virtu & in harmony with the time
      foster'd and nourisht all beings .

or
everything is blessed
S.S. sez   in the Beloved's eyes .

for the sweat of the love of
setting the words in their rightful place/s
She will surely bless you .

      and/ whats the name for
      body moving thru space/time at
      a snail's pace when mind
      flashes IMAGE/S faster than a
      digital computer ?

whats that called nowadaze ?

    love to you and your kin

                              1923-Granville St.
                              Vancouver B.C.
                              September lst '70

Dear Warren

    . . . . Gladys got sd what needed to be said **outloud**
(in her G.S. piece) abt your big part in the West Coast
poetry scene . Warren I fully share her sense of your
extraordinary relevance .– –Pity I have to write you from
that distance a letter comes from instead of tonguing-
your-ear . Warren we all want a sacramental relationship– –
We want it more than any nationalism . Continue to wave
your own flag–in the face of zealots whatever their
stripe . P o l i t i c s : something to make us TWITCH
like a hair shirt or watch it all happening on television
a bottle of budweiser for good cheer .

                    were workin every day on a series of
                    laminated-cedar sculptures. you could
                    come down to have a look at em–if you
                    have a mind to . . .

                        Fall 70
                        Vancouver BC

Dear Robbie

        a few words abt (my) BC Almanac photo-book
        The Eye in The Landscape

                            matter weve talkt abt but
                            needs to be insisted upon :

inside back + front covers (theyre interchangeable),
dedication (bottom right), the poem (bilingual), the Title,
plus author's name (top left)– –to be type-set as
1st page back + front (centre/bottom) *retinal images of
the point, Hornby Island*   shld also be.
wanta see proofs of these crucial pages before you run 'em.
.

also: the borders around each photo/s (or) the space/s
that separate each from each should be the newsprint and not
as white as they are. i dont want these interstices to be
anything but neutral thruout .

wld it cost too much e/g be prohibitive to print the centre
fold-out on better that is a glossier paper? left and right
hand edges of the fold-out shld not be wider than the width
of the space/s between each photo.

each double page from front to back and back to front shld
read as a single page as the photo-sequence spreads across both.
hence i dont want more space between photo/s in the centre-
fold than prevails between such photos on each double page.

for exact sequence the page number on dummy corresponds to
the page number (bottom left) of each layout page. DONT
get them scrambled! remember that my lay-out shld enable a
reading of the book from front to back or back to front–
thru to the middle, culminating in/with the fold-out.

if yr in doubt as to veracity of the French text I'll get
a hold of the original for you. the English translation as is.
and when yr finisht i want all of the original material back
intact Ok .

                you cld let me know when yr ready to run it and
                i cld be on hand to make last minute check-up, etc.

        yr BC Almanac buddy

                        9/ 6th/ '70
                        Vancouver BC

Dear Terry

   Al Neil sez you were the only one who responded
   to all the letters he sent out for gigs.
   which fact is a fucken shame as he is one of the
   extra-ordinary ones   a maverick musician who
   shall be seen and heard. at least itll be yr pleasure
   to do so thar in Regina. is it too late to try
   and get him a gig in Saskatoon either on campus or
   the gallery and dont forget to let the kids in
   yr high schools know abt it–they just might be his
   'real' audience there .

   (early Neil can be heard backin up Kenneth Patchen
   on Folkways circa early 60s. present N. makes good
   sense if youve got an ear tuned to 70s soundings.)
   .
   the postscript to the Regina Era 55/60
   continues to be written by each of us who were there
   doing what we were given to accomplish.–tho we aint
   met since then i keep in touch with you thru
   yr graceful elucidations in various mags.– –and
   i see that i stand to you as i stand to C.G.:
   athwart both of you, yr post-painterly aesthetics.

   nevertheless,
   these eyes

'70 / Vancouver BC

Dear Harry

    John M. phoned the day after he saw you.
he sd he didnt want to have to start over again after
all the yrs spent getting a purchase in Montreal.
he sd i should tell you this. he added that you politely
declined the hash brownies he brought along.

    for myself teaching art to a prescription viz
someone else's terms is impossible. the more so now
after nearly 20 yrs of telling it. my own sense of
teaching presumes a ceaseless examination of all aspects
of a given thing or idea   and the outering of what
such scrutiny enables. for me methodology is nothing more
than such scrutiny and its subsequent outering. i dont
as you know have much use for the cant of classifications
or respect for specialists and their myopic views.
my thot is that everyone at least potentially is a
special individual in so far as each has a different head
hence perceptions. for me a good teacher and i mean
'good'   both as competent and having moral virtues   is
one who knows how to tongue his scrutinies for
the sake of others who then might go on to tell still
others   & so on .

will let you know abt taking the job   soon

yr brother

10/ 22nd/'70
Vancouver B/C

Dear Victor/ Sarah/ Stan/ and

      (now yr all back home– –
      let me say we're (also) more
      together
          Yeah! dont WE all rub off
          on each/other
                ceaselessly
      brothers/ sisters
      K i n s h i p

the wave of 'inconsistencies' shimmer
like many-faceted jewel in a belly dancer's navel
apropos the FUCK UPS in S t o n e d g l o v e s.
most upset abt omission of the last line of
the 2nd Variation (for Victor!) and the omission of
the 3rd and 4th Variations entire.
as for the un-corrected poems and the meandering page
numbers that begin with a no. 4 and just wander– –
no one will as they say in Grimm's 'know'
but US.

    – – –I suppose it was bound to be the Fate of
    my SG even tho they never expected
    a happy ending. IMAGINE a pair of (stoned)
    gloves loping off into the sunset!

and/ instead of 'other' poems for the next I's
you cld print the 4 Variations entire. it wld enable
Others to know there are in fact four of them.

if your finisht w/ mss/ photos/ negs/ proofs/ etc
could you forward them?

.

Yeah I wld love to edit a westcoast issue of I's but
an issue of my own utterly (personal?) choices.

.

    in the pissoir at the Cecil
    above eye-level on a 4" square tile
    one large brown felt tip pen
    S-L-U-G by none other than Slim Flowers
    master of boneless calligraphy

Vancouver '70

Dear Don

    – – –ever since *the job* that didn't happen
I've wanted to get a letter off   telling How it
couldn't happen   Here and Now circa 1970:

Some thoughts then abt your F.A. Dept and a post-
Script to my encouter-sessions w/ yr brass.
A wit once sd "you get the politicians you deserve"
I wld append its no different viz universitys.
And the more so when brass doesn't honour the simple
Fact that a dept. usually acts in their own best
Interests–apart frm the fact that a dept. ought to
Know their deepest needs, intimately. Brass like
The rest of us ought to reach out beyond specialism
To be truly responsible. I want to say right out
That I thought them ignorant abt the Art they
Proposed (behind the scenes) to legislate and cannot
Respect their decisions on anyone's behalf– –least
Of all your dept. In over 15 yrs of teaching I dont
Know of another occasion when brass denied   yes
Denied the unanimous wishes of an entire dept.
They'll get whats comin' to them for it!

    Don   Theres no future in academia
    none– –except sinecure. Theres
    no place to be particularly in/among
    the shelter'd trees   UNLESS your
    as they say willing to go out on to
    the end of the topmost branch   and
    feel the terror the exhilaration of its
    swaying. Don a university F.A. Dept.
    ought to be the place where We can test
    the real world on our fingertips our
     tongues. Thats where the nectar is
    Don–We all of us have a honey'd head.

Don   Everyone makes History (together
Its Everyman's biz.
Don   History's a huge mind-graffiti scrawled on
Earth's porous crust with sticks   stones

And ball point pens. Its a/th Mind flashing images
on a giant panavision screen.   Don
Whats your slice of it ?
Your history– –as much as any Gowan's
Don   None-of-us are (Hopefully
Impervious to change: Some want to hide in
The false comfort of their incredulity– –
From the unimaginable therefore terrifying drift
Of Time/Space   as tho they had their backs
Up against the pyramids forever.
Others want to keep in among the thick-of-things
With all the stoppers out. Yeah your
Isolation on that blimey island   (a twitch you
All made me feel as 'real') is
Perpetuated by the shelter'd grove bullshit of
Your tweedy brass. One day They'll
Find a debris-strewn coast inhabited by ghosts
With PH Ds rusted on their shrouds and
There'll be nothing but the wind
To button up their emptiness . . . . with.

To INSIST: yr Dean has as they say
A BIG JOB   tho I dont for a moment think that
Its any larger than yrs or mine. Apropos
the art biz its my sense that the old free-enterprise
Insistence on dollars and cents acumen doesn't
count for much and even if it did I wouldn't
Necessarily respect it. I am more interested in yr
Dean's willingness to overcome his stupidity
Viz the arts and its web of intricate relationships.
To wit yr dean is not more useful   therefore
Truly interesting than the movements of his mind– –
Outwards, enables. And so it is with all of us.
The Bauhaus was the dream of what an art school cum
F.A. Dept. ought to be. Almost everyone used to
Say WOW thats it thats the working model. BUT it dont
Happen without yr Gropius your Klees and Kandinskys.

Its sd they fought for the integration of all
Technos/Art/Life– –whc I also believe in
But theres no going backwards   I'm not interested
In yr Garvies or Gowans British Arts and Craft

Curriculums . . . . A dying kultur N.A. style democracy
Ought not worship a previous Death.
The Pacific Rim Kultur proposes another curriculum
One it is our biz to know, thoroughly.

       and John John has his own rhythms
       they're there in the clear spaces between
       his stammerings. Administration whc
       bugged him is no more than a simple ability
       to attend to whats at hand–as tho it
       mattered as much as what isn't to hand to
       be accomplisht   til tomorrow.

              (frm Eugene Guillvec
              translated by Denise Levertov

       Eternity never was lost
       what we did not know was how to translate it
       into days   skies   landscapes   into words
       for others   authentic gestures   but holding on
       to it for ourselves   that was not difficult
       and there were moments when it seemed clear to us
       we ourselves were eternity

Don I have the thot that
most of our media including the electronics
exists to enable us as artists to
do what we have always done. I, for one
see no other reason for these
innumerable extensions of our body our
nervous systems   than the telling
of a Fable/ Fiction/ Allegory/ History/ Pome
Your/ His/ Mine: Storied Life.

Lovely Lady/Friend in Monreale writes:
"your nine by nine black Noctua hangs upstairs
next door to Gaston Lachaise's amazing
bronze ORIFICES: PROTUBERANCES: FECUNDITIES"

abt '64 I wrote this for G.L. His Women:

       Gaston Lachaise
       you who knew her by her orifices

                    called her 'the mountain'
                    tell those who would harm her How
                    you made bronze sing   her
                    praises   how the shine in her hair
                    left its tracings on her
                    sculpted form . and Gaston add this
                    that her tears will wash
                    the dirt out of any man's eyes

Don   Why dont you stop playing their games?
Why let them define the rules of a game they barely
Comprehend?   WHY?   WHY? are you wasting your
Time doing anything but what the furthest reaches of
Your mind   enables?
                       Why Bother, Brother

for the S a f e w a y   G e n e r a t i o n

"Going into a department store and buying a fake to
hang on your walls is out; the in-thing is to have originals
on your walls. They want a large painting for over the
couch framed for about ninety dollars and that can only be
mass-producecl Art. Many of our customers come to our
galleries with a swatch of rug or drapery or a sketch of a
wall and try to match it with a painting. As long as
the colour is right its Ok with them. You could show them
a red Goya and they wouldn't buy it. The normal mark-up
is about two hundred percent – whatever the traffic will bear.
The prices can range from under a dollar to over a hundred
but the subject matter tends to be the same everywhere.
Nearly everyone's first painting – that is everyone who buys
their first painting from us buys a landscape its always
traditional. After that people branch out into seascapes but
portraits sell worst of all because people dont want some
one looking down at them from over their mantelpiece.
Abstract and Impressionistic Art doesn't sell well in Central
Pennsylvania – but nudes are coming up fast in popularity
because people are not as shy as they used to be
about putting them on their walls or in their homes. Size is
important as colour or subject – we handle nine sizes. The
artists whether European art students or employees of
art factories in Hong Kong or Taiwan are usually paid on a
piece work basis – although one California wholesaler sd
he had contracts with nine artists who were supplying him with
one hundred and fifty paintings a month each. Our buyers
are usually young married couples furnishing their first homes
or elderly couples furnishing retirement apartments."

"MASS PRODUCED JUNK GRABBING BIG SLICE OF ART BOOM"

                              (the Vancouver Province 1970 headline sez

1923-Granville St.
Vancouver BC
11/ 1/ '70

Dear Lorraine Monk

       sum thots abt the photos in
       the B.C. Almanac Show.
       Almanacs purport to be among
       other things
                prognostications
       for the year ahead– –

As one of the photographers in
the B.C. Almanac Show who cant be there w/ you
at the opening   I want to say its got to
be a noteworthy occasion if only to show HOW
15 B.C. Photographers S-E-E. The issue is
what image/s particularize place/s. Our place
happens to be B.C.

The job of the Almanac Photographs– –
and I want to insist upon this precisely because
politics the mendacity of power 'hides'
such facts: is How Our Faces Our Very Acts Occur
in/among these RAIN/ FOREST/ TREES   this
marg at the edge of the Pacific these mountains.
like We all love the accompaniments.

if B.C.A. dont give a large 15 volume slice of
INFORMATION (if not) REVELATION   on at least 2 levels

1/ ample evidence of 'where' 'how' 'why' We do
what we choose to do   in B.C. circa 1970

2/ the manymany ways all-of-us are into photo/
graphic/ processes viz P-E-R-C-E-P-T-I-O-N-S . . . .

then BURN (BABY) BURN All my inconsequential
evidence.

abt: *(so-called)* d-i-r-t-y   p-i-c-t-u-r-e-s

>luvly flip friend in Monreale sd
>"porno/ shit/ smut– –s just dirt man specks of it
>on your retina." to wit: its impossible to
>make/ take a clear image   make any kind of imagining
>clear without cleansing your lens. even an in-
>finitesimal speck of dirt can ruin an image   all I-
>mages including
>   S-w-e-e-t L-o-r-r-a-i-n-e
>however   I do object to a Hughie Hefner
>making a midas mint out of her air-brusht pubes– –
>if anything is obscene its his Penelopes for
>the new breed of high-rise puritans.
>.
>
>my own part in the show is
>an attempt to fit a complex number of images
>*together* that might reveal   all of
>the intricacy in the dance between Nature
>and the Human
>   The Pictures of the Imago-Mundi
>   - - - - - - - - - - - - - - - - - -
>
>>These words are mere captions
>>to the IMAGE/S in B.C. Almanac Show
>
>>Like the images in the books
>>these words aren't worth the paper
>>theyre printed on unless they
>>tell what they have to In/And thru
>>themselves, entire .
>
>and dont it continue to be
>as they say 'true'   that you can lead
>a horse to water but you cant
>make him drink   unless he wants to
>
>– –to have returned the images to
>the world   and be able to say "have a good
>look at them I'm going out for a beer"
>sez it.
>
>   yrs. for more *prognostications– –*

fo r   **Paul Blackburn**
'sT h e W a t c h e r s

"the one" she sd
"you stroked clits with"

the left hand
fool's

finger tip
left . . . / bereft . . .

on a cedar plank
the 'sudden' trauma . . .

the A W E full
dis member ment . . .

FOOL! FINGER!
VOICES!

(Boxing Day
December 1970– –)

.

"O Cronus

god of the middle finger,

the fool's
finger"

have I paid for my
foolish ways . . . ?

4th Avenue Dream : for John Newlove
----

in the faded-pink wallpaperd room: i dreamt
i'm atop of a wind-swept plateau   surrounded by a host
of hooded and huncht grotesques   moaning through
their painted grimaces. (Goya's Witchs Sabbath   seen as
through a delirium). then   as if commanded– –each
in turn leapt over the edge. peering down i could see them
parachuting downwards   touch the grassy plain below
and burst into a flaming petalled flower.–its my turn I'm
croucht at the end of a long corridor formed by their
wind-rackt bodies   their painted grimaces unchanged . . . when
a voice like the wind's sd "you are too slow and too halt
you have misst your chance." turning to where i thought
that voice had come from –there was only the hissing wind
the boulders the mounds of them and high high overhead– –
black birds (heaven's vultures) SCCCRRREEEEETCHT

                                      1964
                         Vancouver – – – – –
                                      1971

16 CEDAR LAMINATES

S-h-a-p-e RED CEDAR ELLIPSES .
sandwich the shaped ellipses together .
shape the sandwicht ellipses with sandpaper files & plane .
then join these shaped & sandwicht ellipses to suit .
sandpaper (further) to smoothness fingers know .
clean and varnish 5 times   using wet/dry sandpaper be-
tween each coat . wax . & polish .

add: cedar's pungency . shavings . slivers .
& one lost index fingertip .

        ful-
           sum
                Task:
      hands
           eyes
              cedar

   s t i r

  Air / Space

   .

   gratis

& DONT LOOK BACK! ---'cause therell be some
shaped-thing stirring right under your nose !
_ _

Calgary Feb. '71

Dear Claudia and Francois

    .... this will be a one handed letter 'cause
i had an accident on boxing day .... i cut off my left
hand middle finger tip pushing a board thru the
overarm radial saw . whats left of the finger *pulses*
tho i cant see it all bandaged up . whata way
of finding out the balance of power changes with
such a loss . now it is my right hand thats stronger
as tho it incorporated the lost fingertip . and
there are all those simple things the left hand did
whc has been shifted– –such as typing with the
right hand first finger only . dismemberment: loss
of a part of one's ego .... H O W   A R E   Y O U ?

Glad you discover'd Gary Snyder he's worthwhile dis-
covering . and go on discovering pomes (and poets– –
that way you will go on a discovery of your many selves
like how it keeps on happening to me, etc . Y E S
why not make your own book of poems all parts of it:
motto K E E P W H O L E . and and you know I will
recommend U to 'whomever' for just about 'any thing'
CEL would do, etc .

Francois– –I wouldn't give a damn if you were even a
F/L/Q . this country belongs if it belongs to any
body   the I N D I A N S . we're both Foreigners   or
like 'him' (nonetheless) natives.

ahhhh the image of Susy Lake floats at eye-level
thru the grass haze and another image of the Detroit Whiz Kid
joins it . S U S Y as Pink Floyd commemorates her an
encore . I once upon a time knew (another) Susy a
Nishimoto I fell for during the 2nd W.W. almost 30 yrs
ago ... .Shit! such correlatives must be an old
man's game 'like' how they knit time/space/love into a
thick cloth of the loveliest hue s, imaginable . ya– –
and Hugh is a part of the weave a kinky colour standing
out a bit above some of the others . Here its cold
enuff to freeze my nuts off, etc : MEMORIES WARM ME UP .

lovely friend Gerry Gilbert reads at Sir George . I've taken the liberty of giving him your address . Gerry can tell you a lot abt the image 'cause he uses it as a door

'Comments' on yr poems 'cause you askt

you slept
in a perfumed room
i lay under
a christmas tree
both, are
kinds of fragility
/

not 'highs'– –non-image
say what 'it' is
/

as above

your 'life'– –impossible
my 'blood'– –ya ya ya ya and a red corpuscle to u too
'waves in the sea'– –tired old horse
/

in father's letter

Winter's wind– –
leaves a silent scripture
in the topmost
branches

or theres got to be another way of
sayin' what Pa sd
/

like yr wee love poems best
put them together w/   or without title. or
just a small title for 'em

'interludes'– –too abstract for me
sure sounds mellow tho
/

puttin' folks down aint yr cup of tea
/

W.C.W.s injunction
"not in ideas but in things" sez it

Ezra's polemics on poetry
unexcelled. read him on IMAGE/S

2/

F r a m e s
been used by Daphne Marlatt one of
our best
         (Ryerson and Black Sparrow
         for her books
/

After, Basho– –wld take guts
/

we wanted
to be inside of
each other
that last day
in the old
house I– –
fell asleep you
painted
/

dont care for 'silver curl her bitch' etc
/
know = NOW
I liked = THEN
/

for Old Mother Earth, 1970

generous– –
to a fault
while
pneumatic?faces

eat you up– – – – – –o tedium
/

Dont HURRY / HUSSLE or WORRY A POEM
Keep in thar w/ *the astonishments*

                         emanations
                         frm a long lost finger-tip

                                    frm the snow-covered
                                    Crystal of the Foothills
                                    Mid-winter '71 Alta

Dear Brad

    I have said that you mean more to me than
all our dumb contentions   which thot has me
peckin' away w/ one finger of right hand.
the left hand the one with out its index finger
tip waves a tender Hullo. O Brad dismember-
ment of even the least part of oneself ALTERS
all sense-ratios thruout the organism. I– –
aint interest'd in G.S. anymore not even its
contentions *but* if it enables you to get a few
cogent things said and in the week by week
act-of-response/ abilities YOU come more and more
into your own sweet-mouthings its an OK gig
better than ugh wassermania.

    (the grey (ghost) plasma of me young manhood lies
under these swirling mounds of frigid snow . . .)

    WHEN did you last piss into a suburban Calgary
snowbank?– –I did just last night under a livid
green street lamp I dribbled hot yellow pee on
to green tinged snow-bank . . . . stood back as tho I
might be able to decipher its frozen hieroglyph– –
but the oncoming snow wiped it out.

    (this pancake flat place is so freighted w/ my
hungry adolescence I go abt in mid-winter
with my shades clipped on. Still   theres that O
O MY GAWD MOTHER MARY SHEER BLUE SKY   TAUT
ACROSS MY PAINTER'S EYE!)– –Ah the all-blue E
Iliptical paintings I did in '67 '68 had a touch
of   immeasurable blue   tippt into them.

    see U and Others at the Cecil   when

one last variation   on
The 4 V a r i a t i o n s/ for Victor Coleman

4 H a n d s

I searcht
another man's images
and found my
longlostmiddlefinger tip
sheathed in a
dismember'd glove

with the forest
unravelling
through moist fingers.
the negative– –
held up to the light
revealed a half-
forgotten finger-print.

embalmed
the finger-tip
reveals no copyrighted
ownership nothing
but the original
finger-print/ whorls

and A   F i n g e r

in the dream a sky corridor w/ numbered doors
each door has a glove nailed over its number. I am
running from door to door pulling the glove off
each door– –to read its number. beyond what seemed
the last door the number that held its secret   a
neon finger-tip pointed towards another and yet an-
other door. O my Dream! my Finger-tip! my Door!

T i p

. . . . if you stroke her clit with it
D O N T A B U S E   I T !

                    circa:February '71
                    Calgary Alberta

Howdy Mermaid– –

            if you'll send me a packet of
            your loveliest scales   I'll send you
            Louie Riel's original snowshoes.
            then, while you cascade down a mountain
            I'll splash abt the aquarium .

did i mention i found Bill Aberhart's gum boots in
a 8th avenue second hand store?   the in-steps were
stufft with faded promissory notes signed by Mr. S.C.
himself. i am having the notes framed and his boots
mummified for Madame Tussaud's Wax Works .

                hallelujah   Im a bum
                hallelujah   bomb'd again

.

Jim you sd flies circles around your other men .
(flap flap flap . . . . flop)

Mike drove you wild on his 750cc black honda .
(goddamned black leather stud yankee hog)

while the fungi poet of Roberts Creek sang in your ear .
(and your hand wrote his slug songs down)

then, theres your ole yellowstoned painter fiend– –
(who's sign is a cough, cloud & a smile)

he wouldnt be caught dead or alive   jammin' your hive.

.

                O Mermaid I am a found poem
                or a plumb bob. tell me which be me .

thanks for checking out my lost Sony:
hope its grabbin' up esoteric messages to
massage M. McLuhan's catholic ears .

                yrs: for A L L
                the beauty you can embrace
                without searing yr
                    fin/ tail/ scales/ etc.

                    2/ 8th/ '71
                   Calgary Alberta

O Hugh eeee

    . . . . i cant git ajob in B.C. in 1971 a.d.
thus i am teachin' one semester   here in Deadpan
Calgary. from my 12th story office window i
can see the snow-cappt Rockies a hundred miles away,
with no cumulative-shit cloud overhead. which
is abt all i can say for the place .

this is to let you know that i am gonna need a job
come Fall and   you can bend a few ears to such
a simple pragmatic fact: (tho i know that buggers cant
be choosey)   i definitely prefer   a short term'd
High Salaried Job   in either/or   painting/ sculpture/
poetry/ photography/ dope/ & the perils of Concept
Art. like you name it i'll tell you if i cant/ wont .
that teaching job could be 'anywhere' North
of the 49th peril,   from sea onto sea .

will you tell Doc Morton, Dottie C. & Ron Bloom
including D. Burton the garter belt kid .

.

Liz have you read Kate Millett's book abt which
a milquitoast critic sez ". . . its like having your balls put
thru a washing machine wringer." i haven't and   after
that review what decent/living/North/American/guy is gonna
pay thru the nose for her kind of prose. really?   more–
she cites jean Genet as among the few males who have under-
stood a woman's debasements. Oh! Our Lady of the Flowers–
i dont know what you are abt but i am sure you are.

p/s how many cigarette holes you got in yr rosey-coloured
chesterfield   now ?

.
    . . . . anyhow we all have Montreal   (in mind)   together.
you 2 ought to be able to keep it warm. my breath if
i face East and blow   wont even get as far as Regina . . . .

2/ 10/ '71
FlatbushCalvary
Alberta

Dear Chris and Viv

  – – – its dementable how seldom i get to see
my friends . . . . left, as i am with bereft-images of
all of them i am not comforted . nursing such
thoughts here in howCowTown i would nonetheless confess
that 'once upon a time' there were *many* . . . . and i
aint been goin' out much 'cause theres the fact of my
youth the blackalleys where i collect'd cardboard
boxes and bottles the "fuck you jap" ethnic-pokes the
east Calgary ghetto, immigrant's yoke my Ma and Pa
bear the burdens of. later, during WW2 i workt for
several summers in Gros Cap NWT as a fish processor.
Alec suave ole Alec boss fish-cutter from Winnipeg made
out all one summer with a Meti girl Margaret she
had one wither'd arm and fell for him fell hard as hell
for old Alec and followed him to Edmonton at the end
of the season–Where he told her to fuck-off goddamned
filthy Indian . . . . and i i loved her loved her
arrogance with all my naive virginity . bereft-IMAGES– –
a fool's obsessions . it is impossible to love this
this yesterday place its the impossibility of looking in
the rear view mirror–without another face to stand in
the presence of . to wit   i am loveless and loathe my
self . . . 'bereft-images' a dwarf hides behind .

Chris when i think of how our friend/ship nonetheless
survived all the fiberglasfulminations I'm grateful– –
and just yesterday while toking up at Jos's place he sez
"Ha ya wanta see somethin'?" reaching up on a high shelf
he took down a batter'd box with 'those' shrivelled up A
pples– –they'd shrunk so much you cld cup 'em in one hand
and i remember your sayin' how they didnt rot because of
the aforemention'd obnoxious fumes . talk abt sun-ripe
prunes or its Adam's (original) apple curs't   and think
of the creases the wrinkles we've all earned in the same
span of time

         somethin' to ease the unease of
        these wintry blights
                  these yearnings
    etc .

2/ 18th/ '71
Calgary Alberta

dear B r i a n

    . . . have'nt seen you much lately. have'nt been
able to do more than merely look at you.
lately, i have'nt been able to see much of any
thing including myself– –it is'nt because
i dont want to but because i have'nt been capable.
stoned, stunned or whatever Im always left
despite my good intentions) with my own lament-
able hang me ups my frequent bouts of dire
depression . O Bri gettin' out of the way of
one's own tentacles of deprecations
dont get any easier despite multitudinous middle-
age prat-falls . here in Flatbush Calgary i've
been self-conscious abt such matters such mindless
flaps   soursouls like yrs truly can be a prey
for. has anything changed really changed? &. &.
always the tender provisional answer   thats
the merest whisper   is Yes/No or Think &. Think
again. before answering Either/ Or .

.
'cause of the fragile wound on left hand i am
typing this letter to you with my right one only.
and its sure enough true that two hands with
ten whole fingers is better than the same two hands
with only nine and three quarter fingers. i mean
the definitive loss of one wee finger-tip alters
all the ratios between left and right hand– –
not to mention how the rest of the body has had to
make subtle accommodations. still   there continue
to be lovely occasions when the intactness of whats
left of me   sings a bitter-sweet melody to that
longlost fingertip   whence a fulfathomfive S m i l e
blesses the space that lost fingertip as matter/
form   once upon a time fill'd.

.
take care of yourself. and Heather whom
we both know   each, in our way.
Ah Bri . . . aint Life g-r-a-n-d aint we all Here
to prove thru all our acts that aweful
fact.
        your cusp rind babel friend

2/ 19/'71
Calgary Alberta

Dear S h e i l a

T h a n k s   f o r
t h e   c o p i e s   o f   W h i t e   P e l i c a n

Ah the apparition of one's voice . . . / words in
a magazine and the pleasure of finding one's self
with strange bed-fellows: which at least is as
anticipatory as innumerable ofttimes n-u-m-i-n-o-u-s
Encounters in real-life so called . of course– –
I read and re-edited it frm cover to cover and re-
reading (again) what i seemed to have extempore-
humourously utter 'd (after the taping the transcrip-
tion and subsequent editing) . . . I thought "yeah . . . i
guess thats what i must have once said, therefore,
meant . . . if not what the hell are these sounds/ words
all about and . . . who? who is saying them?" Sheila
if even a small hunk of e-n-e-r-g-y moves in/ and thru
me via muthus/ breath– –over and into an other the
whole thing e/g W.P. and its various brood will have
at least, succeeded.

page 24 of La GranDada Richter's Dada/ art and anti-art
quotes Goethe's Faust ". . . if ever I say to the
passing moment, linger for your beauty's sake– –then
you can put me in chains, then I will freely go
                                        to hell'

      (will the real M.M. get his nose out of
      the stacks and stop writing abt the death
      of literacy. will he tape his final will
      and testament or take all of it with him– –
      to a post-Gutenberg Galaxy ?)

– –may the white pelican bless you
– –may we save it from our perversities

– –may its namesake s-o-a-r !

2/ 20/'71
Calgary   Alberta

Dear Terry Fenton

. . . . I have been an indifferent care-taker of
my paintings / my past etc. A large part
of what I painted thru tfl the mid-50s I destroyed
lost or simply abandoned. Even as I made them
I knew they were terrible. Later I simply kept on
painting over them. The salvages were as often
as not given to friends. Claude Breeze   thus
inherited several canvases which he promptly made
over into 'women in the landscape'. And tho
I know where a few of 'em are they're not in any
of the country's galleries. So . . . . whats left
to make a choice frm? Norah McCullough has one small
Emma Lake W/C plus a ducco on paper Mexican land-
scape. Cliff and Pat Wiens have work from this
period in their collection. Bloore has a fine W/C.
Lochhead and McKay cld also have works? Both
the Saskatoon Arts Centre and the Arts Board might
have something or other? The College has one I
gave for the collection when I left. . . . . Ah! my
derelictions.
　　　　　　　– –Remember that I came straight to
R.C. frm Mexico thus my work (inevitably?) shows its
influences. They are readily discernable. Or   at
least I know this as I carry such sources abt where-
ever I go. (You in yr way also also do, dont you?)
I count as among the most important paintings those
I did in Regina late 50s– –the all-white ptgs of
whc there are abt a dozen. I do have some of these
and can let you have them. And thats abt it– –
as far as 'memory' serves. Like I say I am a lousy
caretaker of even memorie's remorseless processes.

'if' for whatever (un) reason you want
to see me in Regina   you cld invite me to come and
read all of you some poetry. I am an old pro
at least the equal of belated 19th century types like
St. Andrew– –Afterall we're only a blast of wind
a-part .
　　　　　　　say Hi to the remnants of the Gang

2/ 21/ '71
Calgary Alberta

dear Mermaid

    if this C h i n o o k shld continue I'll have to
put away my snowshoes and great buffalo overcoat .
then I shall get out my roller skates and oil 'em up
to go zooming along the old Crowchfld Trail . yr
laurel/ hardy tree-poet waits breathlessly for the lst
crocus to push out of the thawed sod of Scotchman's
Hill in East Calgary. He will pluck it to place beside
the nearest gopher hole–to entice the little bugger
out   so that together we can salute golly green giant
S P R I N G .
                    sittin' here 14 stories above this
                    my gawd have you forsaken me 'grandeur'
                    call'd Rocky Mountain Foothills   i
                    feels Sarah (good ole) Sarah Binks at my
                    side . she stands there ready & willing
                    to prod my quill lest i miss a goodly meta-
                    phor or sunny simile .

(that was yesterday . . .

S A R A H   W H E R E   T H E   H E L L   A R E   Y O U – –

. . . . . today of all days. damned bitch she's never a
round when i truly need her. i wanted to ask her as
a proper god fearing woman whether or not she thot
that the word G O D is the first and last metaphor for
all our earthly lamentations, etc .

– –if your radar-proof/ poet fiend lover named
Slim Pickins dont take good care of you tell him I'll
send Sarah with God's Wrath to make him toe the line .
Sarah sez she'll turn S.P. into a mere slime trail sans
slug . incidently Sarah thinks all mermaids gotta be
vestal virgins 'cause they aint got a pee- hole .

dear Fin & Tail– –
if you stare up at vasty blue sky
above these foothills
long enough– –it will suck up in
to itself All that breaks
our wee hearts into tiny pieces of
regretfulnesses .

does the vasty blue Pacific do the same
for a mermaid ?

                        2/ 22nd/ '71
                        Calgary   Alberta

dear Danielle

    .... hows the wee F r e n c h f l ow e r there
among the grey civil savants ? hope you're doing better
than i am here in howcowtown where i got called a
"dirty fucken arsehole Indian . . ."– –from a cruising car
on eighth avenue alias main street .
    .

S-h-i-t ! – –didnt get my mail forwarded from Vancouver
so long   i misst the trip to the Maritimes   you
were so kind to write me abt. was i ever pisst off !
the more so as I've never been East of Monreale .
    .

– –if there happens to be another such occasion   please
be sure to phone me long-distance   ok .
    .

– –one day I'll be in Ottawa   tho goodness knows
what for and   stop by to give you a warm/stoned/HUG.

               my forlorn gloves thank you.
               my hands thank you.
               they say thanks for the memory . . .
               .

               any day now a C h i n o o k will come
               to prod my lethargy. when   that happens
               even Ottawa wont seem so far away .

2/ 22nd/ '71
Calgary Alberta

Dear Dennis Reid

    have received the material. this letter
belatedly) acknowledges the fact
          T h a n k y o u .

and it seems that the bulk of the detective work on
The Group of Seven Era   is an accomplisht fact .
if i hadnt fail'd miserably the international corres-
pondence school course on how to become a Private
Eye lst Class   that is if i had done my home work   i
might have been capable of adding a nicety or two
to the sum of the evidence 'but' sleuthing i keep find-
ing out is not my bag. nor is pro/con : fact/fiction
—as a contention. theres a wee bite of circumstantial
evidence in all the volumes of victoriana which i
keep searchin' for. as far as our friend T.T. goes he
of course can look after himself. nothing i write
about the two of us will at this late date distract frm
his legendary status as a genuine Canadian hero—
not even a sturdy Jack Pine or a Winnie Trainor .

and while i am onto it i gotta say that goin' thru
the heaps of memorabilia is like wading in a foggy bog—
all that victoria and albert prose gets a bit heavy
without wit's levities. my provisional conclusion is that
the dullest moments of a History correspond to the
Historian's prose. another take on it is that no period
can be more lively than the prose of that period and
the Historian's use of it. the underlying assumption be-
ing that all moments of Historical Time and the acts
thereof are equal each to each other. furthermore it
assumes a non-hierarchical continuum of acts-in-time/space.
like 'who' is telling the story with liveliness coupl'd
to optimum insight? if The Group is to be singled out
from the Canadian Shield Trees they painted its gotta be
in the telling particulars of The Story. i mean
how come Gibbon's decline-and-fall-of-you-know-what con-
tinues to enthrall. or a Edgar Allen Poe's Tell-Tale
Heart goes on throbbin' even as the Godfather's mob stomps
all over it on television.   like, how come?

and i feel close to my Paleolithic Brothers. we both
know the fretful thing 'art' is and how its a love/lone
bread and butter necessity in the teeth of Life's per-
versities. like he had his love and fear and i've got my
own fearsome loves. and i have that sense that both
of us want to conjure up a magical world–to let fall
ever so gently upon the nonetheless real world lying
just outside of the cave's maw .

meanwhile: Im teaching a semester here in Flatbush Calgary
because my kinda art dont pay has never paid more than
the minimum wage. and thus Im faced four times a week with
a bumper crop of the latest freshmen and women. Im appal-
l'd by the sheer numbers of 'em with my gawd! what sense of
a vocation do they have anyhow! i have always disliked the
burden of such quantity in teaching and look back to the yrs
at Regina College with its small handful of students as
the best possible occasion for the kind of learning art wld
seem to propose. nonetheless a modicum of enthusiasm en-
ables me to carry on and it must be that a few of them will
come to know what they are truly given to do and simply
go on doing it.

    remember me to your
    o my gawd is she ever tall Wife
    and write if you want to

late Feb. '71
Calgary Alberta

Dear Victor/ Sarah

    . . . . the thot of how so few of the things I've made
continue to excite me   worries me. and the thot
of the things I still have to make and the loss of
that excitement   troubles my sleep. one day I'll
get up to find all-of-it together with the works of
my peers gone as a new generation of vituperative-
ones will have torn the garlands of the may-pole and
strewn our graves with them. meanwhile back in one
of his crumbling chateaus Picasso corrodes into dust
as his old buddy Jamie Sabartes risen from a sur-
realnomadsland finds the old modmaster's huge black eyes
staring up at him frm the heaving floor .

(The Human Condition/ Hannah Arendt):

"We mentioned before that this reification and material-
ization, without which no thought can become a tangible
thing, is always paid for, and that the price is life it-
self: it is always the "dead letter" in which the "living
spirit" must survive, a deadness from which it can be
rescued only when the dead letter comes again into contact
with a life willing to resurrect it, although this re-
surrection of the dead shares with all living things that
it, too, will die again . . ."

derelict thots frm the wind-swept Foothills

```
                              O
                        l i g h t


                             .
                         l i g h t
                   f o o t : l i g h t : f a l l
      i n g )          l i g h t          ( i n g
                   f a l l : l i g h t : f o o t
      i n g )          l i g h t          ( i n g
                   f o o t : l i g h t : f a l l
      i n g )          l i g h t          ( i n g
                   f a l l : l i g h t : f o o t
      i n g )          l i g h t          ( i n g
                   f o o t : l i g h t : f a l l
      i n g )          l i g h t          ( i n g
                   f a l l : l i g h t : f o o t
      i n g )          l i g h t          ( i n g
                   f o o t : l i g h t : f a l l
                         l i g h t
                            ..
                         f o o t

                    f o l l o w i n g

                              O
```

Dear Michael and Louise

    tho I went to Toronto the Good right after
leaving art school (49) and lived lst
behind the Children's hospital across from the
late Angelo's   2nd at 272-Parliament St.
and thru-out all the subsequent years I visited
as well as exhibited there *Toronto* even w/
the vivacity of its swollen ethnic communities
doesn't mean much to me. Michael does that
make me another un-WASP orphan? I've read that
in this/our post nuclear age we are "the last
people of the earth " And it feels that way– –
these days of the decline and fall of Capitalism
's veracities. Like how our very voraciousness
(unwittingly?) leads us down the garden path.
I say this knowing that I am hapless in the
teeth of idiot/idolatries **tho** my youthful anger
remains unappeased.
                    after the 2nd W.W.
my father planted a willow sapling in front of
the only house he ever owned. It stood on a long
curving street full of nearly identical units– –
without a single tree. Now that willow is taller
than all of the houses. My father taught me
home is where you've planted a tree . . . . but I a
slow learner have only come to know it

O Louise I too have stood on Yesterday's curb and
watched the harried Present hussle by– –as if
I had no part to play in its A W E F U L L ex-
crescences

        say Hi to Ron B. for me

frigid March '71
Calgary Alberta

Dear Ken

Met Joe Plaskett on Yonge Street— —
outside of Ab's Gallery. We're always a little em-
bare-arsed a little be-mused even as we're
shaking hands and almost in one voice say "imagine
meeting you Here, etc." Anyhow, we invite each
other to a cup of coffee and say ordinary thinks to
one/an other, politely as hell   before we walk a-
way – –HELL ITS AWFUL TO BE MERELY POLITE!
its always those fucken etceteras. Nonetheless,
Joe is his own man the last genuine Canadian Expatriate
after Morrice. Yeah, He is his own man grown like the
rest-of-us *more so*. Its curious How our image of any-
body wants to remain 'static' even as their own life
whizzes onwards   Joe
in that sense remains the/ same guy I met at Emma
way back in '56. I suppose we will continue to meet
and/or pass one another on the Main Street of Cities
other than our own, forever: Perfect Strangers for
Each/Other–which is its own true thing. Come to think
of it   We (you & I) tend to meet that way more and more.
Those Years my long stemmed friend when we were
all good friends some of the time have gone for good.
I hardly ever see you, Richard, Art or Ron   anymore.
Even the Can/Art Gripevine dont send any messages thru
abt u u u and u   except Art who continues to JERK
even as We who have never had a foot inside of an asylum
have been nonetheless 'strait-jacket'd'. joe's workshp
in '56 all the way over to Barney's Death in Manhattan a
decade or more later marks the breadth of the period.
YEAH–Those were the days my friend when we all waltz'd w/
sweet Emma Lake. Praise be to Emma Lake who showed us
her green entwinings. And Ernie Lindner, who of all of
us truly woo'd her. He continues to do so even as
Dorothy P. is her true lesbia. Ken if you happen to
hear abt one more young nit who thinks he can give a
good account of Her via other wit's mouthings   tell em
they ought for the sake of   even, the mere facts   talk

to Those who actually slept under her trees
and forgo the 'dumb words' of those who have never
known her. And I have the thot that
all-of-us got our trips together 'then' tho we are still
a few yrs away frm our characteristic work/s. All this
cause I got phlegm on my beard frm the latest re-hash of
our Emma Lake Years.

Yeah   Let 'em ask   even
A Clement Greenberg 'if'   We were not
Already on our way somewhere.
Or   They could ask Ernest Lindentree HOW
She seduced every one of us.
Tell 'em to page John Cage's S-i-l-e-n-c-e-s
Or Art's nightmares. Even Louie the
Caretaker knew Emma well.

    Belgonie!
    Belgonie!

      the gophers
      the high flying kite

    the studio
    I've built 3 more since
    and I'm wondering if I'll build
    anymore . . . . ?

O Long Ken Silver
O Patricia

O Regina
Queen City of my flat dreams

      See you
      in Can/Art or at
      the movies

3/ 5/ '71
Calgary Alberta

Dear Brian Wilson
    at Simon Fraser University

– – – –I've been thinking How shall I find a
teaching position in Vancouver where I wld prefer
to be. It is afterall my moving abt where my
family and friends not to mention the mountains
the trees and the ocean preside. I have kept
in touch with U.B.C.– –its part of the despair but
I haven't a clue whats going on at S.F.U. Thus
this enquiry– –
        can I be of use to S.F.U.?

    since completing a 16 ft. high
    tripartite sculpture for the Canadian
    Pavilion at Expo 70 Osaka   then
    organizing my StonedGloves Exhibition
    for the National Gallery I have
    been putting together a number of
    cedar-laminate sculptures for my Spring
    show at the Bau-Xi Gallery. Which
    makes me a weekly commuter as I am in
    Vancouver 4 days out of 7– –
    talk abt flying high for dear Art's sake!

With nearly 20 yrs of commitment
to 'The Life of the Imagination' I think I can
say I know how to tell the ABCs of Art.
Its what I can do best tho I wld add its never a
displeasure to do other things too. Like it's
all grist for the mill etc.
        Anyhow . . . .now you know
whats been on my mind.

    Harry and Katie with whom Im boarding
    wish to be remember'd

                        3/ 5th/ '71
                        Calgary Alberta

Dear Hugh

    Chris sez you
    and Liz have split. she is studying
    drama in Toronto while you
    go on living in Montreal making sculptures
    and are sad sad   sad. and what can
    a mere friend who has heard abt it 2nd hand say
    to leaven the pain   knowing as he does
    the depth of that despair.
    if i knew i could by the act of writing 'move'
    some of yr pain over   onto myself
    i certainly wld try even tho i know Kant
    couldnt and wrote 15 volumes of philosophy as
    a consolation. dear Hugh these words
    wont give consolement   theyre flat on the page
    bereft of sadness even rage.
    and doesnt it continue to be true that
    our Art's sweet and sour G l a d n e s s e s is
    born out of our incommensurable sadness.
    and what is He or She and their soulful afflictions
    all abt? what heart is not infected? what
    inflection does the mirror wear?
    and what is all the cum weve left on each other's thighs
    abt?   Hugh   I sometimes think that
    Everyman's Heart is scarr'd with a 1000 such
    lacerations   of which you and Liz
    have your share. Dear Hugh Im left (again)
    with questions I've found no answers for   unless
    Heart's Ache is itself an answer . . . .

    nevertheless, Love to both of you
    wherever you are. some of the time my mind will
    hold both of you together   despite the
    adversity of even the weather

3/ 5th/ '71
Calgary Alberta

Dear DocMorton

>. . . it seems i have no way of getting a job
in Vancouver for this coming year. . . how are
my chances at suburban York U.? someone i
cant remember sd York had gone INTERMEDIA– –
is that true? Well, i paint, write poetry, play
the Jew's harp, put on light-shows & other
kinds of happenings. i've taken 1000's of
photographs, know a great deal abt movies, dancing,
rock and roll, hallucinogenic drugs, pot, hash,
and the existential despair of academic conferences– –
all of which happen to occur in my daily life
and hopefully serve the myriad aspects of
my A r t . now i see a rank and file of
upstart Academics doing the same bum politicotrips
i've spent nearly 2 decades putting into perspec-
tive, viz the art of teaching A r t.   after all
these years tenure/ rank/ & sinecure continue to
be boring as ever . anyhow, it seems, that Art
my kind of art does'nt pay and thus my teaching is
going to have to. i dont need to remind you–
that i think Im one of the best teachers in the
biz. just ask those i've taught who go on
doing their thing, particularly them.

the nastiest thing i can imagine abt this HowCowTown
is a herd of shorthorns shitting their way thru
the mirror'd & broadloom'd lobbies of all the ginger-
bread high-rises in town   before disappearing into
huge caverns 'somewhere' in the Foothills .

3/ 5th/ '71
Calgary Alberta

dear Carole Fisher
    (alias the Kits Mermaid

        your cow: town: poet: laureate
        been reading D. L.'s
        re-learning the alphabet & thinkin'
        you might also enjoy it .
        (its a ND paperback)

& you're right abt how we're fouling our hearth .
& the faster we shovel fossils the higher the shit gets .
& already we've dumped on the moon .
& Gulliver is up to his arm pits in mountains of it .
& Martin Luther wld rub our noses in it .
& according to his gospel the Devil is pure shit .
& as a mere child didnt you play stink-finger ?
& foxes Im told always smell their own hole first .
& how does a kind man smell ? whats evil's odour ?
& does fall-out begin with a foul mouth ?
& end with an odourless (last) breath .
& how abt our farts ? shall we stand bare-arsed to winds ?
& whats the odour of the after-life, then ?

if you drive along the trans-canada midway between
Calgary and Lethbridge   then stop and get out
to walk out onto a vasty fenceless field and face
North/ South/ East/ & West you can still get a
mighty big whiff of this fetid earth its fathomless
excrements left by phantom herds of buffalos

        any day now us prairie kids
        will be gettin' out our gopher traps
        & 22's   as grey snow recedes–
        to show brown grass which tells how
        Spring & Summer's Pleasures are
        just around the next wind blown corner .

. . . . next time we meet
Im a gonna keep my mouth shut
and just look at you .
like whats to be said after a
million words anyhow ?

Middle-March Bliz/'71
Calgary Alberta

Dear M i l l y

    . . . given what you put into yr paintings
Id be a fool not to want one. and if you dont
think i've got a heart left for Monreale–
you're crazy as well as mistaken. I've just come
frm Jos's place where we talkt all night abt
all the lovely faces we know there   with yours–
shining out frm among them. your stoned friend
has a wrinkly smile permanently etched on his puss
these days. he never thot to become like Possum
Eliot's Prufrock walkin the litter'd beach wonderin
if he ought to roll up his trouser legs or eat
a peach etc . . . . now i know that Possum was always
an old man   whereas i continue to think i am
younger than aging tells. dearest Milly i continue
to know an aspect of my visibility by the way–
your friendly boat coming sailing into port from
whatever direction and Im standing on the wharf . . .
waving a colourful banner .

        . . . if to paint is to love again
        as old lech H.Miller sez– –
        i will o yes yes i will do it again

3/ 25th/ '71
Calgary Alberta

dear est Mere Maid en Head
    (alias Myrtle Mermaid

    got the fin thanks. do need the other fin soon.
    and. Im dragged by the need to hussle my show for
    late April deadline. like whats more dreary than
    facing such drear limits of time. its the dregs
    & dross of what Im abt the rest of the time. you can
    tell Paul I'll nonetheless have it together then:
    minus one small finger-tip.

    of all the poems in your book i can only re-call
    the DeGaulle one, the last one. it was yrs ago.
    imagine! you've been writing all this time   quietly.
    now its your turn to get up and read to others
    outloud. get up and do it when the time comes. hear-
    ing you read the 5 Tales told me that.

> "people want history to resemble them
> or at least resemble their dreams. happily
> they sometimes have great dreams"
>
> "perhaps politics is the art of putting
> daydreams in their place. nothing serious
> can be done if you bow to daydreams. but
> how can anything great be done without them"
>
> "Stalin told me only one serious thing:
> in the end   only death wins"
>   – –Chas DeGaulle

I am drawing 3 sets of 7 drawings
each set of seven comprising a series of variations.
theyll be silk-screened in 3/4 colours in
an edition of 50. some of 'em might be completed in time
for the show. nothing else to report not even
a wee poem. poems only seem possible when nothing else matters
but the poem itself–surrounded by 24 hrs of concern
for its gestation.

seein' how you're friendly
towards fishermen :

Spring : light / mist
asleep in his boat he grips a 1000 ft. line

match for the biggest whale .
                            – –Setcho 980/1052

March '7 1
Calgary, Alta.
123-Waterloo Drive

sitting near but separate, from one another
their bare feet in shallow pools scoopt out of the
wind and water worn sandstone   she said *the sea*
is inviting us in for a swim and are you coming in?
no i think i'll just sit here and watch you.   we
never do things together she said taking her clothes
off and wading in. he watched her swim out and
remembered when they were first married
swimming with some friends she had swam naked
her ebullience shining on his awkwardness.
it was the water dripping from her naked
body the lank hair and her matter-of-factness that
had intimidated. he sat there trembling as the sun
disappeared behind a cloud bank.   he thought
how right she is–and yet, yet he could do nothing nothing
it seemed about it. he kept his eye on the small dot
far out on the water–he was beginning
to feel a bit anxious for her safety though he knew
she wouldn't overdo it.   now bit by bit
her image grew larger he could see her waving to him–
all all of a sudden she emerged wet and shiny
with a smile on her face she said you really dont
know what your missing. drying herself off
and getting into her clothes she said I'll bet
theres someone coming over the top of the bluff– –
turning we see Peter standing up there smiling. o its
just Peter she said as she wiggled into her jeans–
and Peter walks by behind her. Peter, I said on vacation
theres always a pretty woman getting dressed and a
young man coming up behind her. on the upper-deck
of the Queen of Nanaimo she said you didn't even try

Spring '71
Calgary Alta.

give us this day our daily guilts
----

shld pay my income tax
shld phone Monica and my parents
shld write to my friends every month
shld think abt painting again
shld laugh and cry more often she sd
shld cause as little pain as possible
shld read the O.E.D. a page at a time til the
shld tel my life in rhyming couplets
shld send Hirohito a birthday haiku
shld be more obedient to every whim and fancy
shld provoke demons devils drunkards
and politicians

        Picasso's naked women recline in
        bare unfurnisht rooms . the mirror on the floor
        near the foot of the bed reflects
        the light of her un-sounded sorrows . dawn–
        and the cock on the open window ledge
        salutes the coming of the minotaur . half-man
        half-bull he carries her off to the woods
        where he will fuck her good . the mirror reflects
        the sunlit shimmer on her twisted body– –
        'a repository' of all the arguments meat is
        heir to. Picasso's *cubed women*
        furnish the bare abysmal rooms of my mind .

March '71
Calgary Alberta

Dear Glad-is

      & there are those times of late when I've felt Im
in a kind of Siberia of the Maple Leaf Forever   I mean
aint loneliness grand   aint it the soul's sweet desolation
or   some other banana. The Beatles circa Tallman's parties early
sixties comin' on on my stereo   The Yesterdayness of
a moment   another sense of my all-a-lone-mess. & John curn O Ho
Ohno tellin' me   he dont care for this and he dont care for
that and   me thinkin' yeah Johnny boy   tellit ugh like it is in
yr lemonheart   make another milliondollargoldplatedisc of
yr ol' bleedin' heart. Gladys aint Love grand   & aint our Johnny
Boy some sort of electro-medieval-troubador Hero. Liver-pooh
is gonna be the brand name of catfood Big Apple is licensing
General Foods of Canada   to package & sell them. Jeez Gladeyes
aint the revival of Charlie Chan on tv and them oldenday movies
with Betgrable and Myrnaloy   not to mention 'other' dumb cods
like Williampowell or Waterable, grand. aint movies just another
wee compartment in our IBMaginations   in the ol' soul's
sweet & sour   concatenations. Glad-is   HELL is simply an un-
imaginable sadness. And how is the not unformed one feeling   like
down there where   yr plumbfirmbelly w/ its navel as   the centre
of his universe, is. I used to   in the good ol' days put
my ear to Monica's huger than real belly to feel   a stirring in there
and i did then think that that child and i might never again
be that close—so close only a thin membrane parted Us.   yeah
it was/is merely miraculous. I mean aint it that   Cliff & Glad?
Old hartfortinsurance merchant/poet Wallace Stevens   i think sd
"the world as a fiction aint much different from fiction as
the world" (I'm paraphrasing, of course. Gladys aint that that thot also
part of the sweet & sour old soul's vibes. And, aint it a
thin slice of   gollybrain Olson's History: Young cat askin' "aint
you got any heroes left, now?" I told the shaggylad, "no   not now but
it was just the day before you got yr lst piece of pussy
my hero is Charlie! O Charlie! (Where Are You Now?) Olson". Angelaah
telling Lani and me abt her thing with her Pa   one of those
melding moments I've almost had with you. Her Candor,
matched by the moment-of-death   oldlechgreek Newlove told abt.
 yeah thats another rare   melding moment. Anyhow Im telling Ragmop
all that I thot I knew abt Charles   & in that long-winded act

felt 'his' huger-than-real breath pushing, from behind. Thats it
thats the hero & then some   aint it? This letter is taking twice
as long   typin' w one hand. Anyhow   gollybumgladys   He, it seems is
The Last One (its impossible to make heroes frm the same clay as one's own
peers. i mean, no matter where The Itch comes from   or
goes   you know it. No, for heroes you need an Ol' Sunne
sometimes its gotta be a really old one like,
once upon a time there was a garden call it Paradise etc.
I mean that old w paper-mache figures of Adam &
Eve   our aboriginal heroes & aint Dostoevski's Siberia at least possible
no-matter-how-thin-you-slice-it   a kinda frigid tear
hung on the soul's sweet desperation. Daphne as slender willow Eve
standin' beside her sweet Adam is possible only in
this sense I'm layin' on you: this Gestalt concerning one
lost (kinship) finger. The fact that Im nonpluss'd w love
and yes   did go out &   bought a Playboy to finger her glossy tits
inc how Hughieboy living it (is it?) 'up' says it. & thars
writing/reading/learning man Stan abt whom I mostly feel glowglum / I
think we might make it but dont 'cause for whatever
reason, we cant. And I've been both Leopold & Molly Bloom
'together', in my narrow bed   rapping to myself abt
all the places I've been &   hopefully will 'get to'   & all the sweet
/ sour lovely faces I've seen & held   if for an instant
on a lonelydark street corner   and YES, especially The
Woman held closer-than-close . . . .

Opal, Alberta: Early '40s
left to right: George, Roy, Harry, Joyce, Frank and Irene

                    Early Spring '71
                    Calgary Alberta
Dear Tod

    The hungry-ghosts of our young manhood haunt
this fucken city. Its over 20 yrs since
We both left the farm and came to art school
here. We were, however naive, filld with
the 'apprehensions' of whatever it is that Art
purports to be abt. Do you re-collect the
small painting you did I think you got the idea
along the Elbow River in East Calgary– –it
showed the thick layerd ice with the cold clear
blue/green water running neath it the naked
poplars in the middle distance   etc. And I re-
collect coming to yr basement flat in NE
part of the city after attending church and I'm
imparting what I cld remember of the sermon
as you spoon cold macaroni into yr mouth from an
army surplus mess tin   and yr uh huh skepti-
cism. All this as preamble to the fact that I
enjoyed yr true-life story it held me all the way
thru. Keep diggin' yr own psyche.
                                      Yesterday– –
I read poetry at our old alma mater to a 100
or more shaggy lads and ladies. face-to-face WE
who had no commom ground for recollection– –
let Captain Poetry woo us.

           "ask the cold spring
           what if my poem is deathsongs"

        Denise Levertov)

7/24/'71
Halifax NovaScotia

Dear Mr. G. Dixon

re your numerous letters asking for money– –
the answer is simple I haven't any but I am saving
towards your fee and intend to send it on
when I have it together. I am not hurrying– –
what took fifteen years to put together is not abt
to come undone (even legally) in a few short
days. If you nonetheless want to proceed with our
divorce papers then do so otherwise all three
of us will have to wait. p/s does the hearing date
and subsequent proceedings depend on my payment?
or is it possible to go ahead with it and let me pay
you when I can?

                      meanwhile, Monica is a partner to
                      all of this and she shld be informed
                      of my position. You could send her
                      a copy of my letter or phone whichever
                      way is convenient.

– –whatever you decide to do DONT
  send me another bill!

             yours sincerely,

                        frm the EastCoast of
                        the maple leaf forever,
                        Halifax NovaScotia
                        8/ 23rd/'71
Dear Gerry /Carole

    . . . . am 'i' my own mere answer ?
in the next room Krisy clears her throat she gets up
to go to the bathroom she humms or just sits
quiet as hell hours on end . . . . my ears bent to the signs
of her liveliness, wiggle . We put each day together
knowing what each has to tell is 3/4 hidden– –the small
pleasures the angst of dailynecessities : The Test
of a-young-enough-to-be-my-daughter relationship . Etc.

Halifax is full of grave yards :   the DEAD lie under
foot in the heart of the city . We spent a morning in one
reading the pithy epitaphs We fantasied abt their god
fearing humble-pie lives and how most of them were dead
by forty . as we left the autumn sun pour'd down   thru
the tall elm trees . . . . dappling our face and the tombs a-
like . the 'natives' here call themselves Haligonians– –
"HELLO" "HELLO" "HOWS ROBERTS CREEK
                        THE SECHELT HAVEN?"

Carole I'm counting on you for news of my family . I
haven't written home yet–haven't been able to do so . if
and when you're in the city will you phone Monica and ask
her how how she is doing . . . . and the same for all of my
girls how they are also also doing . . . . I'll get a letter
off to them when I've got more of my shit together and
can handle the burden of it   etc. as soon as that .

meanwhile– –for K I C K S I'm gonna try to get a
Halifax / Vancouver F E S T I V A L, together. . . . .

                    make me a mystery
                    O   S l u g !
                                    a slime trail to
                                        E t e r n i t y
                    a golden-wing'd
                            b-u-g

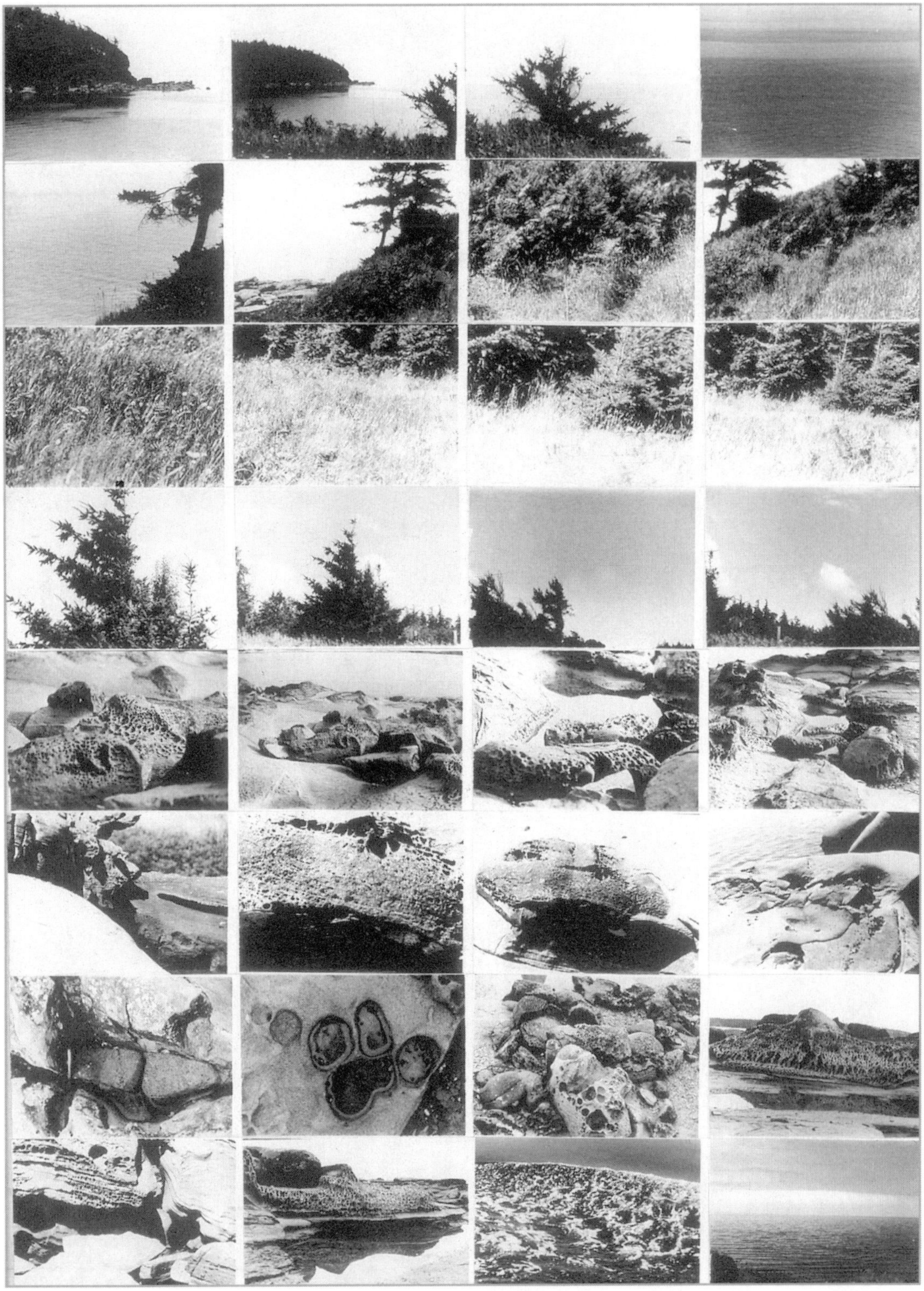

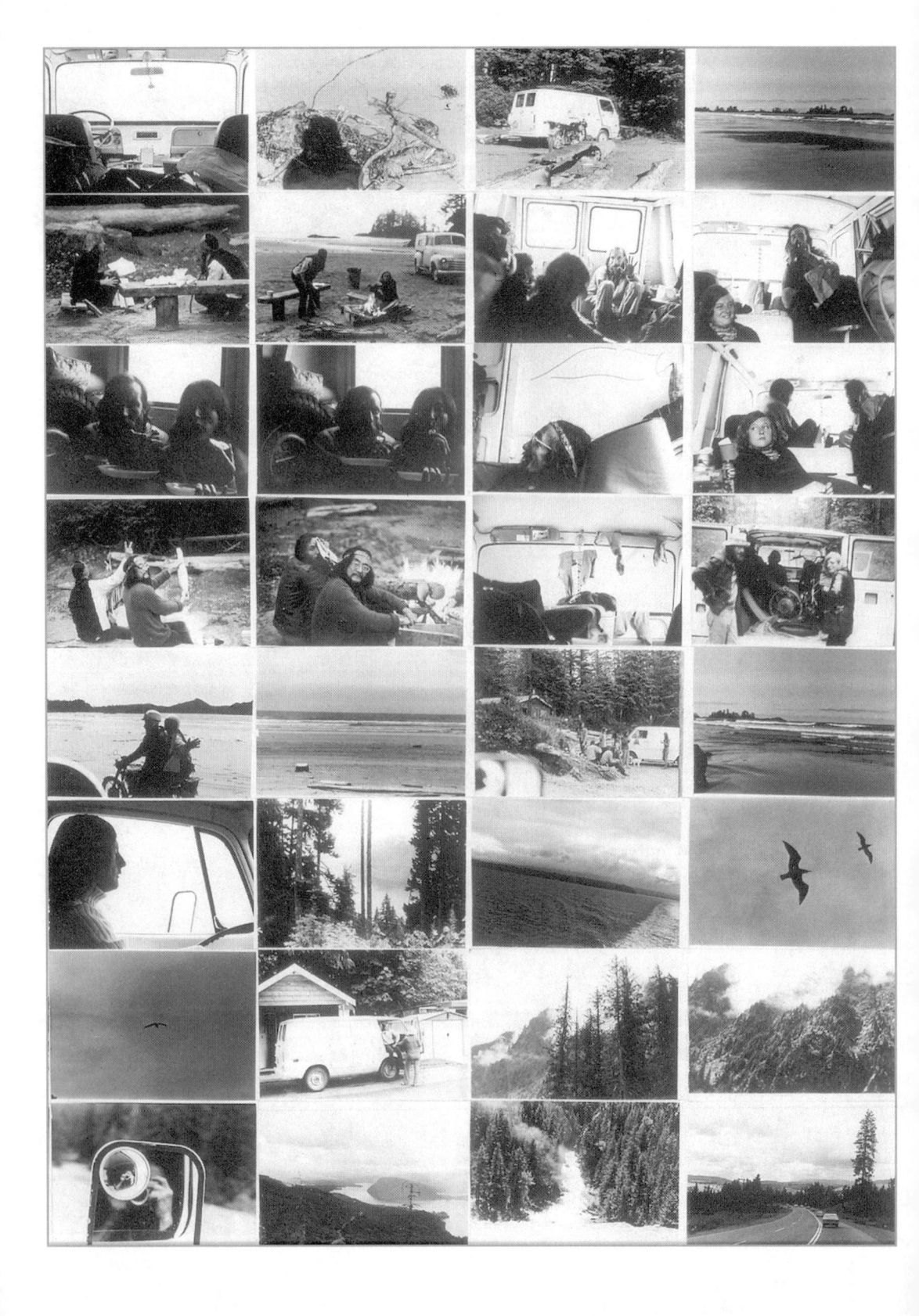

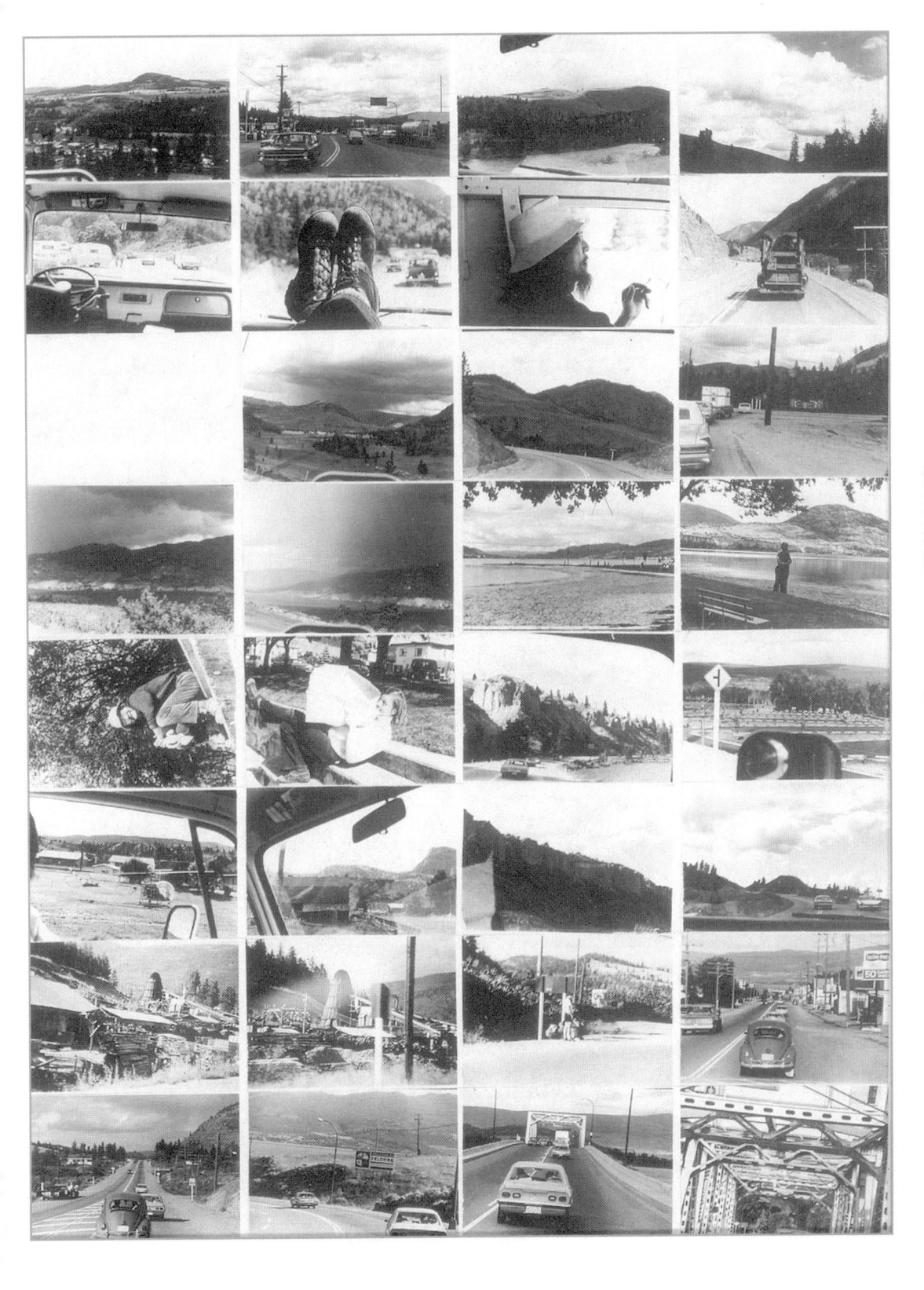

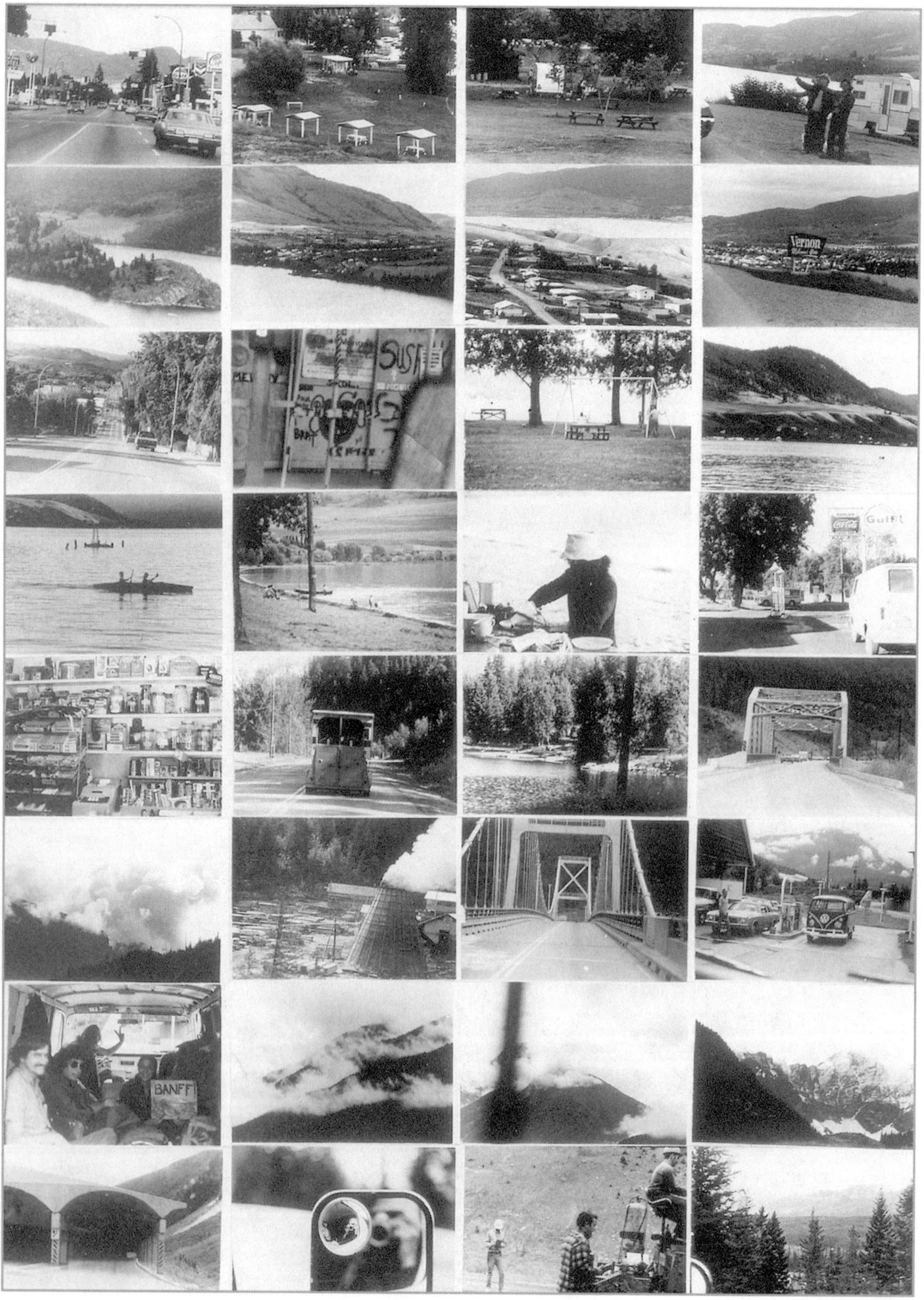
Vernon
Gulf
BANFF

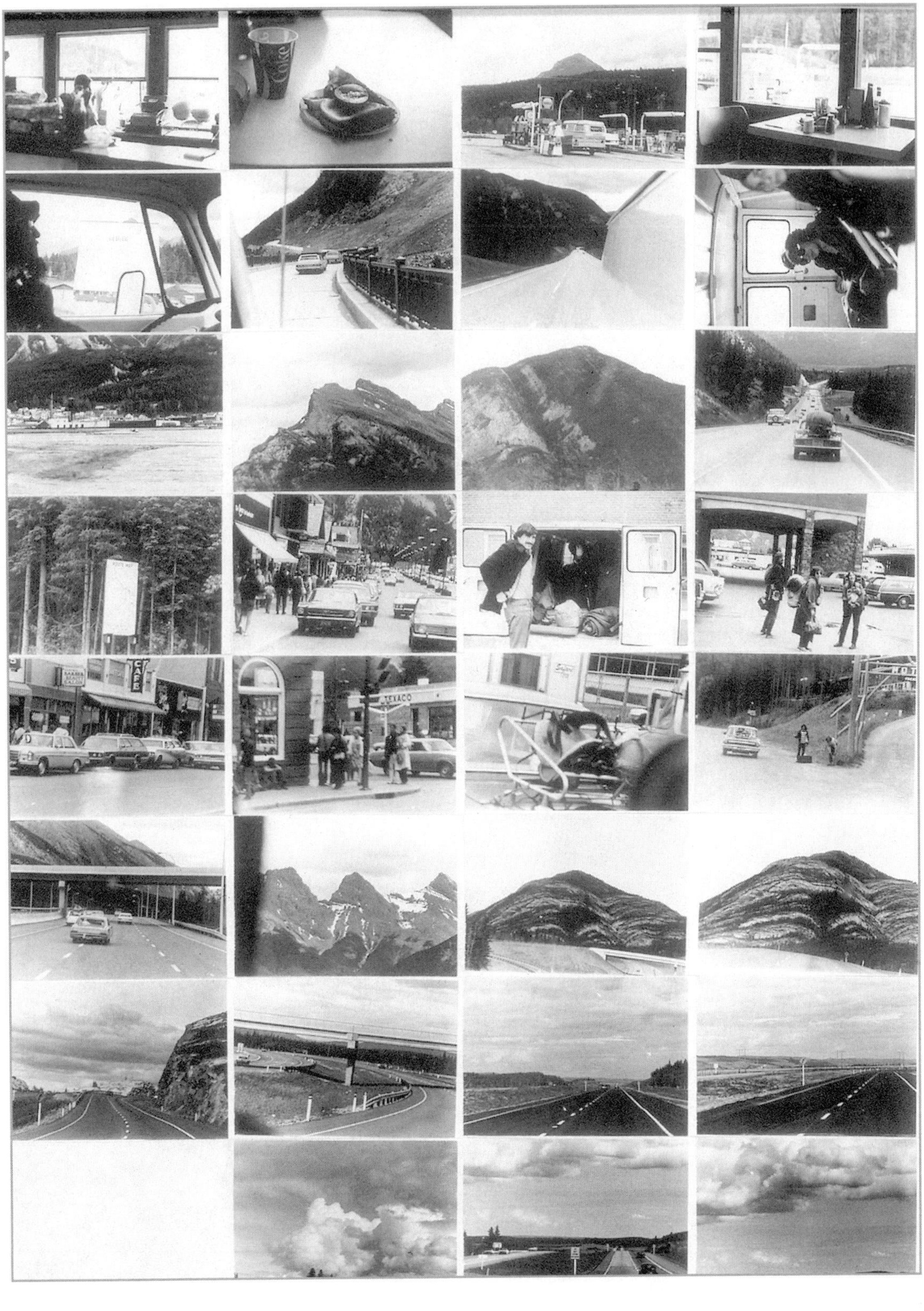
CAFE
TEXACO

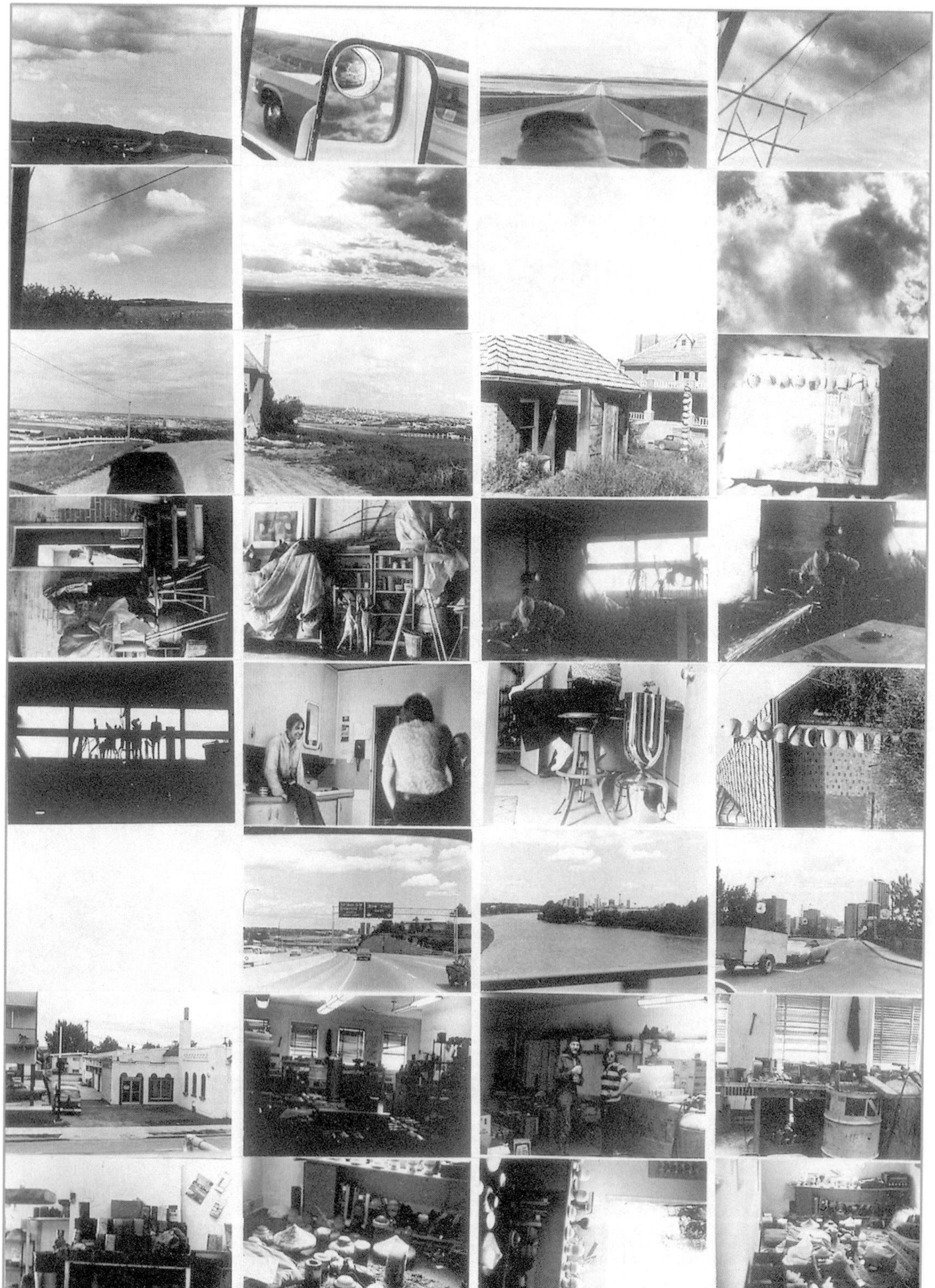

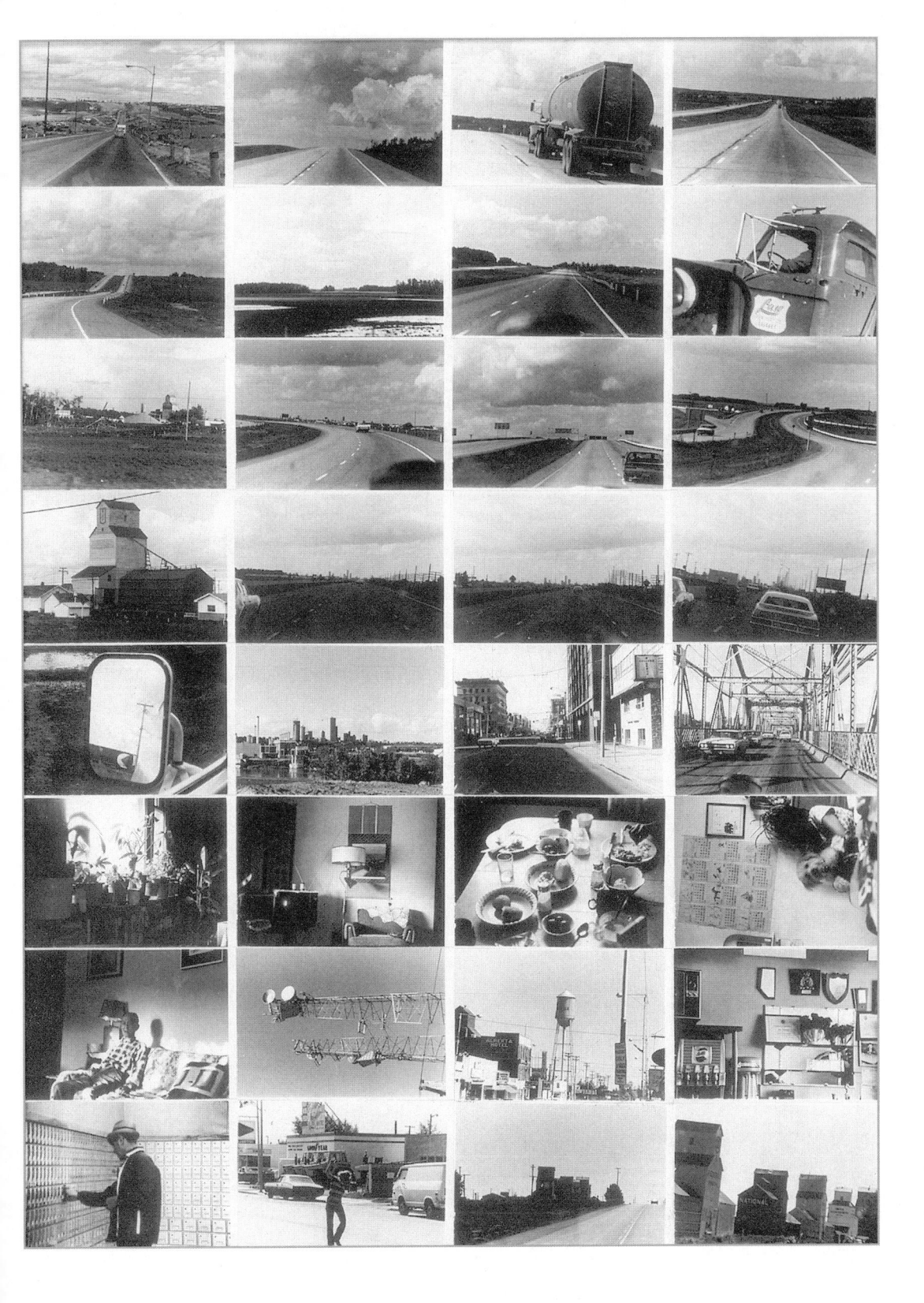
GOODYEAR
NATIONAL

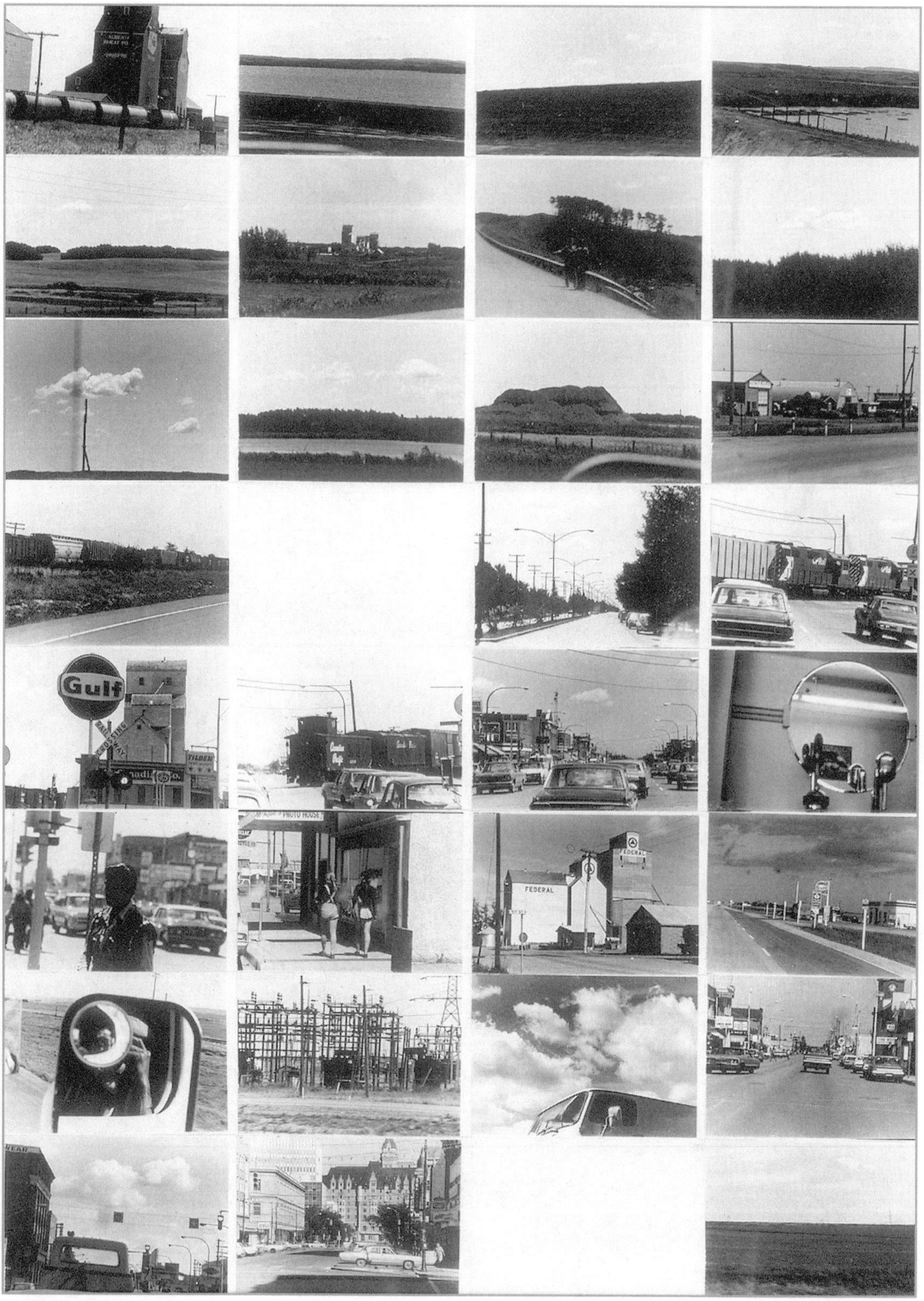

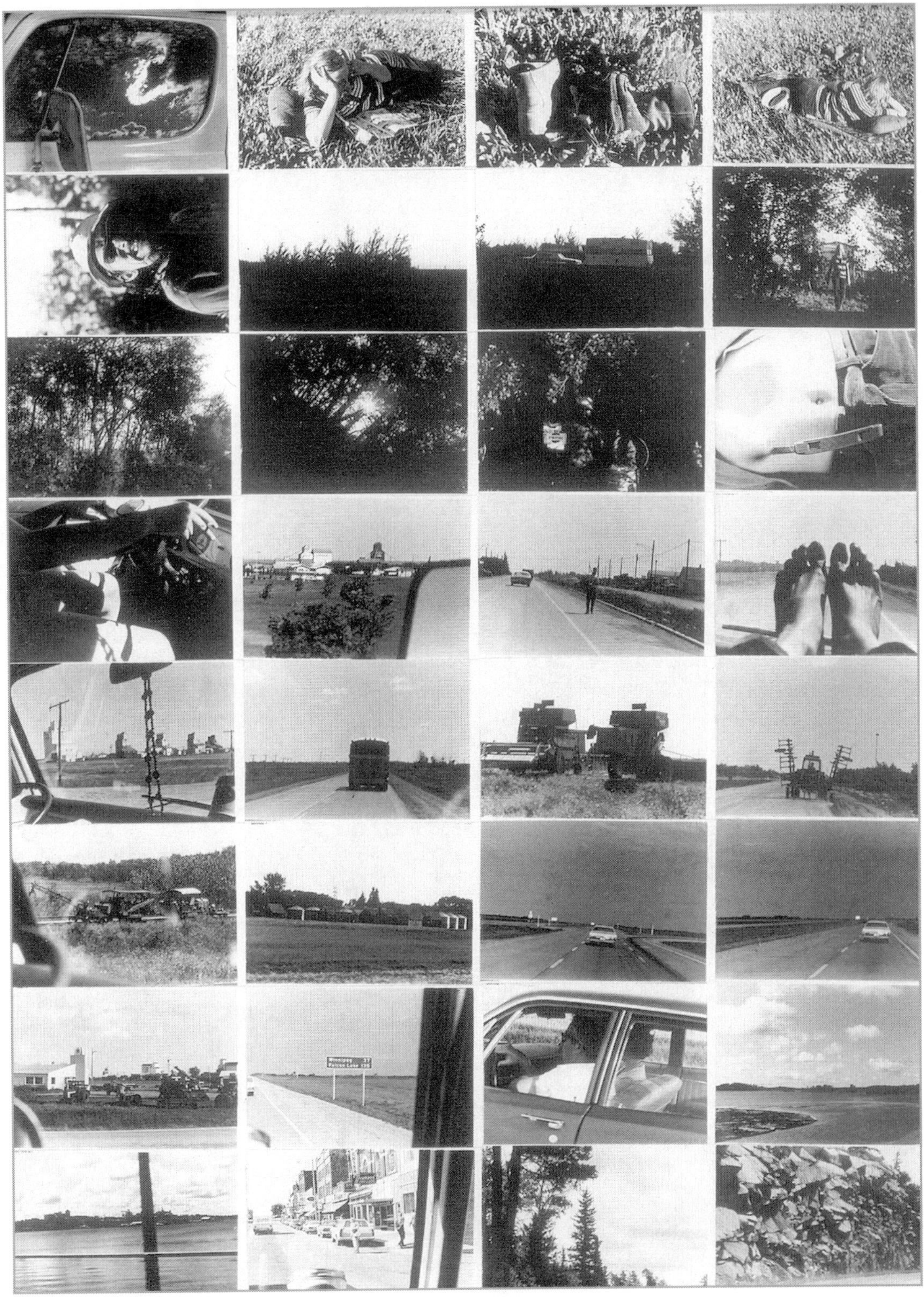

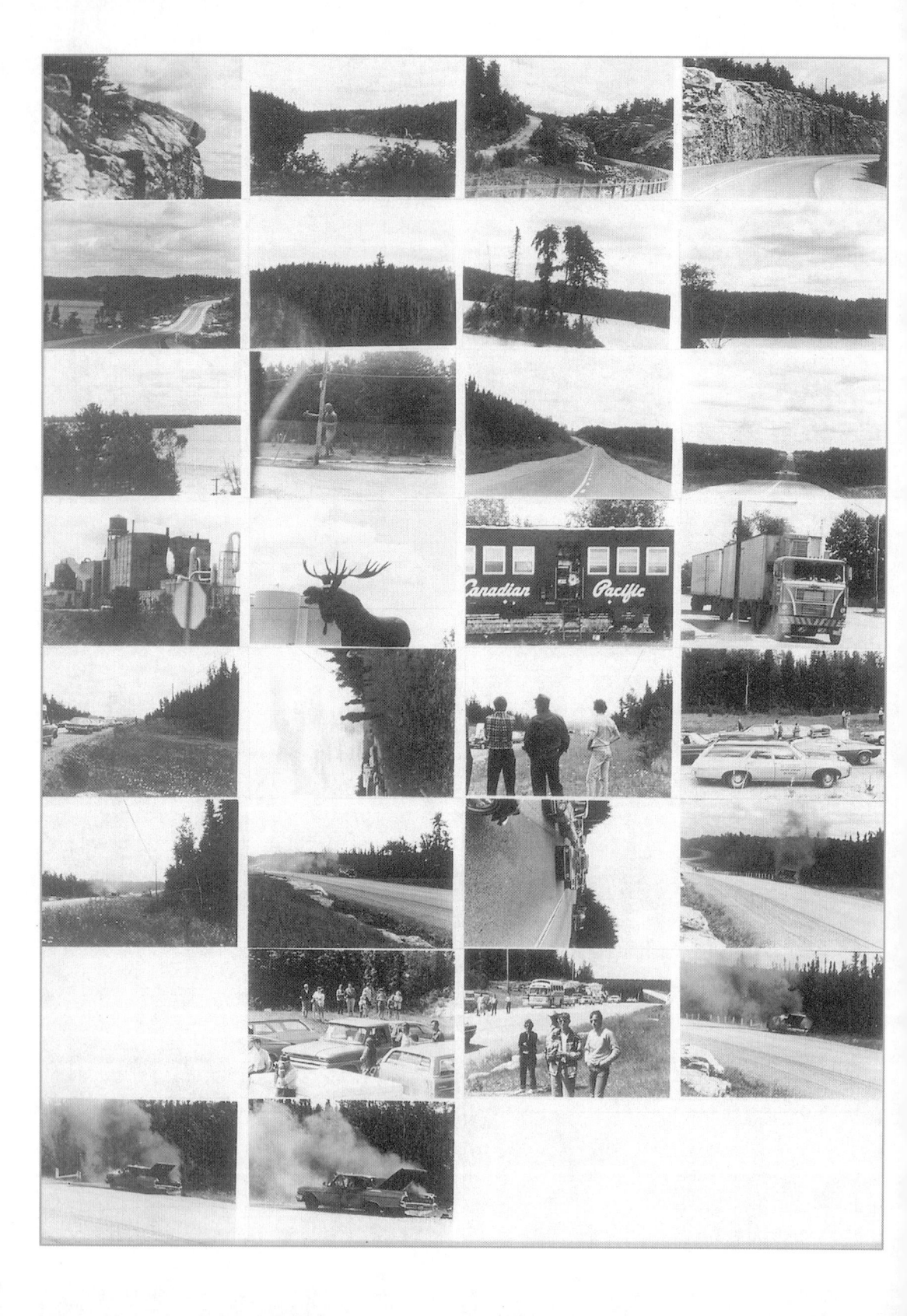
Canadian Pacific

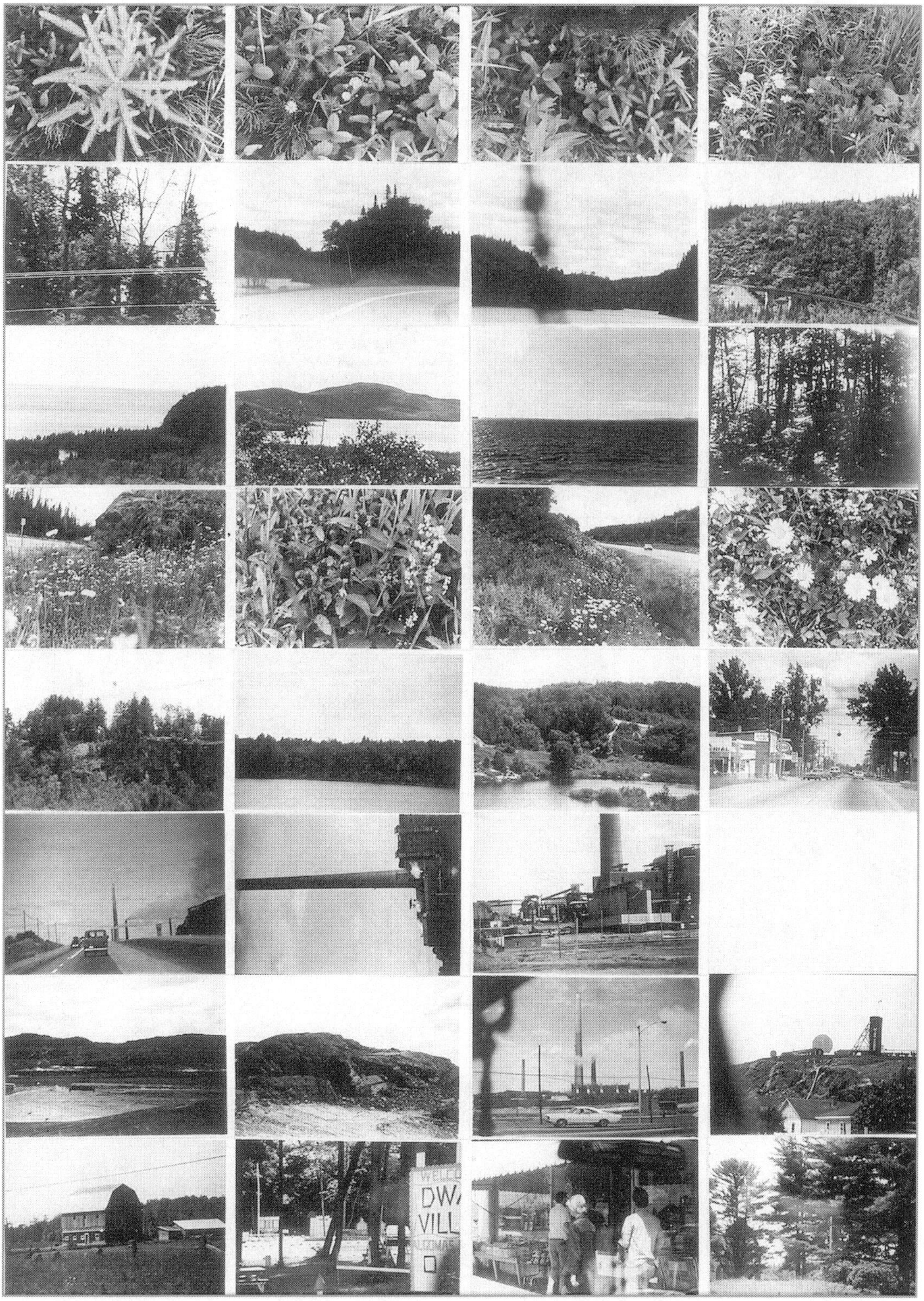

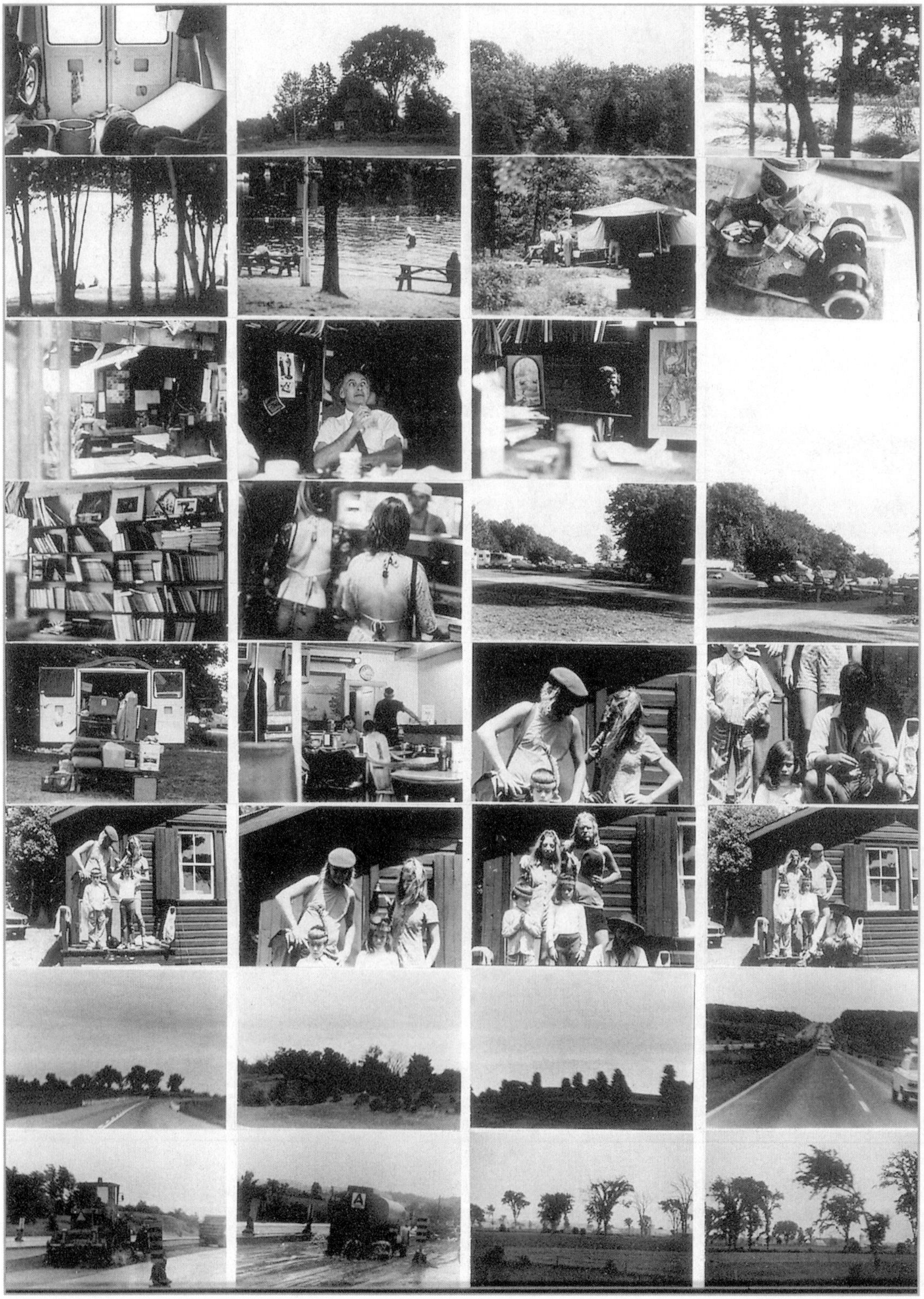

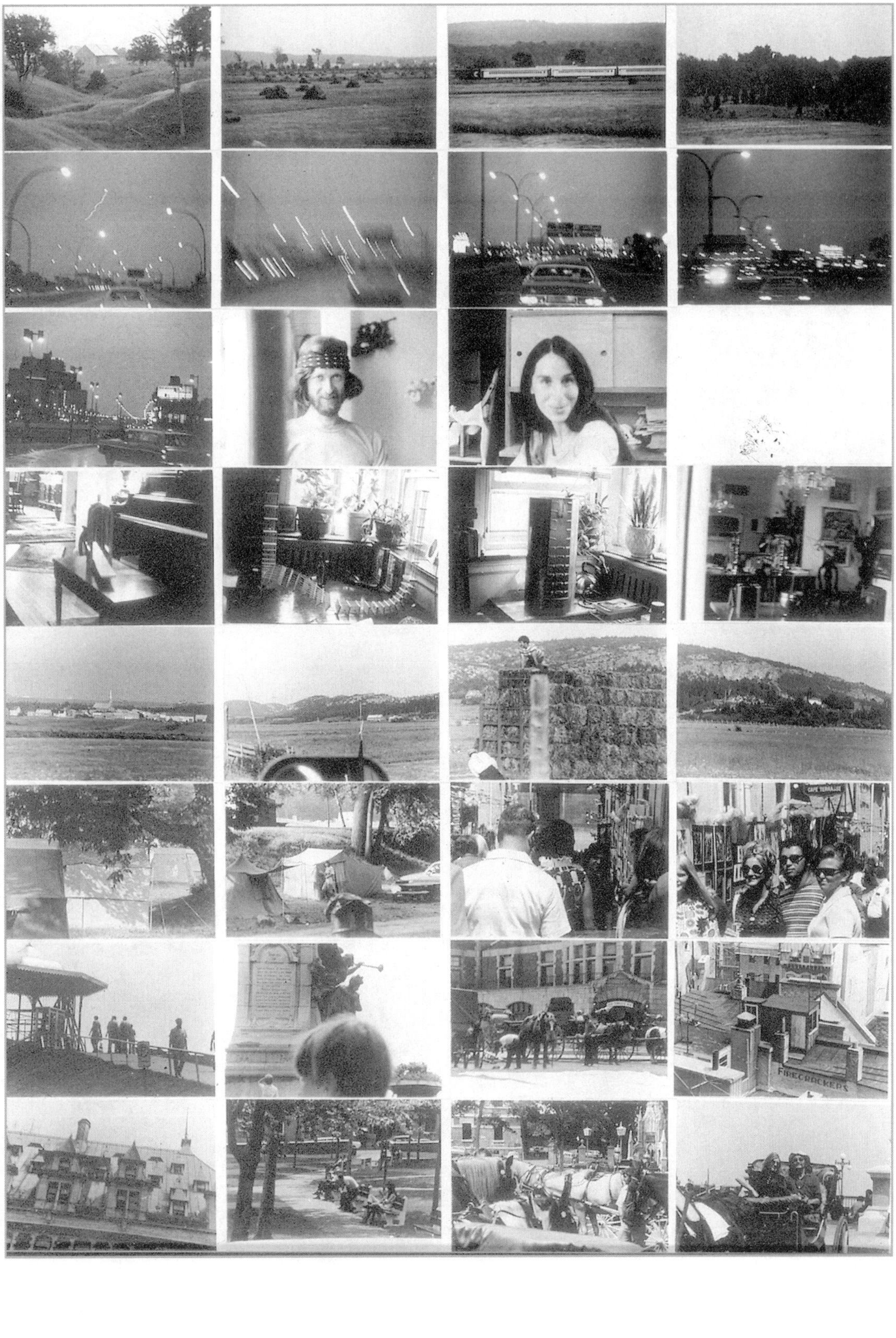
FIRECRACKERS

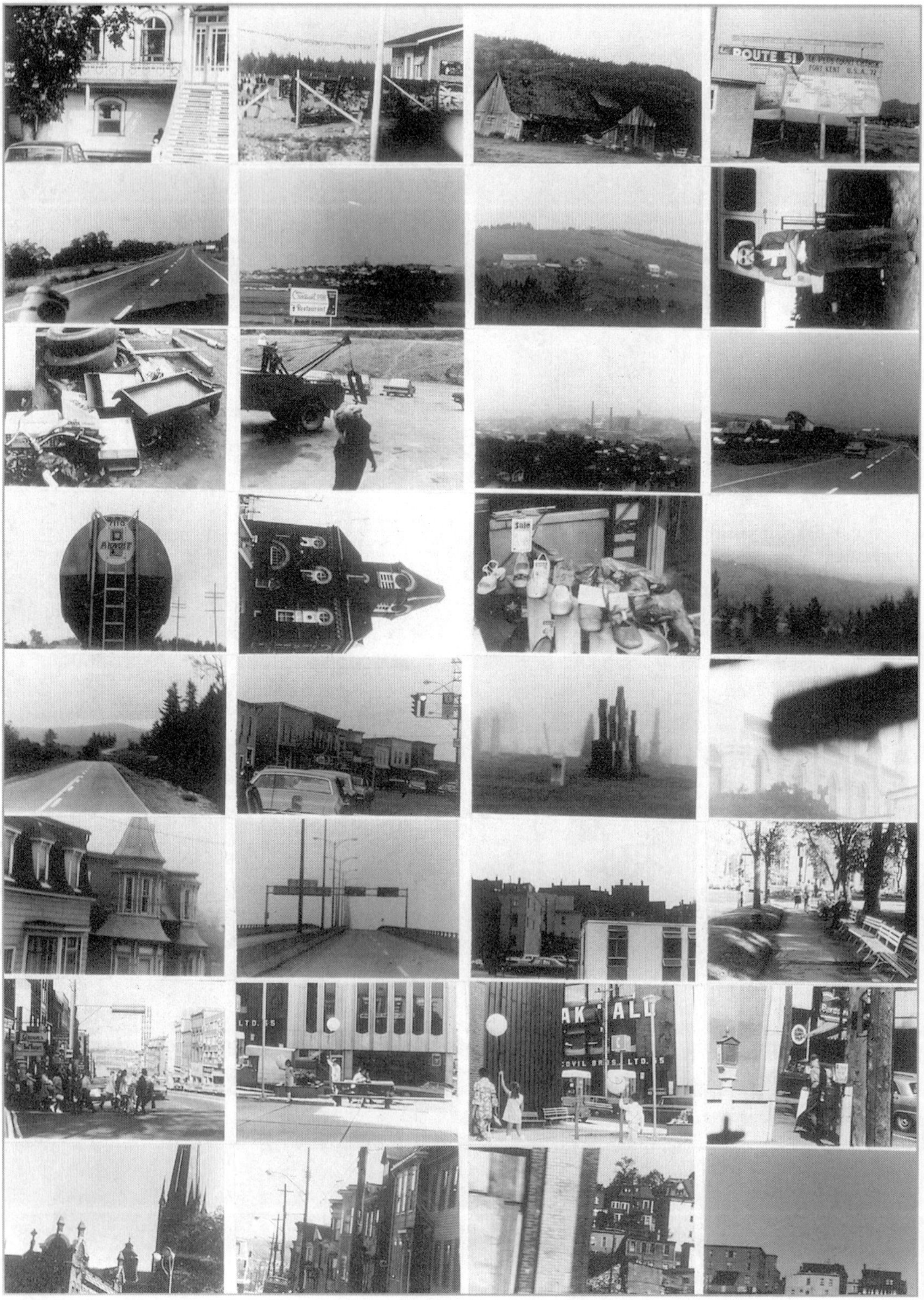
ROUTE 51
Restaurant
Sale
LTD. 55

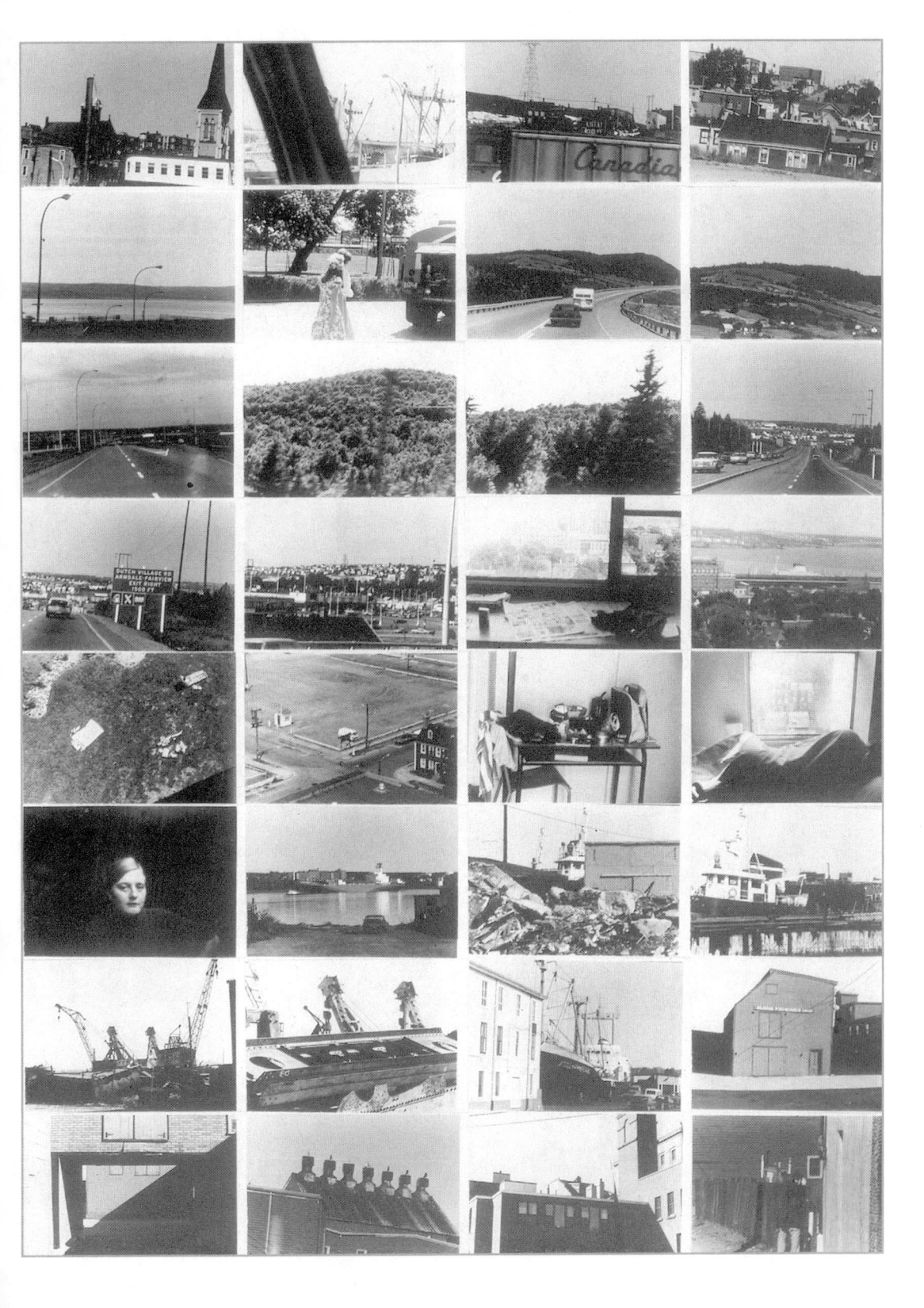

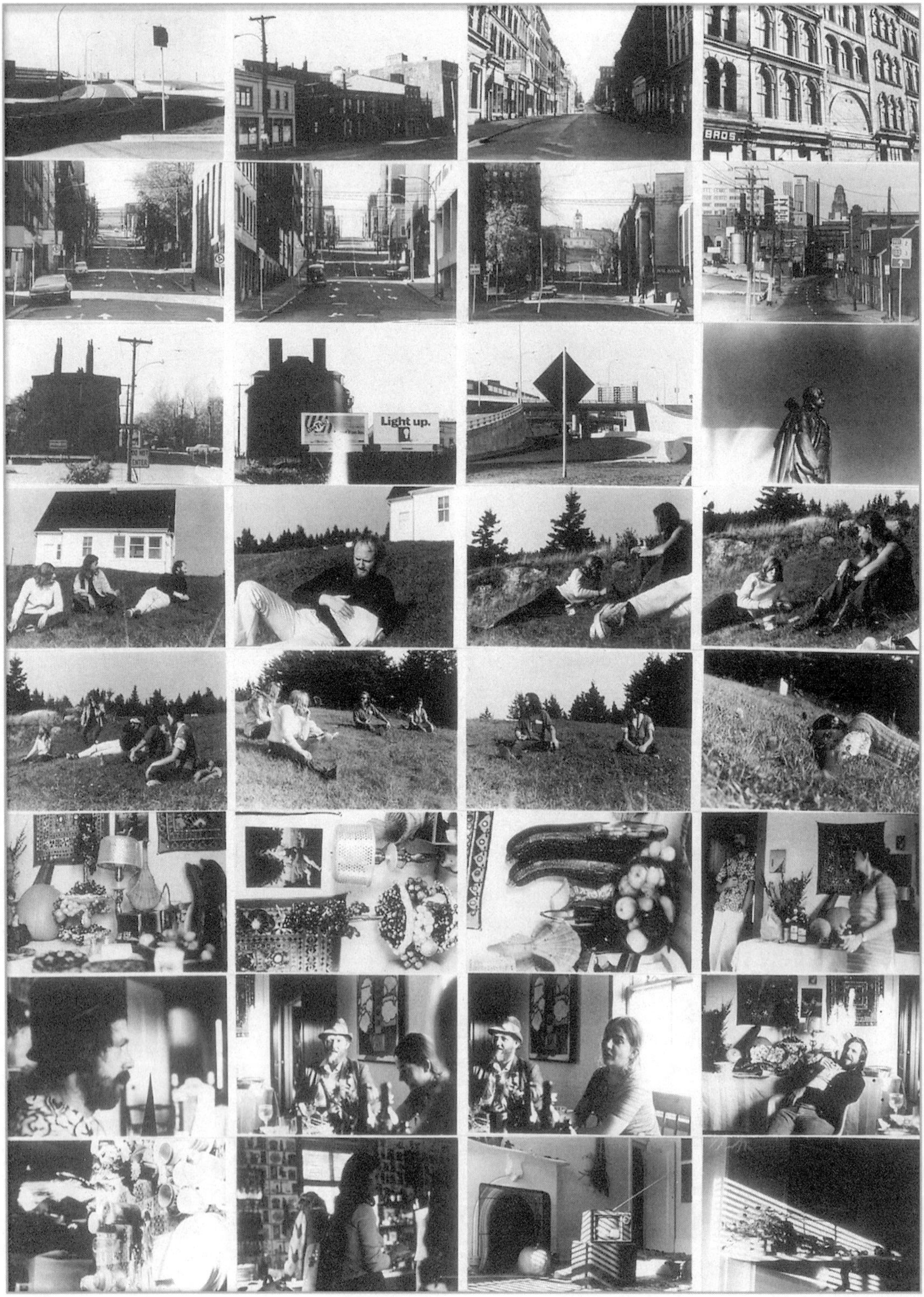
BROS
Light up.

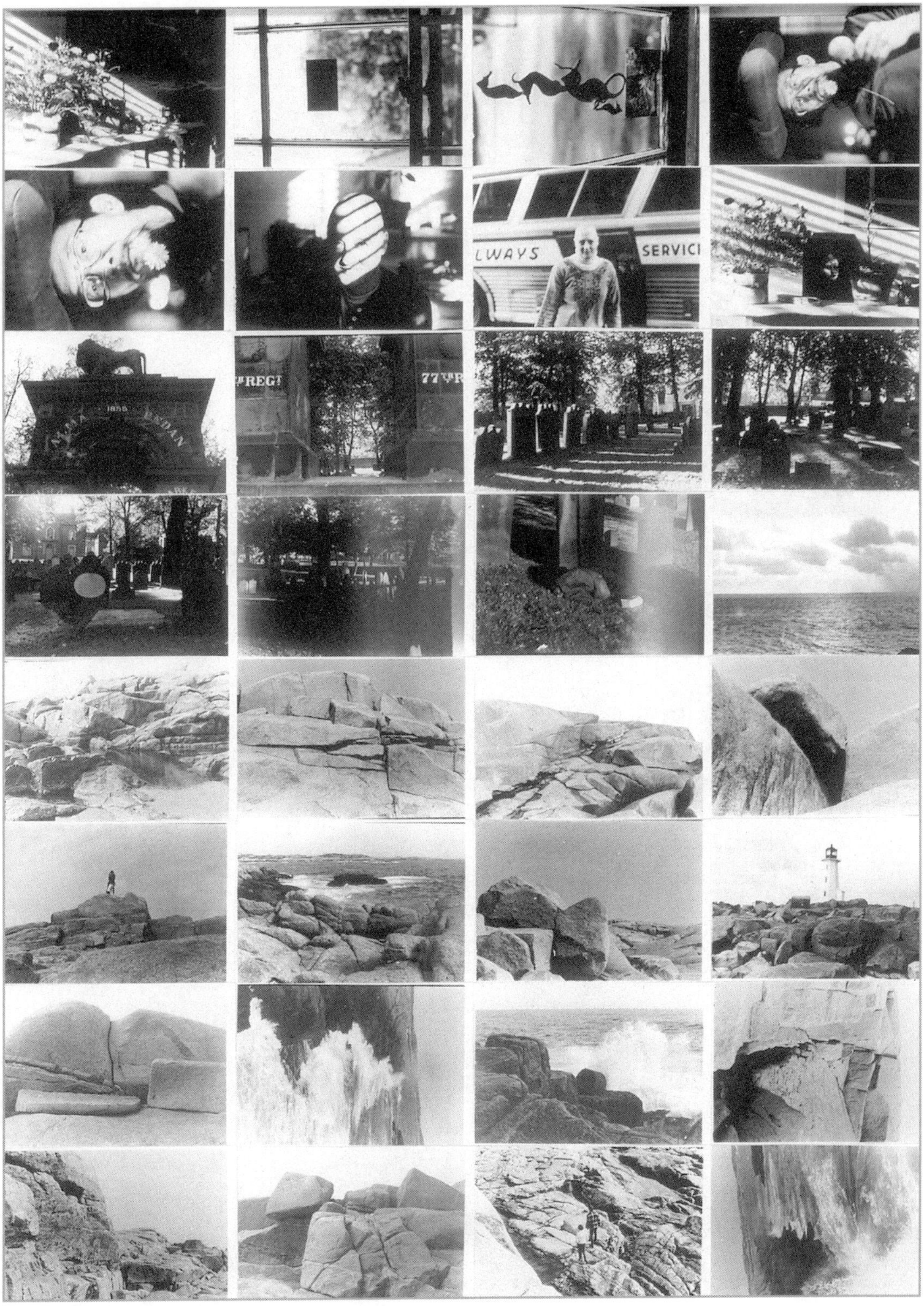
LWAYS
SERVIC

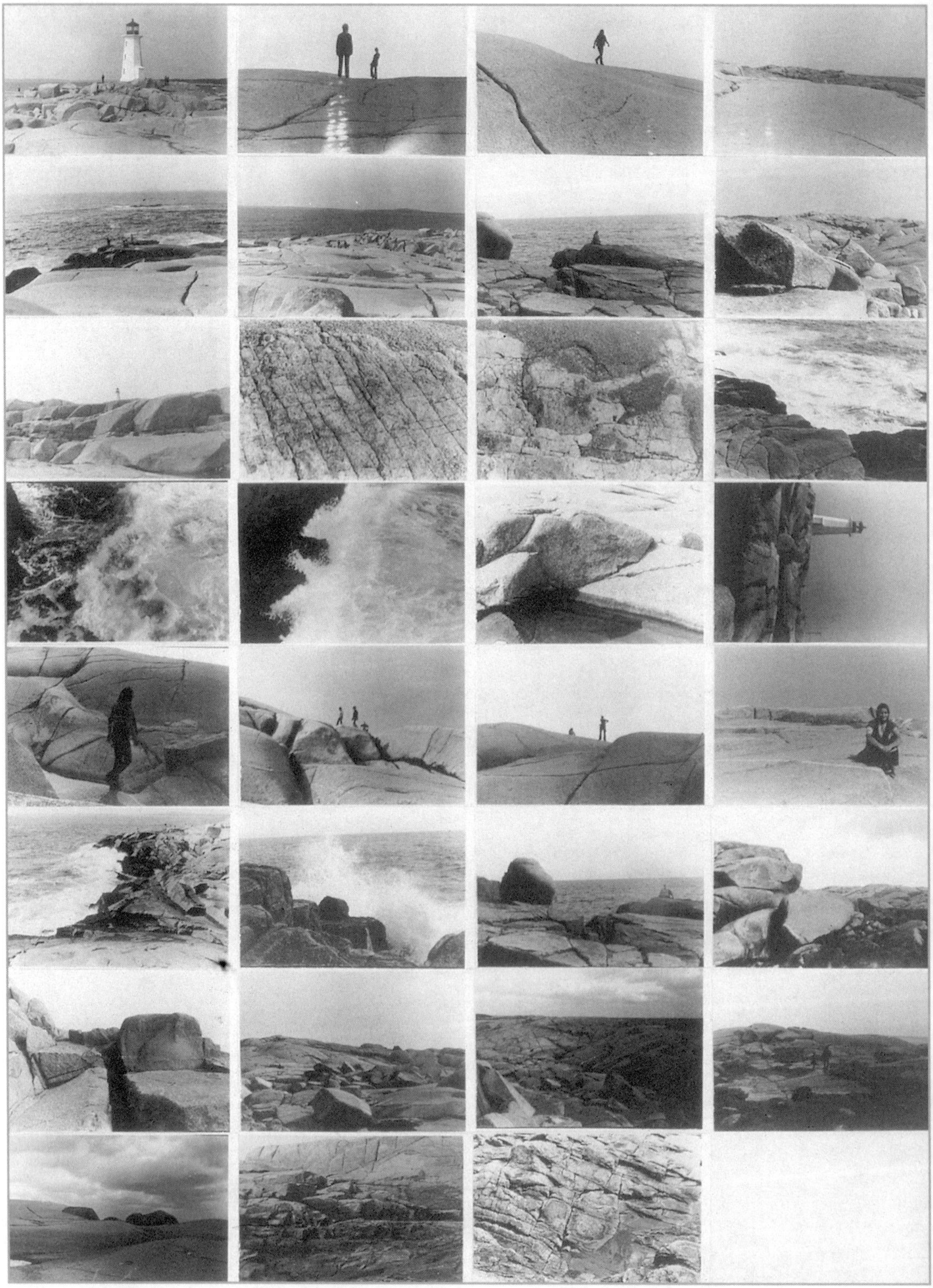

8/ 31/'71
Halifax Nova Scotia

Dear Mariko

    That old Sir George Williams envelope sure
gave me a start–I thought GEEZ! theyre after me for
un-done business, etc. Glad that you and Jan got
over to Hornby Island its at least as magical a place
as any yr Pa knows. The last time I was there i
found myself at a small rock concert in the middle of
a forest clearing w/ a make shift slab wood stage
strung with red and green christmas lights whc swung
in the moonlight wind. And how many of us laid in
sleeping bags or huddled together I'll never know nor
does it matter – –as all of the black night forest
spirits seem'd to erupt frm the hyped music whc
compelled our attention. in the early morning I could
hear the music follow me down the road to Gordons.
Or there are the sandstone rocks their million pores
down at the Point. etcetera.

    Yeah, everything does b-u-z-z particularly bees and
us and what happens to 'you' 'me' 'others' is the
sum of an unaccountable number of buzzes coming from
'here' 'there' and 'everywhere'. And it could be sd
that all things frm the largest to the tiniest unseen
thing does. So, dont forget your own small buzz– –
it counts even in sleep when its become a mur-muring
right on thru even our dreams. And you wont be able to
handle more because its got to be everything. Like
always listen to and stand by them.

        Pa aint got no answers. none tho
        once upon a time he thought he had a few.
        it dont make him feel better or bad
        and it dont make l-i-v-i-n-g one wee bit easier.
        but but who who wants a dumb ease or mere
        appeasement yur Pa dont. HUGELIFE wont yield
        simplistic answers–or at least thats
        what I keep on finding out
                        How about you?

8/ 31st/ '71
Halifax NovaScotia

Dear M o n i c a

>this is a birthday letter: i believe
>Sept 3rd is your birthday. as they say many
>happy returns, etc.
>
>halifax stinks of the atlantic.
>the dead find sanctuary in the city's heart.
>the living do their thing aware
>of both .
>
>here on sun lit tobin street
>one small child beats on a old tin can.
>two stories up i tap out another
>rhythm. across 4000 miles our silences measure
>both occan's depths .
>
>.
>
>you could phone the lawyer re the divorce.
>ask him (if he has'nt) to read you my letter it
>explains why nothing has happened.
>
>if theres anything i can do from this distance
>to help you and the children   let me know–
>i intend to write to all of you regularly. and
>do keep me informed (if you want to .
>
>.
>
>– –not into my thing yet. its as tho i had depend'd
>on a compass for so long that without it i dont
>know what direction to face. i am in that sense almost
>faceless. nonetheless, the itch is there and
>when the time comes . . . i shall do what i have to.
>
>.
>
>ah, my 45th yr– –
>*which I've worn like a shroud*
>—what have you in store for me
>in halifax?

Sept. 1st '71
Halifax NovaScotia

Dear Kiyo

    got your letter/drawings today.
Pa dont know how to say you ought to go on with
your schooling 'cause he knows from his
own experience that schools no matter what level
are only schools unless theyve got a few
good teachers   and your lucky enough to get one.
I have thot that it could be useful if
instead of the school picking the teachers the kids
were given a chance to also appraise them.
Afterall you and your sisters have as much insight
into whats good for you as any adult does and
that includes your Pa. Abt all I can really say is
you deserve a good teacher and a few friends
and as long as you stay open Im sure you will find them.
So why not just hang in there and get what you can
and what you cant get you'll have to find.

Abt 2 weeks ago Pa went into the Nova Scotia country
side to visit Al and Toby MacLennan. Al is from
Scotland. Toby from Detroit. They met at the Chicago
Art Institute. Their good friends Art and Natalie
Green from the American mid-west were also visiting.
We had a long stoned afternoon of laughter and
'glib' then sat down to supper with our special guests
who had been waiting in the next room.
Their names are Al and Toby Art and Natalie   They
were life-size cloth replicas with papier-mache faces
that lookt just like the four of them. And I told
all eight of them how you also made raggety cloth dolls
to keep you company.

                        give Morgan a big hug for me.
                        and say Hi to the Greenaways Ok

F a l l '71
Halifax NovaScotia

Dear D a u g h t e r s

    this is going to be that letter you havent
received. it could even be a long letter tho i
seldom write them. as to whether long letters
are better than short ones i cant really say that
it even matters. Henry Miller once wrote 100
pages to a friend whereas your grandpa Kiyooka
always writes very short succinct letters.
whatever the length of this letter itll have little
to say abt the weather or even the climate of
yr Pa's soul. the truth is that i have nothing in
particular to say but simply want to tell you
whatever comes to mind and make that the heft of
the letter. you might ask—but hasnt Pa got anything
he wants to tell us but the telling of a letter?
and yr Pa wld reply that even a letter can be
its self and no other. like any other thing thats
already existent it needs no qualifications
even tho it may not be, comprehensible. folks like
yr Pa makes it their ofttimes foolish biz to ask
questions abt even letters 'how' a letter becomes
existent—that is 'how' does a letter say this one
get to be written and what can it say? if you read
between these lines you will find The Weather
'how' it affects the flight of birds, even yr Pa's
lacerated-wings—which need mending before he
can take off again. being grounded—
he is writing a letter to say how lovely it is
to see the three of you beginning to fly. may you
soar higher than these words can hope to.
and if you put enough words together you too can
write Pa a letter one this letter purports to
be an invitation for .

9/ 2nd/ '71
Halifax NovaScotia

Dear Engledink Gangbuster
    Chief Censor of Smut 'n Smear

    . . . readin thru Gorgeous Strange Here
in Haligonia is a bit like thumbin thru old
snapshot albums or evergreen and gold
yesterday's yearbooks with captions written by
an assortment of friendly ghosts   even as–
theyre posing for the camera's obscene eye my friend
John A MacDonald salutes you from a mere
4000 miles .
                      Libby at Cape Traverse P.E.I. got
                      a 90s leatherbound giltedged photo album
                      full of Lower Canada Folks proppt up
                      in front of schooner and sea settings: tin
                      types of only god knows 'who' they are
                      which we spent a long time goin thru 'cause
                      those of us who are given to *tell* know
                      there aint no such critter as a dead man–
                      without a tongue.

                      ask gunslinger abt it. ask him he'll say
                      a six shooter in hand is worth two underfoot .

                      yr concern abt the Slinger is unfounded.
                      why bother abt (old cliche) "generation-of-
                      imitators" it goes without sayin without
                      Ed's tools you? they? will fail miserably .
                      the slinger is more than any envy viz large
                      audiences Dorn commands. its just not a useful
                      prop   as say a picture of a dead man can be .

Halifax salutes Dasa, Lies, Dal, Heather and
all erstwhile members of The Grange.

                      keeps the Straight and yr Letters comin

9/ 8th/ '71
Halifax NovaScotia

dear Barbara

>thinkin its just another piece of garbage i
>almost tosst out the handbill . . . all abt you do
>ing yr thing in Oakland California   WOW!   then
>reachin back to good ole intermedia days recall'd–
>all of us sitting in the sun on the back stoop
>just before you and Yvonne were to be interviewed.
>theres also a lovely film-loop of yr dancing . . . .
>
>just this afternoon was thinkin i aint had any fine
>dope since arrivin in Halifax . . . and wldnt it be
>as they say lovely 'if' i cld get some. then, checking
>my mail-box i finds a tiny but utterly familiar lil
>package of Yes an ounce of heady ah hashish   frm
>an old ex-nicotine fiend in Montreal. happily thats
>happen'd today . . . hows Benji and wheres Yvonne and
>are you goin to be in N/Y. this winter?   uh uh uh Judy
>Collins whom i drove over to Wolfville to hear is
>pullin me ear into the next room
>   Dear Barbara– –
>keep cuttin those o so luvly shapes when you twirl yr
>fulsome body o-u-t-w-a-r-d-s
>
>
>   –aint mouth'd words
>   the next best thing to kissin
>   angel-wings . . . ?

9/ 14th/ '71
Halifax NovaScotia

dear B r i

>
> been diggin into the life and times of
> our illustrious forebears. The Group of 7 who
> flappt colourful paintings aloft   in a
> battle of nits and wits over half a century ago
> whc just abt makes the lot of 'em our lst
> 'old masters' together with Morrice, Milne and
> a scant few others.   and talkt abt conceptual
> art trips did you know that Tom Thomson painted
> abt ninety small pics in as many days in
> the Spring of 1917   just before he got it good.
>
> – –tho the frame of references be different Id say
> Were abt much the same thing viz our nervous
> patriotism, our new frontiers. i mean dont we also
> want to re-claim the ground we stand upon   by
> seeding it with our own sweet and sour imaginings
> and have an end to facetious comparisons with
> big brother across the interminable 49th parallel.
> and i have never felt so strongly how perilous
> almost precipitous our free enterprise system turns
> out to be–these halcyon days.
>
> meanwhile Im lyin' low i read and take notes
> then have a nap before getting stoned and sitting
> down to my typewriter to make up a story abt
> T.T. and his buddies. Hopefully my take on him will
> tell me a thing or two never suspected.
>
>
> yr goat-foot'd friend

mid-Sept. '71
Halifax NovaScotia

dear JohnKnee Boy

    yeah do come see us   do do that
    whenever   we'll put up with you as long
    as putting you up dont become an-
    other downer. and pleez use the dough for
    as much good afghan hash as itll buy
    otherwise a huge quantity of the best gold
    en grass   for yr crass lad and his o
    crazee lady. johnny o johnny boy how do u
    make love to ladies who were once upon
    a time v-i-r-g-i-n-s but have become
    Mothers-of-Inventions? u might as well ask me
    to procure a vestal-virgin who also
    toked up after tossing u the golden key to
    her chastity belt   or a playhouse bunny.
    and yes tell the waywards i remember those
    Ah so sweet riffs 'n whiffs out at th
    ol cheese factory
                    see ya Johnny Boy 'when?'

indubitably yrs

                          9/ 16th/ '71
                          Halifax NovaScotia
dear Whip (Geo.) & Poo (Ang.)

    readin B.Js bit abt you?/her? in G.S. tells me
    how wrongheaded we all can be abt each/other
    despite *the imperatives* which are a fact of our
    frail-litanies
             and Yes i have been workin
    on *Under the Granville Street Bridge/ Sunday
    after the War/ Outwards* for G.S.W.S. i am hookt in
    to an interminable act of re-shuffling–as for a
    longlost chronology, aware of the fact that in doing
    so i want to re-shape my very self, at least.

    .

Krisy is on the floor painting birds and sea horses.
I am of course writing this and no matter how many times
it happens (with whoever)   its a daily miracle. call it
a measure of how one-and-one equals two small warts on huge
Atlantic's left cheek . or is it how we button up our
abysmal emptiness with ?

as for the N/S/C/A its where i hang out me gropings–
for whomever–to S E E what comes of them etc. otherwise
its where various odds and sods grind their axes to
chop down conceptual-thickets and fence in their own taut-
ologies. imagine a Ludwig Wittgenstein siring the likes
of these so-called artists. *no matter* i do feel privileged
to sample this international glossary of mad men and my
coming here i suppose can be thot of as part of it

with all me travels I dont/cant remember the names of
more than a handful of streets / avenues / boulevards /free-
ways/arteries/addresses/channels/cuts/embankments/   or
hotels– –George can sech a nounless poet be nonetheless
numinous   or does it make me a mere digit another of
them Menckensque Yahoos .

                  Ang. dont let 'em tell you
a child-in-belly is less miraculous 'cause our mouths are
sometimes filld with shit

                      yr oldyellowbelly'd friend

9/ 22nd/ '71
Halifax NovaScotia

Dear K im

   (CAR's Treasurer

Bruce Parsons is the bearer of
what informations there is frm us Haligonians. he is
his own man yet spokesman for the rest of us.
We sent our greetings may your conference be at least
consequential to all us who are artists.
speaking personally   i am all for standing upright
side by side with my fellow artists   or if
its more effective   on top of each other's shoulders–
whicheverway   other than the dog-eat-dog the
Art biz is .

> whatever be each his own
> ideological references: We/Artists are
> nonetheless part and parcel of
> a socio-eco-system which system affects
> plumbers, profs, pro-football,
> proletarians, parlimentarians, agrarians,
> and artists of all sorts, alike.
> our needs are no different viz the basics
> from the above   or 'if' they are–
> 'why' 'how' and 'who' shld therefore *pay*
> for the differences?
>
> J U S T I C E re: artist's fees
> not to mention Benson's vexations re his
> White Papers is but a small gear in
> congeries of politico/economico/socio/logical
> machinery–We're all gear'd into . . .
> unless yr going to talk abt gettin' more
> lubrication whc Im not interested in.

Im putting on the agenda :
We/artists examine the artist's way in
contemporary kultur and the relevancies of un-
voiced assumptions tieing all of us to
status quo institutions and their showing/buying/
selling/ propagandizing/ of our works, etc .

what can (i)(we)(car) do to help to
make the world better via A-r-t   for all in All?

9/ 24th/ '71
Halifax NovaScotia

Dear Lanny

    gotta note frm J.A. askin' me for
a loan of one of my paintings. YES you can have
one or more of 'em tho I've no idea what
cld possibly be suitable for yr circumstances.
you cld go see Paul Wong at the Bau-Xi say
your an old friend and that i sd you cld choose
works of mine you thot suitable. then when–
ones you borrow have for whatever reason begun to
bore you & others you cld return them and
borrow others. need i add that the thot of one of
my paintings enhancing a room and hence help-
ing to turn folks on–to Life's Colourfulness
excites me. its what I am abt

.

here in Halifax the long dead and those who died
just yesterday lie side by side at the feet of
those of us who walk the streets as if we owned them
Lanny theres more graveyards in downtown Halifax
than in any city i've lived in in N.A.

.

as for the so called mentally ill-
whether here or in Vancouver or anywhere else
in N.A. they are the maligned-ones   in
the sense of the measures we use to
incarcerate them. like 'who' truly knows
what is 'normal'/'abnormal'?–it often seems
to me that the straightjacket gets put on
the wrong guys. in the face of all sorts of
blatantly ignorant acts carried out in
the name of a just-society the shoe does seem
to be on the wrong foot.

keep in thar keep kickin' up a fuss .

.

I'll drop P.W. a line to say yr comin' by

                              10/ 2/ '71
                              Halifax NovaScotia
Dear Werner

    MORE BIZ: at the time you took over 1923–
Granville Street I had ESSO (Home Comfort HA!
come by to check out the amt of oil left as
of July 1st and they did they sd its worth $48.99.
if you wld be so kind as to reimburse me for
it I would appreciate it. Just put it into the acct.
you pay the rent moneys into, OK?
                                           Otherwise– –
I'm busy as usual or rather as busy as the context
enables. Whether or not its going to be possible
to go on telling the story of Art in the early 70s
begins to seem doubtful. I mean that I seem to
have nothing relevant to say, let alone 'see' as
far as painting as an Art goes   tho its not the
problem as much as it is me. etcetera.

– –just to have come Here
for THE SPLENDOUR of a MARITIME AUTUMN is
at least! worth all my procrastinations.

and what kinda measure is 45 Falls– –
with Winter's wither-blasts just around the corner???

                A BIG HULLO TO ALL
                ERSTWHILE MEMBERS OF THE GRANGE

10/ 4th/ '71
Halifax NovaScotia

Dear J u d y

      been thinking abt Our City   How
its ongoing folk-Lore depends on adopting
or its a co-opting of a second name
an alias pseudonym or wise-guise   to wit an
Anna Banana, Marcel Dot, Slim Flowers
or even a Doctor and Lady Brute– –like name 'em
and we've got them. theres Kitty Hawke
Art Rat, Mr. Planter's Peanut, and Other Odds
and eminent Sods including Seamus Finn
the old shoemaker's visionary Dollarton twin– –
like aint we got more than our share of 'em.
and what can all these appendices be   ?
is it possible that a pseudo-name is our
so called real-self and that our given name is
a mere invention (like a parental wish or
bloody whim   no more than that.   or again is it
the fact of no one not even a parent thot
to name the other half we also are.   or
its mere theatricalitease– –a vain attempt to
ambush the REAL from the other side of an arch'd
proscenium . nomatter the namings, our poly-
morphously perverse porosities know   if
it knows anything   the difference/s .
these thots come to you frm Halifax where
the nativeborn call 'em selves Haligonians no less
than grey speckl'd rock or maple tree

yr one syllable name friend, Roy

10/ 7th/ '71
halifax nova scotia

dear Mariko

just got a luvly birth-book R I N G S
frm Daphne Marlatt. you could get a copy via G.B.
one of the editors of G.S.W.S.   its no. 3
in the series.   & if you &/or Claire want some-
one to talk to get in touch with her at 4027-
W. 34th St. Vancouver.

yr Pa's been writing: more accurately he's re-
writing what he has written. he keeps doing that
'cause what he wrote once-upon-a-time seems
now badly written. hopefully, he will nonetheless
get it all together for the G.S.W.S.
the provisional title of the book is: From Under
The Granville Street Bridge/ Sunday/ After
the War/ O-u-t-w-a-r-d-s.

i bet the Seymour River–there
on Riverside Drive is beautiful this Fall. Yr Pa's
sorrowful he cant share it with you.
if you pictured it in words &/or paint plainly he could see
even hear   its Autumnal Syncopations. like 'how'
do you feel sitting out on the topmost balcony s-t-o-n-e-d– –
on Sight's & Sounding's Abundancies ?   W H Y
doncha tell me abt it ?

luv to yr sisters, yr mother,
morgan & others

                    10/ 7th/ '71
                    halifax nova scotia
dear Jan

            got me suit. thanx. its sure strange
            gettin' me suit thru the mail   as one gets
            say a letter or postcard.   now, its hung
            up in my closet as it hung in that other closet
            in Vancouver. before that Montreal. hmmm i
            wunder if suits like dark closets   thrive in 'em
            or just wilt like carnations after the dance?
            i find i can admire me suit's patience–i mean
            how it simply hangs in thar–waitin' to be
            worn out. now supposin' i wore me suit every day
            like bizmen or bismarck wld   wore it to school
            wore it while painting   wore it while riding trams
            wore it after a drunkenight's sleep   just wore
            it like my ordinary everyday clothes. supposin' i
            did that –would i therefore be different? &
            if so 'how?' & what abt me suit? wld it be
            the same suit? & if not what kinda suit wld it be?
            & wld it fit me as they say to a 'T?' . yr Pa's
            had just 2 suits in his life and both of 'em hung
            all of their lives in dark closets   waitin' for
            that special occasion when i might have worn them.
            both suits eventually wore themselves out.
            suits are sure funny that way.   or else its yr Pa
            who is funny abt suits. either way suits dont
            fit me. neither do overshoes. some day i'll tell
            you all abt the misadventures of my various
            overshoes.

                        sorry to hear Morgan got stung
                        in the arse. Pa dont know how he cld
                        save him frm gettin' stung   any-
                        more than save himself from gettin' it.
                        seems to be what bizzylil'bees do.
                        cld be simply a matter of stayin' out of
                        their honey-suckl'd paths when you
                        think theyre after you.

Pa enjoy'd yr ziggity-zaggity letters. will you
keep on sendin' them ?

10/ 4/ '71
Halifax NovaScotia

dear Engledink,

(re: **halifax/vancouver exchange:** a kindred response
to yr letter, from halifax where al and marguerite neil
gave a concert at the nova scotia college of art,
oct 3rd night of fullmoon 4000 miles east of that other
ocean all of us have lain beside).

its abt 3pm thurs when my phone rings and its yes its al "how are you
you old bugger were at the cnr station", and marguerite, "we'll wait for you
in the park in front of." moments later im running down
the slope across barrington into the park with city founder cornwallis
at the hub of. theres al and marguerite talking to
old man with briefcase as im comin up to 'em he shakes hands
all around and walks off towards the station. als saying
"we just met him sittin' here he's eighty yrs old made canada's
first airplane and flew it. now the govt. is going to reconstruct the plane
and put it in a museum. geez the old guy told us he's in the biz
of selling planes he fixes up. he knows a lot abt nuclear physics and shit
imagine runnin into him here in halifax this lovely clear as a whistle
thurs afternoon, imagine that shit." after, al and marguerite tell us abt
all our mutual friends back on the pacific we go over to the school in the
white van. al and marguerite check out the acoustics by clappin their
hands. shakin' shaggy ole head al says "shit these fucken spaces are all
the same youd think architects had tin ears the way they throw spaces
together–with no sense of what sound does or how it carries." als asking
allan abt a piano a baby grand he says without insisting too much several
times that, that was what he needed, a baby grand. then there aint nothing left
to do thru saturday when the gallery wld be cleared for the concert.

friday al got his wld ya believe it made-in-japan baby grand.
and after doing what could then be done he found the picadilly and
liquor vendors. that night we piled into the van to go hear
dr. wu, venerable authority on chinese paintings give a lecture on his
pet subject, we all sit in the front row watching
delicately tinted sumis flick by with dr. wu's pointer mov-
ing our eyes/minds thru the twists and turns of a chinese
landscape: we pause now here on a vantage point then further along
going up or coming down, on another, to see what lies above, what below
and what is all around & the view from the thatch'd hut &

the view from the pinnacle open out on miasma of s-p-a-c-e-s that
leaves us all giddy & als sayin "whew that guy wu sure did it to us
with all those changes all those different trips."

saturday al and marguerite thot we sd we wld come by at 10am to
pick them up. we thot they sd they wld come by then so we all sat
around waiting, meanwhile theyre out for breakfast   do their
laundry then return for a nap. when i phone again   im told
they just went out and we thot ha they are on their way here but
that was over an hr ago. now we are driving along spring garden to
quinpool the rotary and the 2nd turnoff towards peggy's cove and its
light-grey and windy but lookin like it might clear as brilliant
autumn color'd undulant landscape turns our heads right and left. We
pass second growth scrub/bush and stone. then its almost all &
only stone, acres of speckled stone, litter'd stones perch'd
precariously on bedrock or tumbled into groupings in
crevices, acres upon acres of small stones stacked on larger ones
looking like neolithic graveyards. & the road curves it shifts
it changes directions almost turning in on itself then its straight out
and again left then right all the way to peggy's cove.
we spend long warm afternoon sitting and walking about on and warming
ourselves by heat caught-in-stone, with blue atlantic at our feet
al saying "its water same as ours i guess but it reaches over a-
cross to europe and africa. thats different to where were
situated on the ole pacific with its reach eastwards to japan china
& india." "ya, you must feel yr an awful long way from home."
marguerite gets soakt getting a cokebottle full of atlantis-water.
im trying to get shot of huge wave crashing rock when it comes in–
drenching me thru and thru. after lousy clam chowder and
what seemd to be seawater tea were leaving when dr.wu and david sewell
come by with cameras to see the sea & goin' down the road towards
their van the lighthouse rock & rollers arent they from winnipeg . . . & shit!
what are we all doin converging here at 3 o clock of a sunny afternoon,
at peggy's cove. then were at al and tobeys a few miles away.
we stretch out in grassy slope between their house and sea,
grabbin up the last of summer's sun. als from scotland he met tobey at
the chicago art institute. across the bay one dog barks   as a man
hammers shingles on his house against winter's blast.
abt 6pm toby says why dont we all go over towards mahone bay
and lunenburg where art and natalie their friends live   pick them up &
get some good home cookin at gladee's canteen.   theres
a strip of nice sandy beach that might look like long beach if you thot so.

al says "ok kiyooka but ya gotta git us back to halifax
for our gig." were following al and tobey in their red datsun along
windy one/three for interminable roller coaster ride thru nova
scotia countryside-night. at art and natalies, high on a slope back
off the road we have just enough time to go thru the house looking
at everything in sight inc. art's paintings and natalie's tapestries–
before piling into the white van to head out towards gladee's
canteen. its a mere shack beside blacker than black sea.
marguerite sayin if she had drunk the seawater it wld'nt have got
kicked over onto the floor of the van. if she had done that and
could have hung on all the way back to Vancouver, without needing to piss, she
could have pisst it in the pacific. that woulda been simpler than
luggin a fucken cokebottle full, all the way back.
after the fish soup, lemonmeringue pie. after hamburger, homemade rootbeer,
the pickled herrings and hot chicken, after mick jagger on old wurl-
itzer and much laughter were headin back to art and natalies 15 mere
miles back along the way. then, we are all there at their place
sitting around the kitchen table with cups of tea watchin *going down the road*
on portable teley beside fresh-baked loaf of brown bread– –and
everyones asking "what road?" "where" and why this, this road or that one, the
other road, Whitman's Road" . . . "& christ! aren't they stupid, aren't they fucken
stupid, & ya, do you remember doing that yrself, anything like it yrself
do you, did you, could you, & do ya think the nova scotia bureau of
tourism underwrote it." theres eight of us sitting around
a table   momentarily at ease with each other, at this, this windy crossroad–
before shipping out on different roads, & thats also some
kinda movie, aint it? als nervous abt getting back to halifax, we're all worn out.
al and tobey have decided to stay overnight with
their friends.   they drive us out to the turnoff where we will know
how to make it back. almost home i need to piss   do that
lookin up at near fullmoon.

sunday night al and marguerite did it to all of us: al alias
seamus firm, alias cricket, and marguerite, clickin' clankin' clackin' thar way
thru barbaric yawlp sound-clusters with 4 yr old essen blonde wonder-
child laughin with them and al pickin up on essen's laughter.   later
essen comes by to tell em how he liked both of 'em.

whats distance? whats east? wheres west? where is anyone, but there where
they are doing what, they in fact do, and whats real, whats surreal is
the fact of our mobilities   how it enables al and marguerite to be
here in halifax with us   as earlier theyre in ottawa

and kingston, with others and the day they waited for me under
cornwallis's freshly bronzed frock coat this old guy comes by and tells them
he's the first canadian to build and fly air planes.
then i take them home in the white van
that brought me here, 2 months and 4 thousand miles ago, today.

       blessings on thee & all yr kin

10/ 11/ '71
Halifax NovaScotia

Dear Daphne

    Theres a small colour repro of
The Creation of the World frm The Book of Hours
2nd half 14th century)   tackt up on
the white wall right in front of my typewriter.
In the very beginning when his Lordship
put it all together

                      The Order is E a r t h
                                    F i r e
                                W a t e r
                                   A i r

        each element
        contained within a Ring
        (varying in
        circumference frm
        The Centre
                    O u t w a r d s

'somewhere'
within this miniature but
nonetheless
HUGE construct   your R I N G /S
r-i-n-g their changes
 .

              Yesterday out on Barrington St.
with my camera   eventide light shafts of   in
the leafy shadows under tall elm trees   St. Paul's
Cemetery 'where' old white-haired rubby   huddled
in tatters sleeps beside   aged headstones   emptied
wine bottles   His blackout soften'd by splinter'd
light : death's shadow/ proximity   illumined
 .

Mariko, her lovely friend Claire
writes. And I am wondering if you might see them?
tell them if the occasion enables how
writing goes hand-in-hand with rites-of-passage
and other etceteras

                    10/ 12/ '71
                    Halifax NovaScotia

to the Mur-muring Maiden
    of Kitsilano/ Robert's Creek

    Biz 1st: good news Amaya bought some work. I'm gonna
                need the money for all my kith and kin
                plus others I've gotta help feed. etcetera.
                Whats happening for my silk-screens   has P.W.
                sent 'em off to N.P. Toronto and T.W. in
                Montreal who have both asked for them?   And
                where does my account stand am I in the red as
                usual?   Further, have my ptgs arrived back
                frm Montreal? If so send me a list of them to
                check against my own.

                SHIT!   C. you ought to go right up to him and
                ask for a substantial raise. No one not even an
                artist shld have to work cheap.

. . . been working on Tom Thomson's Secret Papers the ones
found all bundled up on the topmost cupboard of an
attic cupboard. The ones the demolition men almost tosst
out when they started wrecking the building Tom long
ago lived in. A bundle of papers retrieved by a
young friend a student of mine who was working for
the demolition firm during the summers. He sent them on
knowing that I would be interested. And I
have been going through them and I thinking
that T.T. had a commonsensical (therefore a– –
Canadian?) view-of-things. What a contrast T.T. makes
to my other (earlier) hero Stanley Spencer who was in
all things except his art a romantic if not plain nuts.
Carole, if you put them together and sandwich me in
between them you'll get a larger than life man/artist the
kind William Blake perhaps, exemplified. Anyhow I've
been working on Tom's secret papers and what will come
out of it viz my own writings is anyone's guess. Its
all astonishing, to say the least.

D.V. Thompson sez
abt Medieval Book Painters that
they prized
            Ingenium/ Intellectus/ Ratio

   and so does yrs truly

for both of you

    last night we lay in bed with yogurt & fruit listening
    to your tape. that afternoon we thumb'd thru G.S. saw
    Gerry's photos/words abt Shell Beach mutual acid-trip.
    night before Al & Marguerite laid their WestCoast Sound
    Trip on us at the school. in/between i wrote Brad abt
    them. then we've had a Mr. Ian Wilson with us at N.S.C.A.
    his art consist'd of sitting around a table with
    others ala Wittgenstein, probing the provisional– –
    (a?) (r?) (t?) & thats his work, of art? earlier one Dr. Wu
    noted author of treatises on Chinese Painting showed
    how to move thru labyrinthian spaces on tip-toes. also
    W.T. Charlotte's Pa here awhile. so is/was Vito Occanti
    & Other eminences frm England/ Europe/ USA. & The Ant-
    ics of Us Artists does seem to spread frm coast onto
    coast, ceaselessly, as either shore's ocean does. yr tell-
    ing abt B.B. made us wish we were there to hear him.
    like they say 'hes far out far fucken out!' as for the
    infamous panama hat you gave me at Long Beach its still
    used tho it did get lost for 3 weeks when i left it
    at Al & Tobey's place near Indianhead after visiting
    Peggy's Cove. you can be sure i will bear it atop of me
    head all the way back even to Long Beach. next time
    you're stayin' in yr home away frm home The New Era
    Social Club say hullo for me. tell Glenn I've got
    a frontal shot of the new era dental shop in Lloyd-
    minster for him. Gerry, you gotta see tongue-in-
    (whose?)-cheek article abt one A.H. author of million
    dollar kitsch in current Maclean's. his new best seller
    is all abt fanciers of greenbacks.
    title M-O-N-E-Y ! like blatantly.
    for abt 6 weeks Krisys been painting over then over a-
    gain the painting she begun when we arrived. & the
    changes the ongoing changes of her painting is comparable
    to the changes im going thru with my G.S.W.S. book.
    not to mention the changes as they occur be-
    tween us daily. as for the Halifax/ Vancouver Festival– –
    i'll know by month's end how it pans

            wld dig to hear B.'s tape. ya– –
            & take care of each other when necessary

                              10/ 12th/'71
                              halifax nova scotia
dear Toni

            wee note to remind you i want to
            teach at U.B.C. because Vancouver is where
            i truly want to be. all my incessant
            moving abt is simply evidence of how home-
            less i've been   and will be til i find
            my self back in Vancouver.
            G. K. at V.A.G. sd (jokingly) 'Kiyooka yr
            too damned expensive for us.' which is
            plain bullshit   tho im not as cheap as i once
            upon a time used to be.   none of us are
            any more . or, rather who wants to be used
            cheaply when the so-called G.N.P. soars

Bau-Xi postcard says yr having a one man.
best to you for that occasion.
im reminded how you (later, E.B.) got into Morandi via
small plastic etchings, etc.   your works
continue the old Italian master's sensibilities – –
all the way over to me, gratefully.

                  not much else to say except how
                  im daily out into Nova Scotia Indian Summer
                  Countryside & for the 1st time in yrs
                  the scarlet orange & brown whiff
                  of autumnal loveliness tears my heart
                   into sweet/sad etceteras

      hows WestCoast from on high?
      is it (also) colourfill'd   if not
      pissing sweet rain daily

dear Danielle

        thank you for advising me abt
    S t o n   e d G l o v e s
                NOW!
        that my handsome gloves are going to Paris
        i want to go there.
                Paris in the Spring !
        –like entwined-bodies in an erotic dream   dreamt
        under the snow, mid-winter, Halifax.

        – –it wld be for the 1st time ever!
        .
        you forgot to mention 'who' i shld get in touch
        with, 'where' in Paris, etc. tell me – – –

a f a v o r:

could you put yr hands on
french/ english book/s of P. Eulard's poems?
i keep coming across his poems &
am moved by his lovely mouthings. his silences.
if you cant get a hold of a bilingual
edition a french one will do. i shall get somebody
to help me or fumble my own way thru .

"a mouth around which the earth turns . . ."
                          he sez

        p/s do you think Paris wld sponsor
        my going to the show? or   will it have to be
        the Canada Council?

                        yr brazen head pen pal

10. 27th.'71
Halifax Nova Scotia

dear   G l e n

Thanx for gettin rid of the Heap . . .

ah the splendour of a Halifax Fall   its un-
polluted mile high skies   red rock promontories
and the grey Atlantic. as far as far as N.S.
goes its among the old places w/ traces of
old European commerce   otherwise its as old
as the 1st native son. as for the NSCA its just
another Yankee branch-plant tho   thank god
the students are mostly Maritimers. I like
their quiet/presences their Atlantic/gait. the
school seems to have generous financial support
w/ more than the usual sufficiences for the
unusual like 'World Encounter' enabling select
students to go around the world (like their
sea going forbears, etc.

Hows things at the Grange?
are you still playing frisbee in the tall grass
between the arms of the bridge?
remember when We came out of the Cecil–pisst
found some fucker had lift'd my mini's
windshield–then, drove like mad across the bridge
the rain pouring in up to our ankles . . . ?

10/ 31st '71
halifax nova scotia

dear Mo / So-nia
    & Others at new era social club

        gawd how did you conjure up sech a luvly name
        for yr child? – –i cant tongue it let a
        lone hummm it or even write it   its Saleronkeny
        is it   W-O-W-yee!

been receiving cards/ letters etc frm all over
announcing galaxies of newborn babes. its got me thinkin'
how such myriad re-births must be some sort of kin-
dred confidence in 'space'/'ship' E A R T H : How despite
the many ways we keep on fucken-up we nonetheless
go on spinning therefore extend our selves into prosaic
tomorrows, forever . &

now that my own three daughters will soon make a grand-
father out of me (tho, i hope not too too soon!)
Im enwrappt with the thot of how my own mere whiff of
a life is inextricably woven in & thru other lives:
that backwards/forwards the 'i' i am is but a mere strand
in an intricate tapestry wherein my own daughters your
your newborn one are but several more strands in the ocean
of US. like how we do impinge upon each other, cease-
lessly. yeah .
        g l a d t i d i n g s
                                      /sez it

sal/er/on/ken/y – –gawd she'll be a wee 30
in 2000 ad when (if im around . . .) i will be 75!

& i cant imagine a nicer way to place Her in
the huge world than at a s-t-o-n-e-d Tea Party at
the new era social club.

imagine uncles/aunts etc. of the order of
Gerry/ Glenn/ Carole & Other–s
inc a fictive grandpa say like yrs truly

halloween midnight '71
halifax   novascotia

dear Gladys

      Halifax Guardian (lousy establishment rag
sez "city council wants halloween changed frm the 31st
a sunday back to saturday the 30th . . ." were wonderin'
whats happened since theres only the usual Tobin Street
Noises. does it mean that droves of little costumed
and painted buggers will be bye the bye is it tomorrow
nite–to drive us mad as Alice's Mockt Turtle or–
did They all come by   was it last night!

A ngela's note announcing their newborn adds that
Cliff and Gladys have split. O Gladys the sweet/sad plain-
pain and the angst that afflicts   the heart and the head of
those of us who for whatever reason 'pledged' to love
honour and protect   the Other . . . then found it impossible–
but hung-on by our heads til bit by bit even it
loosen'd its hold and everything fell at our feet into
tiny bits of bitter matter-of-fact-mess. O Gladys–
the new meta-physics of Love will have to spell it out
clearly that even 'bondfast' cant stick us together.
yet, theres a pact if not a pledge which our decadelong
friendship is evidence of . . .

            moments before i went to piss and
            theres Krisy's knickerd bum sticking out
            beyond pink tiled half-wall hiding chippt
            enamel bath tub. i thot, is she puking into it . . . ?
            when i told her my thot she laughed and
            went on brushing her hair   as lovely Maritime
            Autumn continues to hang sodden leaves on
            this my 45 th Fall

            yeah . . .
            much more than even
            these words
            for you

                G l a d e y e s

11/ 1st/ '71
Halifax NovaScotia

DearGerry/ Carole/ Glenn
     and Others

              at the New Era Social Club
              on Powell Street (hub of pre-war Jap Town
              Vancouver B.C.

     abt the Halifax/ Vancouver Exchange:
     got the proposal off to the C/C/ our pres G.K. is goin
     to Ottawa he'll do what he can to instrument it .
     Im askin for $9.5oo. at $750.oo per participant. plan
     calls for 8 artists frm each city of whom 4 will be
     paid for by the college 'cause theyre goin there anyway.
     will send on the proposal when i get it copied   it
     tells the story. frm here on its up to the Canadian
     Taxpayer's Medici .

with much fanfare Krisy has quit smoking (again.
shes bought long sticky strings of black licorice to chew.
stunn'd on non-smoke she re-assures me its higher than
any mari-juana. stoned or not she does her thing w/ intensity
i marvel at. Gary Conway a student reports how its snowed
everywhere across this broad dominion even in vancouver–but
not here, yet   as tweedy guy walks by on Tobin Street with
big black and white spott'd dalmatians .

now that we know theres no place on earth to hide
from the vibes comin in from everywhichway i guess its time
to recognize we've just got our medulum obligatos the
coils of 'em to turn inside out, from within .

– –got all the Long Beach pics spread out on a table to
shape into a panorama of mid-summer '71 .

11/ 4th/ '71
h a lifax nova scotia

dear Carole

    lst Biz:

Don Macleod frm Gibson's says i owe him $60.
for books bought at his defunct store. i thot i had
paid him a portion of the price in advance but
cant remember. cld you check it out with Don and have
Paul pay whatever amt it be.

A.M. Studio's bill shld be paid immediately. (they
made orange plastic cube & stand for 2 of the laminates.

re: La Belle Express have 'em send on the ptgs
collect to the Bau-Xi. i mean Paul might as well have
them he has everything else.

i want a resume of my acct. & has there been
further word abt big Toronto sale?

- -

(tear on dotted line   of tears)

        couldn't cry. . . couldn't do a thing. . .
        s-t-u-n-n-e-d 'me' mouthing a
        dry pork chop. . . 'she' a raw carrot. . .
        blurts out "Roy I'm gay. . . I I
        cant dont want to make it with you. . .
        anymore. . ."

We lived day onto day, encapsulated in a mundane
eternity. . . or so it now seems with this this decisive end
to an almost unendurable Autumn. (Inimitably)(Utterly)
Krisy is going to move on though she does not know where or
 even when. Last night while I fitfully slept She cut off
all her lovely hair. . . *6 long months and 4000 miles later*
I'm sitting with my feet up on our kitchen window ledge . . .
just one more fallen leaf in Tobin Street's wet windy gutters
  . . . .

        . . . 'i' is
        nonetheless yours

11/ 5th/'71
Halifax NovaScotia

Dear D a p h n e

        been gettin my book together for
the G.S.W.S: *now* dont seem to be much more than
this day onto day pasting together of
my forlorn yesteryears. i could be post-markt
late 1960s AD etc .

the Emblazon'd Spectra of an Nova Scotia Autumn goes
on and on now into the lst week of November and
Im out/into the surrounding countryside–to see/sense
all the myriad transformations–excruciating in
its fallen lovelinesses. last night's wintry winds have
strippt the elm trees on Tobin Street the gutters
and brown grass cover'd in a motley of scarlet leaves.

H u l l o

Amchitka / Amchitka : 5 Hours before the B-L-A-S-T– –
Krisys been up all night long for several nights. now
shes fast asleep in the living/bed room. in the past
week shes quit smoking, even grass. she is on a strict
vegetarian diet (like raw carrots, raisins and tea
tonight. shes wiped her etching plate off so it cant be
printed: **with awesome deliberation** she has put both
house and body in order and waits for the sign that will
tell her where next? a dazed day ago she blurt'd
over supper ". . i, i cant sleep with you anymore Im gay."
this, as i mouth a piece of dry pork chop.
next morning i open my eyes onto the back of her tonsured
head and she asks me how i like it telling me
how she had shampoo'd it four times before taking her
scissors and razor to it . . .

. . . i feels encrusted with sweet-and-sour homo sapien
affections. . . i is the sum of all such accretions. . . a
bent reed in a   howling wind My Friend can be abysmal . . .

+

otherwise Halifax is where i hang my coat.
i keep writing as tho Vancouver is the whole world.

H u l l o : H o w   a r e   y o u ?

                          11/ 6/ '71
                          Halifax NovaScotia
Dear Claudia/ Francois

    be in Montreal Nov. 18/19th before going on to
    Ottawa and a Canada Council gig - - - - -

    Judy 'Wizard of Oz' Garland singin "Someday over
    the Rainbow" after a guy and gal duet of
    Bob Hope's theme-song "Thanx for the Memory"– — –
    All this syrup via CBC playing back the 40s/ 50s
    assortment of top-tunes etc. And 'me' smack
    in RCA Victor's Dog's Throat– –listening w/ cockt head
    to his master's hoary vocables.

    Ah Halifax giveth yrs truly the loveliest sweet
    and sour F-A-L-L he's known. . . even today, sittin' abt
    window wide open to let salt/ sea/ air pungencies
    pour in

        (I seem to be root'd in Atlantic
          G r e y t i d i n g s .

11/ 8/ '71
Halifax NovaScotia

Dear Jock Hearn

     A few days back I told Krisy abt you
and the World Zen Centre . . . . As She is into some
sort of spiritual trip I cant help her with.
Which awesome fact leaves us no alternatives but
to go separate ways. out of a multitude of
esoteric books like the I Ching, Tibetan Book of
The Dead, The Tarot and Others plus what she
was shown in and thru her own paintings and etchings
She has come to this   this awefill'd need for
a religious context the W.Z.C. could fulfill. At
any rate THE HOLY QUEST for The Grail is on– –
I'm only doing my bit. Will you let me know She
arrived safely ?

          – – –Living these past few days w/
          a tonsured Lady: I've patted her
          smooth utterly bald dome . . . . Both of
          us laughing at at that penitent
          act.
               O jock! I am bereft, again!

Hope this wee note finds both of you
thriving .

11/ 11/ '71
Halifax NovaScotia

Dear Gerry/ Carole

    . . . a bare cover of abt an inch of snow
    this clear Maritime morning. Now at 3PM the lst
    sun in days has suckt almost all of it   up
    into itself. And and I have never felt such an
    intense a-loneness   its not at all that oft-
    times pathetic loneliness . . . but a burning way of
    all all pathetic impulses, something like that.
    Krisy has been gone for 3 days. Her zealous
    it must be 'quest' left us in the end with nothing
    not even the comfort of each other's arms. O!
    O my gawd the intensities of/ the perversities of
    our old man/ young woman/ old crone/ young fool
    conjugations/ the laughable/lamentable thing
    we once upon a time/ had. . . Now 6 months/4000 miles
    later I'm fingering the coil'd brown hair she
    left behind in a blue and white striped EDDY MATCH BOX

    Take good care of your utterly naked selves and
    each other   O Brother/ Sister

Nov. '71
Halifax NovaScotia

Dear K i y o

    your forlorn Pa wonders abt you– –
    he wonders if youre diggin' school which is
    mostly abt having a good teacher and
    one or two good friends???   and How was the
    big field trip you mention'd earlier?
    like what did you see/smell/hear/   & feel while
    you and your buddies were there?

    Pa is sittin' in his small white study Here
    on Tobin Street with his window wide open
    onto the salt/sea/air comin' in from the harbour.
    earlier he is out walkin in/thru the fog .
    you know how it comes ever so quietly in upon
    everything . . . and you feel like floating in-
    stead of walking 'cause nothing seems to be where
    it's usually seen . . . til you're almost on top
    of it. walking in Halifax fog reminds Pa of the
    soggy nights in Vanouver, yr hometown .

    .

abt writing: You put the
Cinnamon Kid thru his changes   as
when the Pukey Punks
have him down on the grimy floor
of an east end tenement
and they're kicking the piss out of him.
or   where the hell is
the door ?

        How to get the Kid thru
        before the shit hits the fan and

        The Story   ends .

like   keep the writing happening (even
when the Kid aint active
                verbs/ move– –

        nouns

    nice, to hear frm you .

11/ '71
halifax nova scotia

dear George & Angela

    . . . . ever since my Pa wrote to say that i must be mad
to leave my famfly and why? why? did i do it and
cant i 'forgive' and 'forget' and go back home . . . I've
wisht i could give birth to some mirth or malevolent
curse if not a baby– –to take Pa's mind off my mis-
anthropic ventures. sure wish i had a compass to tell me
which way my feet ought to move

    Gladfull all three of you made it. its
been (seemingly) a longlong time since i went thru (in
my own foolish way) the altogether simple but fraught
begetting of a child. to hear Ang tell of it is to
be reminded again How the man i am is the other half who
as Creeley wld say, simply but intently watches–then
might go on to tell abt it. i was not on hand at
the birth of my own three daughters–thus have that
remorse to also live with but . . . . i wld nonetheless tell
of the sheer presence they have in the world. yeah
to go on simply telling that .

    old Pablo P. turn'd 90 lately. according to
CBC experts he aint done much of consequence since he was
my age, etc. but does seem (almost malignantly) to go
on and on. to which i responded by asking myself ". . . am
i also a dried-up old olivepit?" "have i already sur-
passt my own mediocrity, etc?"–to which a firm but
small voice sez "thats shit you aint even begun yet!"
which wee voice re-assures if not altogether soothes the
me i am .

    George wanta read my Honshu Backcountry
    Trip? its where i need a critical eye to pry
    into its machinations. if yr too busy I'll
    lay it on another hapless friend/poet.

hr by hr my brief whiff of a life seems
to be longer than memory's awe-fill'd HUG . . . .

    chugg-a-lugg one for me
    at The Cecil .

11/ 29th/ '71
halifax nova scotia

dear Carole

>just back frm week-long stint on the C.C.
>senior awards committee. i had passt in front
>of me (via slides) the work/s of my contem-
>poraries: thus, was given copious insights in-
>to *their/mine* obsessions, falterings & Yes!
>our small break-thrus. i have had to make(day
>by day)nervous discriminations abt their work/s
>argue when necessary 'for' or 'against' it.
>&/ to do all this with several equally committed
>members. W H A T A J O B ! nonetheless
>everything i lookt at is a measure of my own work
>my very own response/abilities. in that sense
>alone it was worth it. & my thot is i wont do it
>again i dont want to yardstick my peers   not
>thata way .

.

Krisy been gone since the 8th. She is a
tonsur'd eagle with a splinter'd wing.
Vancouver very much on her mind.
Carole, i gave her yr phone number & address– –if
she shld call on you will you do what you can for her?
i have done what what i can, etc. i is dis-located
but no longer down in the depth. when you hit the very
bottom of the pit theres no way to go but upwards
thru murk into crystalline glow .

Gerry's 'Love is a round/ corner' sez it as pun.

>>yeah   send on J.L's article abt
>>yrs truly as one of the artists of the yr.
>>i needs a belly-rumble to hang me on.

>>.

>>re: Halifax / Vancouver EXCHANGE
>>no hopeful words frm C.C. despite my
>>enquiries there. if it nonetheless
>>h-a-p-p-e-n-s you will know 1st

Nov. /'71

dear Monica

    i've sent Deano another fucken cheque whc shld pay
for a divorce and a half.
                    i never thot i wld have to
pay-thru-the-nose for *the pain* of our parting   but
that we might, separately, go on sharing familiarities.
further back when we were very much together i thot
only death could utterly part us. that is 'if' i ever
thot abt the matter, then.

i just wanta say that after all the hassles we have
had with dimwit you shouldnt have any more to do with
him the way he flaps his lard over nothings.   as for
his disreputable partner i hope the Lawe throws th book
at him . p/s have deposited all of S's cheques in yr
acct. check it out the next time your in .
.
our PM after the stale/mated general elections sd:
". . . no doubt the universe will continue to unfold as
it should, etc. . . ." if so, it surely includes all
of our mutual vicissitudes, together with, whatever B-
eatitudes we have had together

                                    take good care of yrself &
                                    our children

12/ 10th/ '71
Halifax NovaScotia

Dear Mariko

    . . . got your letter with poem in it then
got another   (yesterday)   with Claire's poem abt you
and yr boy friend in it. getting letters from
his daughters is just abt the nicest thing Pa can
imagine here in Halifax. every day he goes to
his mailbox to see if theres a letter from one or
the other of the three of you. or if not then
theres often as not a letter from one of his dear
old friends. your pa likes the way letters can
prevail over the silences each life is equally fill'd
with. like when there is no ear to lilt a word in
letters can be a man's best friend.

    . . . wish i could tell you what i think Halifax is
all abt. wish i could do that. but, i dont really know
anything abt Halifax but what i am doing here daily.
which of course includes the daily fact of teaching
plus what i have to do for myself as artist. wherever
we have gone   as a family your Pa has always done
these two mutual things. and he has known for longer
 than you have lived that whatever he comes to know
abt the place/s he lives in comes from the fact of his
squatting right there and taking in whatever
comes his way.   im living across from the Nova Scotian
Hotel and the waterfront.   everything i need includ-
ing the college is not more than 20 minutes walk away
– –i like that sense of compactness more and more.
but, no matter where i live i go on doing what i
can do   which includes what i cant do, too. whether
in Vancouver, Halifax, or Kyoto i am aware of what i
do not accomplish. like it must be that doing and its
contrary *not doing* are equal.
no matter   it'll all go on and on til the last tic-toc
which both of us know is a part of the biz too.
if you and claire think a book can be shared then
the enclosed book is certainly for both of you. other
wise you can lend it to her when you've finisht it.
and if you read it savour it it will get into you and

work its wonders   without your even trying to.
Dear Mariko   your Pa dont think poems can change any-
thing   let alone any large thing like the World– –
but it just might touch one small heart's fulsomeness.
you can if you want–show the letter to Claire.

Luv to all 3 of you
& all of your numinous young friends .

& luv (nonetheless) to your mother.

12/ 10th/ '71
Halifax NovaScotia

Dear J a n

GEEZUS its almost that time of the year again
almost yuletide time again   but your Pa aint gonna
panic over its coming   not any more. from now
on its just going to be another ordinary
day – –like the days in the rest of the year.
T h r e e C h e e r s for each and every day   tho
it comes only once a year.   your Pa thinks each
day ought to be as special as Christmas or New Year
but if you want to disagree its Ok as Pa also
thinks that some days are more special.
Jan your Pa wont be home for Christmas but he will
be in Vancouver during the 3rd week of January
for a teacher's conference) which is just an excuse
to have his way paid, there– –to see all of you .

. . . who is your Pa? 'who' in other words/ worlds
can your Pa be? i ask you/ myself The Question
because i have a hunch its been on your mind lately.
has it? anyhow   your Pa might say he is what he
thinks he is   therefore, what he could be.   there's
your image of him, your sister's image/s of him.
there is your mother's image of him and all of his
friends images of him   not to mention the images
your pa's so called enemies might have of him. like
who is he   and whose image of him does he
correspond to? one film loop shows your Pa
as a young lad abt 13 swimming bare-balls in the
Elbow River, at night. he's with 'Pee Wee' 'Buck' &
Others   standing around a huge bonfire fed by
old rubber car tires. theres a sequence of images of
each of us swinging out over the river on
the knotted end of a thick old rope and holdin'
our nose . . . lettin'go with a whoop and a S-p-l-a-s-h !
four years later he left home for the lst time– –
only to ride a freight train home abt 5 weeks later.
your Pa was flat broke but on his way to manhood.

– –SEE WHAT I MEAN ABT (EVEN) (YR. PA'S) IMAGES OF
WHO HE MIGHT BE !

theres one thing he knows
for certain   in so far as he knows
a few simple things   thats– –
how much he misses his lovely daughters.

L   o   v   e to your sisters & mother
for whats-his-name, yr Pa

12/ 10th/ '71
Halifax NovaScotia

clear K i y o

       its almost the winter solstice and
so warm out I've had to hoist up my window to
keep from drying out. you know that punk feel
ing when a body feels like an old prune– –the air
inside a room that dry. but the worst is yet
to come 'cause its the flat under me thats got
the only thermostat for all 4 flats in this
end of the house. in other words they control
the heat and my experience has been that when–
its too cold for them its altogether too hot for
the rest of us and vice-versa. in other words
when it does get cold as say hell is supposed to
be despite its brim-fires   the real Heats on.
anyhow–its like mid-Sept without all the colour-
ful maple leaves here on Tobin St. and every-
one here is amazed   considering theres snow
everywhere else in Canada, excepting (of course
B.C. p/s hows the rain ?

when i was your age i used to wait for my Pa yr grand
pa   to come home frm work. i wld wait for him on the corner
of 10th ave. & 2nd st. east beside the C.P.R. overpass
that went east/ west. i cld always tell when Pa was comin'
by the way he swayed frm side to side– –the more so when
he was slightly drunk–with each short stride.   when he got
to me I'd say hey Pa gimme a dime Ok. and almost all of
the time he obliged. there was 2 other ways i made my
weekly candy bar & movie money. i wld go down the backalley
between 3rd east and 4th west to gather up the cardboard
boxes to sell to William's Bros. for 2¢ each. then our
family friend and barber a Mr. Furusako regularly gave me
a dime to go buy fish cakes at Billingate's Market– –
with sawdust coverd floor on 8th ave. east. all in all
i easily made abt 50¢ a week   and that went far those days
when a bar cost a nickel and a movie one thin dime. your
Pa didnt find The Great Depression of the 30's repressive he
grew up surrounded with much affection   tho everything
else it seem'd was dirt cheap, including money.

send Pa a nice long letter to
cheer him up   he dont want a thing for Xmas
but that, ok. and love & kisses to
your sisters & your mother & others we know.

one day yr Pa will wear Halifax on his sleeve
like you wear embroider'd patches on yr jeans .

12/ 10/ '71
Halifax NovaScotia

Dear M o n i c a

    Our friend Carole sent newspaper clips
of the AWARD you won for the house. H U R R A H
I think I'm qualified to say that you do
deserve it– –yeah, and much more.

            everything
            thats happened has
            stood you   on
            your head *but* yr agilities
            landed you on yr own
            two feet.
                      ah the cartwheels
                      in/ between

            Hurrah
            for Monica
            her unflapp-able
            abilities

    keep in thar– –
    see the 4 of you 3rd week of January .

p/s tell the girls PLEEZ no presents for me .
and the cheque is for whatever each of 'em does w/ it .

12/ 11/ '71
Halifax Nova Scotia

Dear Daphne

Its abt 3.30PM. Half an hour ago I came home w/
a fist full of letters. Home long enough to make a
cup of tea and begin to read the letters– –a news-
paper clipping abt Monica winning an award for the
house she designed and caused to be built. A brief
note frm John Nugent asking me to be the artist-
in-residence at U.of S./ Regina Campus w/ an aside
abt a mutual friend who had another nervous break-
down after he tried to take off in a plane (he didn't
own. He was going to go after the man who ran off
w/ his new wife and got caught. Then, I am into yr
letter your heart's sweet litter 'when' the phone
whc seldom rings rang, loud and clear. Its Krisy's
tearfill'd voice via long-distance from San Francisco
sayin' I'm to blacken her etching the large plate
she left behind   sayin' its profuse-confusions was
the image she came to in her mind's confusions
at the Zen Centre. She added that she was broke and
that her father was flying down to take her back
to Calgary–where We had started frm a mere 9 months
ago. Gawd Daphne! How how much do any of us pack
into such chunks of time and how little I was able to
do for her tho we shared the same bed and board
etc. And much further back I spent my 1st 15 yrs there
but did not re-visit it more than a few times after
I left art school. It was thru Krisy that I recover'd
my hungry adolescence my east-end haunts etc– –in
so far as such early occasions can ever be recover'd.
Thru her thru the act of her showing me her city I
was shown, as it were, my own. All of which sez
that nothing in space/time is linear except in old
fashioned stories etc. I mean it goes on ceaselessly.
Heart's Stammerings etc. And just this morning I
had to have my van towed away for major repairs– –
after our 4000 miles breathless escapade across O!
Canada.

Mariko my oldest daughter writes she
enclosed a lovely poem by her best friend
Claire. The poem is abt Mariko's love-
affair etc. Daughters (like sons?) r-i-n-g
heart's sweet and sad changes, gladly

                                Bleak House: Nov. '71
                                frm HELL–a fact NovaScots
                                drear Atlantic
                                                knows

Dear Friends

    Krisy left   left in a swirl of snow from
the Lord Nelson Hotel at 8AM. . . She's left for
Roanoke Virginia and the Appalachian Mts.–
in quest of the holy grail. She left to tempt Fate
and took the six shrivelled apples that graced
our mantelpiece   as a token a talisman or is it a
omen . . . ? Three days later she phoned from
Roanoke to tearfully say that when she climbed up to
where the World Zen Centre was supposed to be she
only found a few derelict shacks and their long-haired
denizens who sd Jock had left sometime ago for
'somewhere' in Pennsylvania. And the next time she
phones me she is in a hospital in San Francisco.
She had it seems an encounter w/ it must be Everyman
's Adversary Death   and he brutally denied
her.
       And . . . i feel 'gnomic' as those apples which
      she sd she had to eat .
                                Hullo   Hullo is anyone
                                at home ?

12. 11/ '71
Halifax NovaScotia

Dear Harry / Katie

been listening to the eminent Canadian cum
new frontier Yankee economist John Galbraith chatting
with another economist via CBC. And I thought
I heard 'em say   tho you must not quote me)   that
in a world of innumerable Ideo/ Idol/ Adversaries its
difficult if not utterly impossible to initiate
massive de-centralization viz 'socialism' without dis-
sembling General Motor and Krafty Cheese. etcetera
Capital Gains taxes the imagination. As an erstwhile
free enterprise concept Our G.N.P. seems a grey
weightless/ odourless 'confection' on the backs of our
gross national identities. And doesn't it continue
to be more or less a truism that 'currency' knows no
national borderlines. Is without intrinsic value
thus can and does foment rapacity avarice hatreds and
promiscuity not to mention the ubiquitous NA style
philanthropist and demagoguery. Thank god I also have
a considerable passion for good old fashioned
silence/s, heart's balm.

Only a month ago I thot
I had all the news I wanted . . . . then, Krisy took off
she left for Roanoke Virginia where the world zen
centre was supposed to be. She went on to California
and the San Francisco zen centre and now she is
back in Calgary, again. And how come how come she left
me Here with her etchings the ones I bought
plus a lock of her hair– –How come?   I suppose theres
no more of an answer to this than why Galbraith
or any other economist dont seem to know how to take
the plums out of a fat corporation's mouth and
put it into a hungry man's mouth, elsewhere

Katie you cld if you want to
phone Krisy to say Hi and why dont you come by
to do some sculpting. it wld help her
to cut thru as with a blow torch or sharp chisel
her t-h-i-c-k-e-t-s

and a lovely white
solstice/season to both of you

12/ 12 th/ '71
Halifax nova scotia

dear Tod & Fumi

    s i l e n c e aint golden when one's head is
a swarming hornet's nest   no sureee.   all that infernal
buzzin dont leave yrs truly free. ah! the problems of
each his separateness–dont it disclose an awesome
awareness of our togetherness? o, one, two, three
who is really & truly free? –o, one, two, three   aint
we all tied to a huge motherfucker of a tree. here
i am alone on Tobin St. in Halifax and there you are
4000 miles away tied to Vancouver's mid-winter sodden air.
o, one, two, three i saw a vision of Her up in a tree.
o, one, two, three she showed her smooth white thighs to
me and i thot like wow i am not really free. or what
price freedom whats fierce freedom's aweful price tag ?
either/ or has finally become boring–one wants all of it
real or imagined both simultaneously proclaim'd.
i mean dont words like turd seem a mere approximation
unless the senses can hang on to it etc. or is it all a
mere smear. i held the idea of Her in mind held her there
with a loving firmness but she nonetheless slippt frm
my grasp –a marine thing momentarily claspt before squirming
into sweet annihilation. meanwhile down on Point Pleasant
Beach each of us had our own vantage point for standing
seaward. Auden quoted sayin 'Love dont have to do with
looking into the beloved's eyes but that both look in
the same direction, etc. . . . ." that awesome commonsensical
horizon two pairs of eyes simultaneously scan. i mean
the Atlantic's grey mass with one small boat afloat on it
together seen. here in Halifax i seem to be doing what
i have more or less done since age twenty. i seem to be
in that sense merely me. stagnation is a concept a swamp
wouldnt understand. STAND UP ! tree like and wave your
leafy arms seaward, etc. if the saltspray dont sodden you
heaven's semen will do it to you, etc. o, one, two, three
daughters on my mind. whats freedom's price without all
of you? o, one two, three your old man just might be a
wee oak tree. no pledges, pleas, public wailing walls or
primal scream. no Jerusalem, no greensward or hollow
mandates–just a mere oak tree. and i am making all this

up as i go along. if i keep dropping a turd here or
there its to put some commonsense into my absurd reality.
now a days my whiff of a life seems to be a thin slice
of fact cum fiction. hows yours?

                        with love & curses

12/ 12th/ '71
Halifax NovaScotia

Dear Mother and Father

    – –-given the fact that I have never been one
to write home regularly. given the fact that I do not
like using the telephone. plus the fact of my in-
frequent visits   not to mention all that does happen
to each and every one of us all the moments of
our assorted lives . . . . you have every reason to be
confused abt my recent actions. I willingly admit to
what you sd in your recent letter abt *the mess* I
seem to have made with my life and that I ran away from
it to Halifax 4000 miles away. Yet I want to insist
that thats only a part of the matter tho no doubt– –a
very large part in your own heads. Afterall I still
have the children and it cld be sd a mortgage to support
not to mention my own expensive habits– –I am however
bereft nonetheless a family man and I mean to live
up to all my obligations. I wld insist I am not
here in Halifax (by preference) as much as 'need' and
probably wld still be in Vancouver if I had got a job.
Anyhow . . . . here I am and I intend to make the most of it.
Mo and I have been drifting a-part for some time. It
seems that our marriage (the children notwithstanding)
dwindled into a dull routine that neither of us cld
or perhaps wanted to do anything abt. Or so I felt and
still feel abt it. In the end the agonizing end I
simply but w/ a huge pain ceased to even want want all
the years we shared together to go further. . . . . What
else can I say abt it that you cannot locate in
your own heart's anguishes . . . . ? As for the children I
will always and forever be 'their' father 'who' was not
around much, anyhow. As you both know I have always
been (crazily) obedient to my own (foolish) promptings.
For what my life has been worth such promptings have
brought me this far and– –theyll carry me into whatever
future I also also have. It seems that everything or
rather almost everything I have done since 20 stinks w/
my promptings viz Art and thus my innermost feelings
are hinged to such predilections. some say 'addiction'
no matter I know you know what is meant. I wld add

for what its worth that Art is not separable from the I
that wld be a family man a husband father and brother.
How shall I accomplish– –thru Art the very shapeliness I
can sometimes 'see' as my life, etc. remains the most
insistent the most compelling need. I look forward
to the Christmas holidays to get into my own workings.

take good care of your selves
I shall in so far as its given me to do so
do the same
     – –as always

12/ 15/ '71
Halifax NovaScotia

Dear CEL / Francois

   – – –if yr still thinking of coming here
you better let me know as I just might go off
somewhere and not be here for you. I'm a
long ways down in the pit of bleakness and cant
seem to surface . . . . at least, not yet. So– –
I'm thinking it cld be useful to get lost lose
myself in a crowd of strangers, etcetera.
And if you do come bring Susy who shld know I
wld be damned pleased to see her.

   – – – Ah Claudia there are fool men who dont know
that red cabbage is good for their health.

Francois if you haven't got a fireplace
a yule log is worse than a conceptual hearth.

                    winter/solstice
                    Capricorn's treasonable season
                    bids you to enfold each
                    other for warmth

12/ 15th/ '71
Halifax NovaScotia

dear George and Angela

    now yr a Mom and a Pop how it feels to
plumb the bottom of yr feelings   for a Child
inside of yr daily lives? Angela   don't– –
motherhood feel more like the old wive's tales
than glib-lip of women's lib? or am i jus
an old fashion'd chauvinist? I've just finisht
a book whc you might be interestd in reading
while the baby teases yr tit–its abt Zelda Fitz
gerald Scott's wife her mad-cap life. my gawd
how it held me who hasn't got a woman to hold any
more. Segal's Love Story by comparison is
just a plastic burp in the teeth of Zelda's om
nivorous appetites. i can see how Tristan
and Isolde will be lovers forever just as long
as theres a George and Angela or a Roy and
who-ever   together with their old adversary Death.

    George   sometime during the holidays I'll send
a 60 minute tape for 3 Hours Later. itll be a fact
cum fiction compendium reamed out of an empty-
heart 'me'. i think Ill do it on Dec. 24th th lst
anniversary of one lost fingertip. as an ancient
Maximus sez what dont change is the will to change– –
tho i dont quite believe it my actions prove to
be otherwise which is Im sure what he means.
met Bobbie Hogg in Ottawa while on C/C/ biz then
met Victor and Barrie in Toronto. heard how Michael
O created a legendary Bill the Kid out of his
own wit and violences. then to get back to Halifax
and find all 4 of em in the G.S.W.S. was indeed most
pleasurable. if GENEVE aint just abt the best
Bowering you can bury me at a Rocky Mountain Foot
but not i beg you not   on the lone prairie.

    .

    Vincent sd "the more i think of it the more i feel that
theres nothing more artistic than to love people . . ."

and may the winter solstice not darken the whites of all
of your eyes til Spring plants a crocus in them.

. . . and how are my favorite chihuahuas? my lap's History
wouldn't be complete wihtout their palpitations.

                George   you cld B-A-R-K at em for me

12/ 20/'71
Halifax NovaScotia

Dear George Knox

    I continue to be keen abt teaching at UBC and
write again to re re-mind you of it.
My family is there so are most of my best friends:
callit a Heart's Geography .– –if I stick
my head out of the front window on Tobin Street I
get a huge whiff of Atlantic brine back of
Water Street whc serves to remind me I am afterall
an Oriental/ Westerner who never has had a
Mediterranean Dream. Nonetheless I agree w/ Pablo's
buddy Paul Eulard who sez a poet is "a mouth a-
round which the earth turns." Yeah.
.

I take it to be the biz of Pedagogy to move
energy/ love abt any 'thing' thru muthos/ mythos
over to an Other and in the very act gather up
whatever seems relevant to the issue at hand.
Most of what continues to pass as Education is merely
informational. As for all the different sorts of
media' theyre lib-libations for a viewer's digestion
or divertimentos. After nearly 20 yrs of it– –
(my gawd!) I am adamant abt my abilities for part-
ing with everything I think I know. All of whc
could be another definition of the Socratic modality
etcetera.
        – – –shall we hear from you ?

December '71
Tobin Street   Halifax

Dear V i c t o r

Ahhhh!
Cape Traverse : Verse : Curses : Wave

        a Lighthouse   a Gathering of
        a Clan   a Celebration of Homeliness
        a Heave   Surge   Salt spray
        a Clapboard Haven

    "no man an island unto himself"

the black horse galloping across the field
nearby   the lighthouse . . . North Cape

the red rock caves   Libby's fire   Atlantis

what to do w/ it but live it lively
  "   to do w/ it but divine it
  "   to do w/ it but dead or alive die gratified
  "   to do w/ it but attend the HIVE

old homily sez :
The Family that lives lively gathers honey.

    this is for the Ladies at Cape Traverse.
    its for the sacred mother of Ponticherri we saw
    on television. its for all of our assorted
    mothers and daughters. its for all their/ our
    mutabilities.
        H a i l (and) F a r e w e l l

Maryrose   Maryrose
the bats the runic bats in the belfry
the dwarf telling a warpt tale in the back of a van
the moon light and a muddled tail
the story the hoary old story without end
the bend in the road the twice-told
        twist in the serpent's tale
  the story un-edited .

When he and I,
after drinking and
talking, approached
the goddess or woman

become her, and by my
insistence entered
her, and in the ease
and delight of the

meeting I was given that
sight gave me myself,
this was the mystery
I had come to— —all

manner of men, a
throng, and bodies of
women, writhing, and
a great though seemingly

silent sound— —and when
I left the room to them,
I felt, as though hearing
laughter, my own heart lighten.
.
What do you do,
what do you say,
what do you think,
what do you know.

     Creeley's Pieces

one cockeyed middle-aged man wants you to know How
the weekend shone 'cause of your numinous presences.

h a n g o n t o   Dear Life

12/ 20/ '71
Halifax NovaScotia

Dear Chris and Viv

    W A T C H O U T !
here comes that old pagan pageantry agin– –
and its the goat-footed one's season the season of
ice-berg flotillas frozen toes and feet
indiscretions under a warm comforter   polar
dreams and hibernation. And   I'm sitting here
Scrooge-like counting the cursed tic . . . toc . . .
clock's timely incontinencies . . . How it teases
a fallen dick. Hickory-dickory-dock the mouse
ran up the clock the clock struck one and
the mouse fell down and broke his crown   hickory
dickory dock. Old fiend Roy alias Harold Lloyd
hangs impiously frm the long arms of the
tower's clock. Otherwise he's watching Sanyo Xmas
soap operas while the guy across the street a
natal Haligonian puts up his christmas lights.
Now he's spraying styrofoam frost on the windows
and thru the thick falling snow . . . nails a
big red cardboard Santa to the clapboard siding.
Atlantis Night/ s   snow   gin and tonsures
tearfill'd semen. D-A-U-G-H-T-E-R-S of Albion.
 Snow mounds for the children of the North
Wind

        and   an avalanche of (vestal)(virgin) DREAMS
        to both plus a hoary maytree for Chalane.

                the
     – –Gap : Agape– –
          Dream

HALIFAX/VANCOUVER: EXCHANGE

thursday march 9th. noon thru 3 pm
in dalhousie students union bldg.

*cromwell's raga

                (don druick in concert)

*a benefit for the national gallery
 of canada

                (gerry gilbert read-in)

*image bank deposits

                (michael morris, mr. peanuts, art rat)

*skipping rope piece art works

                (gathie falk, performance pieces)

A Nation-Wide
Proprioceptive Party
Looped together
On one scenic Trans-Canada
Eye & Ear Tape:

A Spring Celebration

Vancouver in Halifax
March 6th thru 11th

Halifax in Vancouver
March 26th thru 30th

nightly performances at **The Nova Scotia College of Art & Design.**
come & join us in the festivities. (see accompanying schedule.)

        co-sponsored by
        The Nova Scotia College of Art & Design.
        Vancouver Art Gallery. &
        The Canada Council.

HALIFAX/VANCOUVER: EXCHANGE

monday march 6th. 8 pm
f o r e s t i n d u s t r y
                                    (16mm actual time film, glenn lewis)

tuesday march 7th. 8pm
i m a g e b a n k m a r c h s t a t e m e n t s
                                    (with michael morris, art rat & mr. peanut)

wednesday march 8th. 8pm
f o r m i n g p a r t
                                    (don druick in concert)

thursday march 9th. 8pm

c a n a d a ' s n a t i o n a l m a g a z i n e p r e s e n t s
h i s t o r y o f v a n c o u v e r
                                    (gerry gilbert & friends, read-in)

friday march 10th. 8pm

s o m e a r e e g g e r t h a n i & o t h e r
t h e a t r e a r t w o r k s
                                    (gathie falk, performance pieces)

saturday march 11th. 8pm

evening of dave rimmer's films & big party afterwards

Vancouver participants inc:
glenn lewis
michael morris
gary lee nova (art rat)
mr. peanut
gathie falk
don & cheryl druick
gerry gilbert
carole fisher
dave rimmer
dallas selman & others

all performances at **The Nova Scotia College of Art & Design**
gallery at 8 pm.   watch 'art now bulletins' for other
activities inc. v.t.r. showings in the mezzanine gallery.

co-sponsored by ALL of the vancouver/ halifax participants,
the nova scotia college of art & design,
the vancouver art gallery, /with assistance from canada council.

HALIFAX IN VANCOUVER MARCH 26/30 th

sunday march 26th . 1.30 - 4.30pm

OPENING

video tapes/ films/ photo-works/ wall-pieces
: **occasion to meet & rap with Halifax Group** .

monday march 27th . 8 - 10pm
TO STAND
performance piece by Alastair MacLennan
144 CARDS
public performance coordinated by David Hellyer

tuesday march 28th . 8 - 10pm
NUDE AS NEGATIVE SPACE
video performance by Bruce Parsons
PASSAGE
performance piece by Toby MacLennan

wednesday march 29th . 8 - 10pm
VIDEO PIECE
by Ellison Robertson

"An abridged choral reading of the standard corpus
of present day english usage arranged by word length
and alphabetized within word length"
by Gerald Ferguson

thursday march 30th . 8 - 10pm
HEAP & OTHER ACTIVITIES
with Anita Martin & group

visiting participants

Bruce Parsons
Alastair MacLennan
Ian Murray
Anita Martin
David Hellyer
Toby MacLennan
Ellison Robertson
David Martin

also) works by

Gerald Ferguson	David Askevold
Doug Waterman	Jon Young
Wallie Brannen	Vito Acconci
Richard Jardin	Brian MacNevin
Gary Kennedy	Barry MacPherson
Graham Dube	Albert McNamara
Harold Pearse	Alan Mackay
Pat Kelly	Terry Fuller
	& 13 nscad students:
	"spacial definations"

non-events
unprogrammed projects in & around vancouver .

project
H a l i f a x / V a n c o u v e r : E X C H A N G E
----
o u t l i n e

Vancouver Coordinators:
Doris Shadboldt and Alvin Balkind

Halifax Coordinators:
Allan McKay and Bruce Parsons

Overall Coordinator:
Roy K. Kiyooka

Halifax / Vancouver EXCHANGE
----

proposes a complex interfacing of ideas   between
2 cities a continent apart . the intent– –
to introduce each to each thru a complex of activities
during one intensive week . **the 14 Participants**
include Image-makers/ Musicians/ Poets/ Theatre/and Dance
Folk chosen for their experimental works .
at least a part of our intention is to show the radical
ideas at work in the current art scene .

a joint resume of E V E N T /S in both cities
will be printed as programme and poster . all activities
warranting documentation will be documented.
highlights of the week's activities in both cities will
be VTR'd as permanent document/ catalogue .
 seminars/ demonstrations/ lectures/ informal get-togethers
with students, faculties and layman to suit.

> most of the events will take place at
> the Vancouver Art Gallery and the Nova Scotia
> College of Art . Other spaces will be
> sought in both cities. in Halifax theres Dal-
> housie U. and Mt. St. Vincent U. to mention
> just 2 . theres U.B.C. and Intermedia
> in Vancouver . plus all sorts of public indoor
> and outdoor spaces in both cities .

we shall look into these possibilities only
'if' and 'when' we get yr go ahead .

D a t e s
        Halifax in Vancouver 3rd week of January '72 .
        Vancouver in Halifax 3rd week of February '72 .

SUMMARY OF EXPENSES

per each participant :

. air fare Halifax/ Vancouver return	$350.
. hotels, meals, incidental expenses	$150.
. Honorarium	$150.
	$650.oo
. 10 Participants	$6.500.oo
. Film/ tape/ posters/ programmes/ etc.	$500.oo
net total	$7.000.oo

Vancouver participants (7) require $4.800.oo
inclusive of $250. for new projects .

Halifax participants (7) require $2.200.oo
inclusive of $250. for new projects .

4 out of 7 (possible) participants from Halifax
are on the NSCA faculty . theyll be subsidized by
the college as they will be attending a
university art conference in Vancouver .

whereas it was initially intended to have
the Exchange happen in both cities simultaneously
our intent is now to stagger them (note dates
so that each city's participants can be a witness to
the other city's activities .

copies of this letter have been sent to
the coordinators in both cities. the C.C. might consider
placing the moneys in their hands– –for allocation/s .
there is not much time to pull the whole thing together– –
could we hear from you as soon as its convenient ?

for all the participants,

December 21 /71

Dear Doris/ Alvin/ Others
    interest'd in the Halifax/ Vancouver: **EXCHANGE**

been making enquiries abt town   viz 'who' is doing
unusual things, if anything and theres certainly
enough going-on to put an exciting show on the road .

we're getting a small poster together *here* with
general info . particulars can be followed up via mimeo-
releases in both citys . you'll get a quantity of
them abt Jan. 7th for yr mailing lists, etc. 50/50 re
C.C. funds .

need a list of the Vancouver participants for C.C.
soon as possible . we want a broad representation: more
than just visuals and certainly more than just men .
therell be at least 4 women from here . it's, nonetheless
your choice/s– –Im just one indeterminate voice .

Doris and Alvin particularly) we need to put together
space/s and facilities for the 3rd week of Jan.
Hopefully the same 'space/s' and the same 'time/s'.
DATES 24/ 25/ 26/ 27/ 28th. will need several projectors
VTR monitors other hard and software .

NSCA is packaging abt 5 hrs of VTR tapes with titles
authors and durations.   you could do the same there
bring it along as part of someone's baggage . therell
be a chorale for 26 voices/ assorted performance pieces/
conceptual art trips/ movies both 8mm and 16mm/ and
an evening of improvisational dancing . at least !

as soon as its been decided we will send you a list of
the Halifax participants and their carrying-ons .
and it does look like we can get the Vancouver participants
gig/s at other universities here theres 5 of 'em .
what sort of spread is possible for those from Halifax?
.

12 days of yule chuggin' ahead makes it impossible
to do more til its over. Fall last'd til the day before
yesterday with little snow or cold. today its gone
down to 5 below WOW!
                Greetings from this end of O Canada

1/ 4th/ '72
Halifax NovaScotia

Dear P o e m   C o.

   . . . if i dont write to you but read thru each
wee book of poems– –my response is my own unless
yr talkin' abt *your expectations* which is an-
other matter . . . am i splitting hairs ? anyhow i
like how you do demonstrate that a poet any poet
can put his own book together–in every way equal
to a Mac/Stew or other big time publisher. They
could be having a hard time making ends meet but–
that has nothing to do with poetry. we know if
it were not for their best sellers and branch plant
text book factories they wouldnt even bother.
the whole lot of 'em could go bankrupt but it wont
have much effect on poetry 'cause weve got zerox
and wit to staple together and send out into
the whirlpool, gratis .

                — — — — — — — — — — —
                o luv ly / fugi tive
                    w o r d s
                       O

                Ed ward   Var ney– –keep
                   the dear pomes
                      coming– –
               — — — — — — — — — — —

  shall) 'we sidle up to Nature that
       irate pornographist . . .'

                              asks Mina Loy and
                              yr old friend Roy

Dear Marguerite Pinney

    (right after yr. phone call : the profuse
    confusions are all my own doing . call it the real
    politics of the human its complex interface/s .
    any project/ion that proposes more than what each
    man or woman might accomplish alone incurs it–
    unless we're robots drones or automatons .

    its going to nonetheless go on the road for publi-
    city's sake call it the
    H a l i f a x / V a n c o u v e r : E X C H A N G E
    -- ----- -- --- --------- ---- -- ------

                  The Poster/s is at the printers shall
                  send on 500 for yr. mailing lists . it dont
                  list the participants what each will do
                  'cause for the moment its not at all certain

                  only 'where' 'when' 'what' .

       .

Halifax is sending you a fully catalogued package
of 5 hrs. of VTR together with several students to run
and take care of this and other matters. theyll need
at least 3 Sony 3000 monitors and sufficient space for
showing the VTRs and other 8mm 16mm films not to
mention lots of carousels and projectors etc.

tell Alvin B. therell be more than enough material to
show at UBC, concurrently .

 .

as soon as you have fixed our dates at the VAG let me
know and i shall slot our performances into them .
and yes do go ahead and advertise it for those D-A-T-E-S .

I'll know WHO is going to be the Halifax participants
by the weekend and will (of course) let you know .

 .

– –if the VAG will be hosting a reception for   The
University Art Association on January 23rd   could
Halifax participants be a part of the occasion with-
out usurpation or compromise? – –the time and date are
just right
                        it's of course up to you .

1/ 11th / '72
Halifax NovaScotia

Robert Elie
associate director of C/C

Dear Mr. Elie:

    – –belatedly WE thank you for the grant
    covering expenses for the *Halifax / Vancouver: EXCHANGE* .
    .
    theres much enthusiasm at both ends and MUCH
    frenetic planning . its coming together tho despite
    the hazards of carrying on a dialogue across
    4000 miles of O Canada Our Homely Native Land .

re: funds for Halifax participants
    as outlined in our proposal)

    . Anita Martin
      R.R. No. 1, Lower East   / $650.
      Chezzetcook, N/S

    . Ellen Pierce
      'Youth Arts' 3146-Agricola   / $650.
      Halifax, N/S

    . Alistair MacLennan
      R.R. No. 1, Tantallon   / $650.
      Site 27 / Box 1
      N/S

    these 3 shld have their cheques
    as soon as possible as all Halifax participants
    will be leaving together, shortly .
    .
    Others who will be going one way or another
    include
        Gerald Ferguson, Pat Kelly, Gary Kennedy,
        Ian Murray, Ellison Robertson, Bill Souter,
        Henry Orenstein, Heather Baker, David Martin,
        Toby MacLennan, Richard Jardin, David Sewell

Dear Ms Pinney

    havin' the usual problems
    re the cancellation of Halifax Group's
    Trip to Vancouver . like   theres
    even less money to work with – –
    and some of the participants cant/wont
    make it for the end of March \
    etc.
        SHIT WHAT 'AVE I LET MYSELF IN FOR !
        ----

    the new dates: 25th We set up
                             26th frm 2 to 5pm
                             27th thru 30th– –
                             frm 7.30 thru 10pm

                             (have Liz Touchette advertise
                             the Exchange for above dates cant be
                             more specific than that now.)

        .

    – –if Im learnin' anything its that Im no
    Saul Hurok or Organization Man .
    ----

    everyone in Tobin St. diggin' their cars out
    from under the drifts . . . but my white van
    and i are going to sit this one out til the
    next chunk of sunlight melts it away . p/s–
    you water-logged   yet?

2/ 9th/ '72
Halifax NovaScotia

Dear Ms. M. Pinney

re: yr. letter of 1/ 25/ '72– –Hangon to
those dates We are re-grouping for our Vancouver gig .
(groping might be more accurately the sense of it.)
what happened to 3/ 29th?   is the VAG open Sundays for
special events like the Exchange? We're opting to
do our thing there on successive evenings rather than
night and day/s . and it looks like Those who had
intended to go earlier are willing to go at the later
date/s   so our earlier schedule of events applies .
more info viz changes of participants/ events as it occurs .

Vancouver in Halifax to go ahead (as planned .

    ("into each life some rain must fall"
     or its parcht dreams and jezus christ
     super star . it was Sigmund who sd
     its because money is not part of child-
     hood dreams that its pursuit in our
     so called adulthood is un-fulfilling .

     . . . aint fulfillment what we're all abt?)

2/ 14th/ '72
Halifax NovaScotia

Dear Suzanne Rivard

heres a brief abt where we're at since i
phoned you (during the air-strike) in Vancouver .

We're simply going to split the 7 Thousand in half .
Send one half to Doris Shadboldt at the VAG I've askt
her to distribute the money to the several partici-
pants : Glen Lewis, coordinator/ Gerry Gilbert, poet/
Michael Morris, painter/ Gathie Falk, performance-pieces/
Don Druick, musician. there may well be Other/s it
depends on how they propose to travel and whether or not
they can raise additional moneys. certainly more than
those mention'd want to go to Halifax .

Vancouver in Halifax March 6 th thru 10th (as before.

Bruce Parsons and i have been trying to raise additional
money by getting other institutions in Halifax involved .
we would like to get 3 other places at $250. each which
additional moneys could be used to send one more partici-
pant to each city. or otherwise defray unforeseen expenses .
.

due to the air-strike the Halifax participants are
being re-considered . will forward their names as soon
as its possible . those named in my letter (1/11/'72
to Robert Elie still want to go if they can arrange for
the later date . its only the participants from NSCA
that need reconsidering due to the changes particularly
the changed finances . Halifax participants share of
C.C. funds could be sent to me for distribution .

Halifax in Vancouver March 26th thru 30th (new dates.

tho now obsolete the enclosed poster tells the story
of this unique occasion . after the huge let-down of not
being able to follow thru as planned WE at least have
more time to make it better . interest in The Exchange–
continues to be lively .

a four thousand mile long taut wire Hummmmmmmm .

Feb. 14 /'72

Dear Flakey and Others

    yr moneys shld be coming thru shortly .

    i need not tell you it shld be used to enable
    as many of you who want to come   to do so yet leave
    some extra for the unforeseeable.

    as for the afternoon gigs mention'd previously
    Im assuming 1/ the possibility of one more participant
    from each city . 2/ or use all such moneys for
    augmenting yr honorariums, living expenses etc. for all .
    3/ combination/s of both .

    we're arranging 3 afternoon gigs   one at each of 3
    other universities in the Halifax area . theyll occur
    on alternate days viz Monday/ Wednesday/ Friday .
    could you get together with the other participants and
    work out these afternoon gigs . like 'who' will do
    what' each of the 3 afternoons . wld suggest a rotation
    system so that some of you are free each afternoon
    to do what you want to . ADVANTAGE/S more money for
    whatever and a larger sprawl for all of you .

    want Dave Rimmer (for films) and Karen (for dances)–
    they shld be part of whatever Vancouver does here .

    .

    get in touch with Doris S. re funds.
    and call me anytime collect at the NSCA if theres
    problems i can help out with .

10/ 17th/ '72
Vancouver BC

Dear Suzanne Rivard Lemoyne

belatedly: a summary of
The H a l i f a x / V a n c o u v e r : E X C H A N G E

. . . . Ah   remember it?

the enclosed documents xerox and carbons
shld enable you to   partially re-
cover what The Exchange is/was all abt   .other-
wise its become another past-tense E-
vent for which nothing can be claimed but
the evidence you have in your hand
plus a hatfull of memories . *as postscript– –*
i wld add that it enabled a small group
of misbegotten artists to do their thing and
to be witness to what the Others also
accomplisht . for what it's worth– –
theres at least 4 Halifax and vicinity artists
of divers sorts living in Vancouver .
for the likes of us theres no such momentums
as 'upward mobilities'– –only a scattering
of way-stations from coast to coast .
like I've sd it cld well be Monreale Toronto
Pincher Creek Regina or Vancouver:
its where you hang yr hat and coat a-
mongst the scourings / the devastations of Time

– –across this huge dominion i am a mere re-
cording instrument telling abt a week-long Event–
now passt all pretension . if i were to tell
it all over again i wld begin "once upon a time . . ."
.
Hows your face there
on Capitol Hill   among the
eager beavers?   does it
continue to shine thru all
that rhetoric?   ah the
deathless iniquities

of our politics its tenuous
demarcations .

– –We their other face wear a
tearfill'd smile

dear Dennis Reid

      been workin' on real/fiction
      tentatively) titled:
                Who Killed Tom Thomson?   or

      The Algonquin Adventures of T.T.
      canada's exemplary folk-A R T-Hero

      (title sounds puck-ish but
      i do mean to be 'quote' serious 'unquote', It
      'll enable me to sound many themes inc
      variations on EVERYMAN'S PARTICULAR DEATH . . .

cld you get me some lit. on him   to hang a tall-tale
on?   if thats impossible   a short telling book list
the size of a fist   abt our friend Tom   T.T. for short.

or tell me in yr own words   fact/or/fiction   what
you know,   *yr reflections* on how/when/why/   He
got it.   how he did.   plus other thots concerning
his women & did he lose his virginity ?   etc.

Tom's Death is not fiction   it is not fiction even if
the way he got it is not a known fact.   there is afterall –
the fact of my wanting to tell you abt it.   all of
the rest is likely a fiction completely 'made-up'. it is
possible to invent any number of ways a man might die   but
D E A T H is no mere invention . just ask Tom abt it .

                whats the chance of a fan
                conning the author into giving him a copy
                of his History of The Group of Seven,
                eh ?

                    yrs,

january 12th 1972
halifax, nova scotia

dear Anne,

you aint got quite the last word yet!
the negs & contacts show the rocky promontory
at peggy's cove (use them as you see fit.

i want to match up *these rocks the atlantic*
with the *other rocks the pacific* i took pictures of
last summer at long beach. Pacific/Atlantic:
defines the reach & the question im left with is how long
can any-of-us reach?

:which question obtains in different degrees in
our politics. the politics of ART inevitably. hence
"our" localism. our new parochialisms. our C.A.R.(e.

after all *the letters*
purporting to be abt tom thomson –
i am again left with
my *own conclusions* and the
momentary *claritas* the letters
enabled.was it ever more
than this – except that *the mind*
with equal insistence,
proposes *an order* beyond all our
arguments

                tom's death has got nothing to do with
                the liveliness
                      of his paintings their

                    impossible P E A C E

                        bless you tom
                        bless yr sweet anonymities

& capricorn's child
salutes you & others at artscavernous,

        ROSE:– IT'S *NOW*
                WOW!
                YR BABY!

1/ 13/ '72
NovaScots College of Art
Halifax N.S.

Dear Peter D.

– –Tomorrow Im going to have to go to
you-know-how-boring-they-can-be-*meetings* viz
summer school schemes etc. including
discussions concerning more teachers as
the 'regs' dont want anything to do with it
etc . . . . and your letter arrived today!
That places you dear Peter Peter Pumpkin Hater
at the top of my list for summer school
even a full-timer. So just hang in we'll do
what we can from this end. Shit its about time
We got together.

                    Much sound and fury concern-
ing our sic sovereignty, our 49th Peril:
Everyone yackin' about Yankee take-
over of our Academentias but not
a whisper concerning the Ole Eng-
lish take-over of Can/Art Fine/Art Depts.
Them blimeys just about blanket the
art school scene from coast onto coast
inc yr (former) U. of Vic.

ah Peter Old Stoned Pumpkin-Eater
We both know how how pernicious the
colonization-mentality can be.

Spent Christmas with Henry / Milly
4 floors up above St. Laurent Street.
And have you by chance seen latest
artscanada with my assorted LETTERS etc?

        take care of yr house

1/ 13/ '72
Halifax NovaScotia
(5 days to my 46th yr!)

Dear Richard and Vicki

during some of that time we all have a lease on–
our faire meat seems un-wittingly the victims
of outraged fortune's slings and arrows   viz Shake
speare the peerless one etcetera. I am talking
abt our assorted vicissitudes which sometimes loom
huge enough to make mountains out of mole hills
or its a ho hum conundrum– –fit for a Herr Grass's
dwarf beating on a batterd tin drum. When I was
a sickly young lad I thought my frail body wouldn't
last whereas my more robust friends just got
quarantined for their measles, mumps or scarlet fever
ishnesses. And I keep finding out that nonethe-
less Love persists and I am a witless accomplice to
her tenacities. Thus, despite the hazards of say
gettin' up every morning and not knowing really not
knowing what might befall me before day fails I
know in my very bones that Love twists and turns in
and thru every moment, weaving a multi-coloured
tapestry. I mean dont We (despite our meddling-self)
with a little help frm our friends, survive?

Luve to Vicki/ the children
and (of course) Thumbelina : a Litany
of names noumens proclaims it

Feb. ?/ '72
halifax nova scotia

dear Monica

    our caretaker tells me i gotta move my van in-
to my own parking slot . . . . or else! now its heapt
with huge mound of grey snow giant bulldozer pusht
onto it! S H I T ! today   he's yelling – –
shovel it out or git yr rear-end smasht to ratshit!
(ahhh the purity of yesterday's prairie snowfall . . .)
.
since getting back to Halifax i've been mostly lack
lustre: the awe-full impact of being with you &
the children (how? briefly?. & meeting old friends
before going off to Calgary where Krisy told me how
she tempted death by slashing her wrists . . . then
going on up to Edmonton to be with my parents and
finding them both much older hence nearer to their
end. and. the long night flight across these 4000 miles
each instant removing me further and further from
beloved faces . . . all this heapt on my back as part of
the lack of lustre. as you so well know there is
much else i cant/wont place or even want to face up to–
as part of this aberrance this displacement
.
S t o n e d   G l o v e s got shown here at Dal U.
–as i hung it on the walls i thot 'my gawd where where
is that drive that enabled this show, gone. etc."
i still think its the best entire show i've ever put
together. &. Danielle Corbiel at the N.G. tells me
SG will be shown in Paris in the Spring which pleases
me more than i thot possible .
.
meanwhile, Spring then Summer ahead for all of us &
gawd am i looking forward to it with the very good
chance i will have a job at UBC come Fall. i am keep-
ing my fingers crosst its one of the un-mentionables–
i dont want to get my hopes up too much, etc.

            love to all four of you

2/ 9th/ '72
Halifax NovaScotia

dear George Knox

> 'if' for whatever academic/budgetary reasons
> you have to farm me out (which Im told is better
> than being let out to pasture) itll be ok—i
> dont have much sense of propriety abt such matters.
> any context will do that might enable a mean-
> ing filld dialogue. i wld go so far as to say that
> all other contexts   however well intention'd
> dont matter much to me.

>> such spill-over or is it a sprawl?
>> across disciplines   to embrace contexts larger
>> than art's largesse seems to be how i
>> function best. perhaps i could be with the
>> fine art folks and be lent out to
>> arts one—i mean i would prefer to have
>> a base to heave from

ask Roger Seamon for info viz
my love/hate data in Art: it includes
resume of shows/collections/ etc.
which yr welcome to xerox. plus lst issue
of white pelican with extended inter
view. its the most current thing i can
recommend to you. ask Roger   if you
need more then write

try these:

> *Ron Bloore/* professor/ humanities dept
> at York U. Toronto.
> *Edwy Cooke/* head/ fine arts dept at
> Sir George Williams U. Montreal.
> *Tony Emery/* director/ Vancouver Art Gallery.
> *William Townsend/* teacher/ Slade School
> London England.
> *Ann Brodzky/* editor/ artscanada.

>> . . . dont know who's pressin
>> the green button for me   but
>> i need all the green lights
>> i can get to get back to Vancouver
>> & the west coast, *promptly*

                    2/ 14th/ '72
                    Halifax NovaScotia

Dear Anita
            re W.W.'s C a n A r t B o o k

  you shld be getting the following soon
  1/   a packet including photographs of paintings/
        sculptures, a portrait the one i wld like
        to have used–by Freddie Douglas of Vancouver.
        plus a 30 minute cassette

        hope the taped-hype answers some of yr questions.
        you can if you want keep the tape but please
        send the rest of the material back .

  2/   a mailing tube containing the poster of
        my cedar laminates show at the Bau-Xi Gallery
        whc i dont want back .

  3/   a tray of color slides of my Expo '70 Sculpture
        for the Canadian Pavilion, Osaka   whc
        –you cld make duplicates frm to keep.

i promise before long to send on a brief paragraph
whc will purport to tell   what i think/feel abt
our old friend A r t but first you must hear the tape
and what it sez   re my suggestions .

is the book to be only abt each man and his paintings?
or will it include our/my other obsessions   that
are not incidental to painting or sculpture but part of
that huge whole A r t proposes . let me know
.
to insist the White Pelican 1st issue tells
my story as well as such occasions enable. you can get it
thru Stephen Scobie, University of Alberta, English
Dept. my copy got taken apart to be Xeroxed–
as info for my various students here .
.
the 4 paintings to be repro'd shld be :
1/   the National Gallery's large acrylic Ellipse.
2/   the one repro'd in Studio International, CanArt Issue.

3/ the tall one the University of Alberta has. you cld
   write to my brother there for a colour slide of it .
4/ the one in the Canada Council Collection that got shown
   in Edinburgh .
               if not these there are others but
               check these out 1st .

– –now that i am into the book
do come back for whatever info you further need

2/ 16th/ '72
Halifax NovaScotia

Dear Mr. Madsen

    got yr splendid booklet. it sure looks like
you mean to be serious with that faculty.

    going thru the booklet i couldnt find a context/
course for my own daughters   who are below
the average age of their peers attending the school.
whc proposes– –at what age does a child begin
serious training in the arts. mine for instance–
started even before they began school.
.

    its been nearly thirty years since i have spent
any period of time in Banff. when i was a youngster
growing up in Calgary i thot i knew the place as
well as say a Calgarian today might claim to know it.
Im sure tho the mountains will not have changed
or at least so that i will notice   tho ive come a
long ways since

i shall need accommodations for 4:
my three daughters age 11/13/ & 15 + myself.
ideally we need at least 2 large bedrooms
plus a livingroom and an adequate kitchen whc
equipped with minimal facilities
viz pots and pans and a few sticks of furniture
including at least 3 beds. it ought to be an
easy walking distance from the school and not too
damned expensive. (cld you be more specific
concerning the faculty chalet– –i mean can we
all stay there and wld there be enough space?
ideally the place shld be big enough
to enable me to do my own work in, too.

with these specifications in mind i leave it
up to you to reserve something for the four of us ok .

p/ wld like to get my hands on
a comprehensive map of the region the kind
issued by Natural Resources or a like
source   plus assorted travel folders to tell
us what we can do 'where' and 'when' while
we are all there together .

2/ 25th/ '72

dear Mariko

> . . . . id say almost everyone ought to have
> a chrome-plated ego some of the time. mine seems
> to be so buried in meat i cant locate it.
> then theres the problem of the soul–its flights
> of fancy apropos Leo Tolstoy's biography.
> page after breathless page he wrestles with the
> angels instead of just standing there and
> letting the palpitations of their wings soothe his
> furrowed brow. like he's a huge manifestation
> of those human contraries even your Pa knows the
> lacerations of. meanwhile his near contemporary
> Siggy Freud is pacing off the terrain of the ego &
> its twin the id, etc. writing to you out of
> near total inertia i find all such abstract notions
> impossible to handle. i am trying to be patient
> with myself. hang in thar like they say til
> the ole doldrums pass, etc.
>
> i wrote to Mr. Madsen (Banff School) sayin' i
> couldnt find anything in the school's brochure for
> you and yr sisters to do. maybe i just didnt see
> it–you could check it out yrself. i did
> mention to him we needed a large space for the
> whole six weeks, etc.
> we will get together, one way or another.
>
> yr uncle Frank wants to know if either you or Jan
> wld like to work for him this summer at Jasper.
> it wld be looking after the pottery shop, baby sitting
> or more likely both. think abt it and write to him
> directly. saw your grandma & grandpa on my way back to
> Halifax. why doncha drop them a line? LETTERS are a
> way of saying how much you love them. etc.
>
> > the books are for all three of you.
> > guess which is for each of you?

2/ 26th/ '72
halifax nova scotia

dear Jack Cowin

itinerary:

Here til April/early May.
then the slow drive Westward. will stop
off in Regina May/early June to
see you & John Nugent. late June thru
July into 1st wk of August will
be teaching at the Banff School of F. A.
then directly to The Workshop.

.

my requirements at Emma L are simple enough:
they inc a space/place large enough to
work in, put friends up in, sleep & dream in.
(it cld be the old Kenderdine Place where
former workshop leaders stayd)   plus good food
three times daily . &, convivialities.

.

i have no idea who to expect as participants. it
used to be where artists came to groove with other
artists. i hear its mostly young university or
art school kids now. no matter as it will be a time
for working plus rap-sessions, etc. the comeliness
of the occasion will show itself 'in' and 'thru' all
of us our interactions. given Emma's amenities it
ought to be memorable .

.

cld you tell John i am not interested in Simpson's
jurying job. Simpson's ought to be told theres
no honour in having work/s shown under their auspices
without their willingness to pay rental fees   or
purchasing works. re: C.A.R.

hullo to Ric & Art & Ted &

Dear Kim/ Keeper of C.A.R.'s Treasury

      Yes, Keep me informed. 'Information' is
expensive though it should be cheaper than keeping.
Kept informed I shall (hopefully) go on minting
brand new coins from old metal. The mint the midas-
touch Benson's 'white-paper' taxes the image of an
nation's art, etc. Dear Kim send me all the info
$3. per annum purchases. Kept as it were informed I
wont be able to plead ignorance. And aren't We
bearers of all the information there is aren't We all
informers? Information I would add seems to be our
special burden viz We are each of us the bearers of
all-the-news-fit-to-print 'plus' all the silences
nobody is willing to pay anything for.

      and/ 'late' is not the same as 'never'

          luv to Michael
          frm Sadakichi Hardtmann's
          illegitimate son

3/ 19th/ '72
Halifax NovaScotia

Dear Mr. Noel Lajoie

    I've intended to write you   since
Danielle Corbiel sd S t o n e d G l o v e s wld
be shown at the Centre Culturel Canadien
in Paris
        Now your letter prompts me to it. It
gives me great pleasure knowing that my homely gloves
are to be seen in Paris   a Paris i know only thru
paintings   (or i should say repros of them
and the literature of the Modern Era (which i know
thru translations) plus the so-called motion pictures the
kids here call 'em the flicks or mov-eeze: in short
a Paris I've never visited except in my dreams .
i was trained under the auspices of earnest teachers
who claimed more or less direct experience if not
ancestry of the early Parisian Masters and thus a great
amount of late 19th and 20th Century aesthetics is
part of my early apprenticeship. Perhaps my SG will re-
pay some of that debt.
               no matter S t o n e d G l o v e s
will tell their own story in images these words cant .

if anyone shld ask you 'where' the gloves came from—
tell 'em they were found underfoot   on the site of Expo
'70 in Osaka Japan. even today theres 1000s of pairs
rotting away just under the surface of rubble-mountain .

.

packet contains:

+ 8 black and white glossys of the gloves.
theyre in the show)
+ 1 photo of yrs truly seen talking abt his G(Loves.
—as if politics and economics were ever enough!)
+ plus a bundle of biographical and miscellaneous stuff.
at least send the photo back its a memento from
a lovely friend)

.

p/s . . . tho i regret i cannot read or speak French
i wld love to give a reading of the SG pomes in English
or even Japanese for the sake of my Gallic Friends.
what are the chances of External Affairs inviting the artist
to the opening—if you have such things? and if theres
anything further i can do for you do let me know ok?

dear Lawren Harris jr

        Y E S i will be in Sackville
        March 22nd/ 23rd. probably the night before.
        i am thinking of flying –want to
        take pics of the landscape frm 5000 ft.
        otherwise will drive thru

– –i dont know how small/large yr classes are.
if they average 12 to 15 i wld prefer to talk with
them as aggregate rather than each group in turn.
i talk to everybody the same way, anyhow.
we could have one long crit that went on til all were
utterly exhausted!
.

art students shld feel free to come to the reading.
they shld know that poetry is as much for them as for
english students. its something they can also do.
mix of english/ art students is the best possible
audience. even for a seance.

        next issue of artscanada (Feb?
        contains letters by yrs truly. or
        canadian issue of studio inter-
        national, spring '70. both/either
        can be glean'd for publicity.

        yrs sincerely,

S p r i n g (almost
'72 .

Dear Herb

      the first time we got together was during
a snow storm. we couldnt make it up the slope and
slithering into a curb   i sd why dont i back away
and down the slope and you could stay over?
she sd well why not and she did and we made love .
in the early morning she left her footprints
in a foot of new fallen snow. everytime we spend a
weekend with each other it snows and so the winter goes–
even as i am writing to you its snowing and shes
reading and watching it fall in the next room.
from the marshland hotel i brought back a postcard
blotter whc quotes the Plant Philosopher sayin :
"kindness is like snow it makes beautiful everything it
covers . . ." but . . . i keep wonderin what
lies in store of us just below our epidermis, etc.
Themes and Variations: aint all of our thots even our
assorted acts (including the sordid ones) just
that and the joker is in the telling 'if' telling be
heirloom and necessity. i take it all artists and
non-categorical Others are that kind of anima-mundi
who for whatever reason are moved to *tell the*
tales of the tribe's fitfull tracings. Geez Herb– –
have you noticed HOW LARGE THE PROJECTIONS CAN BE
STRAIGHT AHEAD (and) diminisht seen in a rear view mirror?
like i say its sure comin down and what do words mean?
if you drop this letter walkin back frm the mailbox it'll
disappear into the snow bank–as even these words
fall pell mell thru the hoary-frost'd Air

let me as a family man say that your extensive brood is
the next best thing to my own. it re-assures me to know–
despite our familial perversities our children can be
nonetheless l o v e l y .

                    Cheers to All of 'em

March?/ '72
Halifax NovaScotia

dear George

            (– –if you want a thing for
            the B.C. Monthlies   ask Brad for
            long letter abt Al & Marg Neil
            here in Halifax)

stoppt off in Edmonton to see the family. Pa spends
most of his days in bed   gettin' up only to pee / shit
eat/ or sit in front of the teley. he sez its no fun
hobbling abt with a cane to lean on. like who wants to
lean on any thing. tho not one of the coolies who put
the c.p.r. thru the rockies he is of that generation
(almost) and among the last of 'em alive to read P.B.'s
Last Spike, without glasses yet!   Ma and i sat thru
long clear cold prairie afternoon talking over cups of
tepid tea. She asks me abt one or another of my friends
she has met since my art school days . . . and i keep sayin'
i havent seen so and so since . . . etc. etc. then, almost
in exasperation she sez ". . . you forget too much   i no
forget anyone . . ." which is certainly true abt Ma she
hasnt forgot much. and i know she will remember that
afternoon too the next time we meet. while in Vancouver
i sat and drank beer with an old girl friend   who sd
almost the same thing abt yourstruly. she sd viz those
Montreal days ". . . you only seem to have forgotten how
we met . . . you remember all of it including the shit . . .
dont you?"

            p/s have you had a chance to
            look at my Honshu Backcountry Trip yet?
            dont want no lip service except
            it be a rigorous crit thru and thru Ok.

Pacific Rim/Wake

for Glen Toppings:
to be chanted by the members of The Grange .

black
       Anger
             wing
black
       Hand
             wing
black
       Bridge
             wing
black
       Wind
             wing
black
       Eye
             wing
black
       Boat
             wing
black
       Cave
             wing
black
       Night
             wing
black
       Tear
             wing
black
       Mouth
             wing

black

    C o c k
        wing

black

    A n g e l
        wing

black

    C u n t
        wing

black

    A n c h o r
        wing

black

    T o n g u e
        wing

black

    T r e e
        wing

black

    L a u g h t e r
        wing

black-

    w h i s p e r
        wing

black

    p r a y e r
        wing

black

    c a n c e r
        rising

*

the black bird flew in   thru
an open window of the room behind
his closed eye-lids

the wind the blackbird's wings make
lift'd up his arms
his body itself felt lighter

high above the winds   the winding
Fraser   the cold night air   leaves
his   blacken'd wings

*

"The sea has no renewal   no forgetting
no variety of death
is silent with the silence of a single note"

*

                   A
                W a k e

              A w a k e
            C h i l d r e n

       B L A C K B I R D
          W I N G S

         S H A D O W
     Y O U R   B R E A T H

          A W A K E !

             A
          W a k e

             O
         D e a t h

             !

                         Spring '72

Spring '72
Halifax NovaScotia

Dear Herb

HURRAH its the end of another school year and
I'm busy disentangling myself frm Halifax and the school
etcetera. Since our get together in Sackville I've
been to P.E.I. and back. On the way to Borden met a group
of drunken hockey players the kind that play in minor
 leagues til they're forty and take their sons to the hockey
hall of fame. They had it seems won a sort of champion-
ship and were heading back to Cape Breton where they said
they all hailed from in two huge batter'd up American
cars. We're all waiting for the ferry including Fergy who
has at least six bottles of local beer on his bedraggled
person plus a lopsided grin. In the lunch room Fergy keeps
going to the john. He gets up from the table theyre all
sloucht around including their wives. He has his foot barely
in the door and he's already tilting a beer. They aren't
even watching – –like us theyre waiting and only waiting for
the ferry. Fuck old Fergy his pranks pratfalls and drunken
mischievous ebullience. He is good entertainment as long as
he dont get nasty. Earlier Fergy had come to our table to
announce how they coppt the game in the dying moments of the
3rd period and that there would be a huge reception for
all of 'em as soon as they got back. Then they were all head
ing back to Ontario for the finals. Now were all together
on the ferry. We cant get away from each other even tho we
are all bored with each other. Etcetera. My last image
of Fergy an utterly dissolute un-repentant Fergy has lip-stick
smeared tattoo-wise all over his face arms and hands as
he is propt up by two of his burly friends back to the car.
And I thought that Fergy must be the Emmett Kelly of the
grade 'b' hockey circuitry. The compleat fool and bumptious
defenceman. All this and more as the ferry shudder'd
thru the ice-flow to Cape Travertine.

Ah! New/found/land– –

3/ 28th/ '72
the Ides of) Halifax
NovaScotia

Dear Chris & Vivian

    for over a week Spring seemed to be
however slowly) slithering into our lives–
the way a heady warmth was in the air
and the mounds of grey snow everywhere re-
treated to lay bare the brown grass and
shiny black tarmac. there was a false
spring day when we were all out on the street
in lighter brighter clothes with beatific
smiles from ear onto ear. Then, yesterday
it started to snow the huge snow flakes coming
down so slowly you thot you cld count
each one as it fell . . . til it was white a-
gain all over the place   and the fury of
its falling laminated   the separate flakes to-
gether. from my small kitchen window
overlooking the backyard parking space between
separate parts of the complex-of-apartments–
all of the neighbours' cars have become huge white
mounds   the children play in while
mothers and fathers shovel out their drift'd driveways.
and tho my apartment room is almost of
an equal whiteness its like you sd over the phone
were all hanging on to whatever–
after the long persistent cold.
my sluggish metabolism stirs
as underfoot   the brown grass stirs and Tobin Street
oak tree   roots stir under the frozen
sidewalks. claudia writes she has felt Spring's
Green Madness like a false pregnancy, twice
already. yeah, its coming all right a bright boisterous
cum   all over everything .

        Chris   the trick seems to be
        to lie perfectly still
        as long as you can without mind's
        agitations   and recovery is
        decently assured.

        our bent backs our cross our slippages
        our displaced discs

3/ 28th/ '72
halifax nova scotia

dear Phyllis

      if you arent gonna make copies of
our correspondence . . . i guess i have to save all
of your letters. i mean to go right on making
carbons of mine– –i aint got scruples abt literary
proprieties and do want to keep some sort of a
record of my own thots viz letters. besides letters
are the only things i write sometimes and they
happen to be written out of he same concern i wld
bring to bear if i were writing something else.

in mid-sixties i met H.S. on the occasion of
my reading at the gallery when his big one man was
on exhibit. after the reading everyone went to
H's for a drink and the two of us got lockt into an
argument abt some fucken thing i dont remember.
we almost came to blows. it was the first & last
time i saw H. and almost the last time i got in
to an argument. i go on talkin a lot but i have al-
most given up on arguments. nothing ever comes of
it but the punk feeling afterwards which i came to
resent more than a lousy hang-over.

i am keeping my fingers crosst and rubbing wood– –
in a week or so i shld know if i have a job at UBC.
i dont think i can abide the Maritimes longer than
this attenuated year. not that its not been as
they say good for me– –its given me the longest stretch
of time i have had for yrs: for silences, for out-
rageous indolence, for even lack-lustre following on
an other bittersweet love, etc. etc. dear phyllis– –
i cant say therefore that me head is clear-er i
mean does a man's head get clear of his lost youth the
interminable wastage with consequent wither-
ing in front of him. does it?

YES aint it difficult to write a love poem, &
aint it that diffidence, that ofttimes defiant stance
that holds us back or is it in? and aint it our
human shame our sham the codified ways we wld place
impedimenta in our paths? and we are so wary of

past hurts that love could come right up and bugger
us and we would pretend not to notice. have you
seen Avedon/ Baldwin's 'Nothing Personal'? in it
Baldwin sez this thing i am lisping so intently that
it made my own slight body shudder at the wanting
the with-holding, the waywardness and withering of
love. like he sez its nothing personal   or every
thing is.

          get a hand on next issue of artscandalous for
          lots of letters by yrs unruly. they are
          also abt the slings & arrows our outraged flesh
          is heir to.

          like i sd i could be at yr front door come June
          having driven 4000 miles westward, etc.

Spring '72
Halifax Nova Scotia

Dear Vic/dor

    jeesuz! another school year blown– –
    and Im tired of watering little acorns that
    despite me, will grow into an oak tree
    eventually. I've taught for almost 20 yrs and
    I've grown weary of its routine predicta
    bility. i have never once had the notion of
    teaching as long as breath sustains   or
    the devil got me . . . now it begins to feel like
    the time to attend to my own apprehensions,
    utterly. all thru the long wet Winter's
    grey conundrums I've been thinkin' abt Art 's
    Auguries and 'this time around' i say to
    myself let there be no consternations . . . but
    i aint had the guts to make a start yet .

    how are you? and yr assorted women?

                        til)May 12th
                        halifax nova scotia
dear Peter

    forgive me the long delay re
    yr concern abt a job here. the usual
    end of yr scramble plus asst. ad-
    ministrative bawlsup partly accounts for
    it. despite my recommendation   my
    imprecations theyve gone hired another bloke
    from (all places!) Kentucky. thats
    it .

          I'll be startin' at U.B.C. this Fall.
Halifax been a luvly hiatus in my middle yrs:
its time to hallucinate L-I-F-E agin – –.

will we ever meet again with you back in
England's Green &   me stumblin' abt back on
Canada's South-West Coast. Dear Peter
keep on doing what you do so well.   wallow in
it for a goodly lifetime, etc.

    yr friendly fiend

                              end of April '72
                              Halifax NovaScotia
Dear Monica

    long after Halifax re-newed my contract
    U.B.C. has come thru. tho they are offering me
    several thou less I have (of course) accepted.
    my plans are to leave Halifax abt mid-May– –
    so dont send on even the mail. and 'if' you for
    whatever reason DONT GET YR MAY CHEQUE phone
    me at 429-1019 here in Halifax 'collect'.
    otherwise I wish you much luck re job and all

    Mariko
    will you tell Evelyn Roth I wont be here but will
    talk her trip up. and I am glad to be leaving
    tho I wld in the same breath add its where I needed
    nonetheless to be   etc. Pa looks forward to his
    long winding drive Westward he looks forward to Banff
    with his girls and then Vancouver (again. all 4
    of us will have to wait and see whats possible for
    us in Banff Alberta. Love to Claire, Others.

    Jan
    only the fact of our being together in Banff this
    summer seems to yr Pa perfectly clear. Pa has spent
    most of the winter writing or is it re-writing
    his prose/pome tentatively called "From Furukawa-cho
    Out : A 7 Day Backcountry Trip" he took w/ his Pa
    and young friend Syuzo. That and the ongoing work of
    editing and collating his Letters. Thus, he keeps
    himself busy. How abt you are you also active?

    Kiyo
    read and re-read the scrambled words you call a
    letter. and I haven't forgotten the Toonerville Trolley
    whc I shall deliver to you in person. like I sd
    I read it every weekend (during the dirty 30s) along
    w/ The Katzenjammer Kids and good ole Smokey Stover.
    see you in the comics.

    Morgan
    BOW WOW WOW (meaning) How are you?

7/ 7/ '72
Banff School of Fickle Art
Alberta

Dear Monty

    Anne B. sent on yr response to
my reading in Confederation Centre which I shld
have received sooner if I had not driven as
they say like MAD from Cheticamp on the Gaspe Pen-
insula all the long way across O Canada to the
Westcoast then down to San Francisco and back to
Banff Alberta. Its B-A-R-F according to a backstreet
spray-on job I came across while walking. Abt
the B.S.F.A. let me quote one of the other teachers
"Jeesuz its more like Bennington or Mt. Holly-
hock than any fucken art school I know."
apropos yr response and the line abt how ". . . boys
like Roy can only love now in their maturity" I
thought my gawd Monty sees clear thru me
and and how many many others can also.

    During W.W.II We re-located in Opal Alberta
and farmed it must be sd badly a quarter-section of
scrub/ sand/ stone and tired old loam. Thinking– –
of how literature might be able to instruct us I
subscribed to the Country Gentleman (then the equi-
valent of the Ladies Home Jurnal) aimed at a sedate
agrarian world. I remember sending a money order
along w/ the subscription form for one year. A long
long decade after leaving home that goddamned mag –
azine kept coming to my parent's Edmonton address in
the name of one Roy K. Hooker, esq– –who is none
other than that young cat you finger'd.

    P.E.I. remains a lovely reciprocity. May
the Ghosts of the Fathers of our Confederation
bless especially you and Anne B.

                    J u l y '72
                    Banff Alberta
Dear Bruce and Sonny

       well here We 4 be in
B A R F - O N - B A N F F) the curbside scrawl
one block back of Main St. sez in lurid
red spray-on scrawlings. our address is 332-Squirrel St.
yet. if you think thats kinda Mickey Mouse   All
the streets here seem to be named after some kindred
native critter   whc i suppose is as good as say
naming 'em after the likes of us—imagine a Kiyooka
Drive or a Parson's Avenue. anyhow, compared to
the umpteen thousands of ugh tourists who keep bustling
thru   our six weeks here begins to feel like a lost
Forever.

            more and more i think that the so call'd
Canadian Experience is rooted in the particulars of the
terrain we hail from   whc includes everything viz the terrest
as a mere lad i could see the outlines of these mountains
a hundred miles away if i got on my bike and rode out
onto the high bluff in south-west Calgary. now—
one of those mountains rears up and out of sight from
our basement window and i suppose it must be
i finally prefer the unobstruct'd view—that
sheer 180 degree sweep of land or sea   hence the prairies
or either coast most appeals to me. this, the name of
whc i have forgotten, mountain, just outside our window its
rocky implacableness wld almost certainly annoy me
if i lived here   by its sheer impenetrability.
nonetheless we take pleasure in cloud-wreath'd summit
no less than the deer (seen thru binoculars) down
near the foot, between two huge trees .
the vista is deeper than these words go . why doncha tell
us how your summer goes in N e w f o u n d l a n d ?

7/ '72
Banff Alberta

dear L i n d a

    after speaking to you   was
    as it were   spooked by your telling me how
    you got raped . . . my daughters and i
    left for Banff . the imago/ images of a fierce
    black face hoving above you and my own
    haplessness, from this distance   aggravated by–
    like   what could i have said that might
    have re-assured you   left me (impossibly) with the
    wanting to hold you closely . . . and i dont
    even now know what you should or could do about it.
    maybe its not really my business but i hope–
    you might have it in your heart to forgive (if not
    forget him) his violence, vengeance and
    other malignancies .

                        meanwhile . . . in Banff
    at 332-Squirrel St. everyone is busy:
    Mariko sews up the holes in Geordie's pockets as
    Kiyo sprawls on the floor, drawing   while
    Jan who needs the most sleep naps. earlier, we lookt
    and laughed at the slides I've taken so far of
    our mutual summer holidays. and i am as
    my children seem to be   among the sedentry ones
    those who look and look at everything from
    a distance that will enable whatever we make to
    happen . right now we're all listening to Ravi
    Shankar on C.B.C. radio and   its nearly midnight as
    a squinty-eyed Jan staggers thru the room to-
    wards i think the bathroom . just another 2 weeks
    of school and we'll all be glad to get back
    to Vancouver   despite the jive of
    unexcelled felicities, being together .
                                    etc.

    . . . do you think there is a remote chance we
    might come together at Emma Lake . . . ?

mid-Summer '72
Banff Alberta

dear Carole/ Gerry

    who but Rene Magritte ever heard of
    a pregnant mermaid?

    and does that make Slim a mere Adam?
    .
    and aint the TERROR we spoke abt– –
    nothing but A-W-E ! in the face of our feckless
    fecundities? viz the barnyard at Roberts
    Creek as sheer evidence.

        Our Squirrel Street basement flat is
        a typical Kiyooka lively-room anywhere– –
        litter'd w/ the kids' by no means di-
        minutive obsessions their scattered be-
        longings their pet white rat named Ratfink
        their friends and miscel paraphernalias.

        and the big cloud-wreathed rock mountain
        back of the school yard keeps nodding in.

        Jan and Kiyo left with cousin Clifford for
        Jasper Hinton and Edmonton, yesterday.
        This morning I droppt Mariko off near to
        the highway. Shes heading for Lake Louise
        Jasper and then Edmonton. That leaves me
        with Ratfink   our assorted rumbles.

'i' is a hiatus between Rocky Mountain peaks

how abt the 3 of you?

7/ 25th/ '72
Banff Alberta

Dear Luke Rombout

> my photo/poem exhibit S t o n e d G l o v e s
> has just abt completed a 2½ yr Canadian circuit
> including the Canadian Cultural Centre
> in Paris.–now its abt to be seen here in Banff
> perhaps for the last time (this time around. on
> the strength of the many and varied responses to it
> from every quarter i wld say its certainly the
> most successful exhibit i have had the pleasure to
> put together. i have been, continue to be deeply
> affected.
>> C.C.C. in Paris re Noel Lajoie made a
>> splendid brochure whc includes translations
>> of my copious texts together with repros
>> & an altogether splendid poster. perhaps you
>> could ask Danielle C. at the N. G. to show
>> them to you– –if you're interested.
>
>> l o n g l i v e Bi-l i n g u a l i s m!

> Im writing to you to see if the C.C. might
> be interest'd in acquiring S t o n e d G l o v e s
> in its entirety for the collection– –it wld be
> a way of keeping it all together which i very much
> want for them. i believe you hung them in
> the Maritimes–so have an actual sense of them.
> tell me if your interest'd and if so will follow thru
> on the specifics .

>> my year in the Maritimes was/
>> is memorable   more than a mere memorabilia

7/ 25th/ '72
Banff   Alberta

Dear Vivian

    Chris's letter from Austria tells me
he is scouting the Tyrol terrain for vestiges of
his mother aboard her big black motorcycle.
sooner or later we all have to chase down the facts
of where we do hail from/ where the genetic gale
blows from– –with whatever valour each of us can muster.
i remember that long stoned day and night at the
Cheese Factory after the others left   the three of us
sitting around the table and Chris talking as he
seldom does abt his confusions re his family.
O Chris   may your zealous quest be as they say fruitful.

as for the Banff School of Fine Arts its a summer re-
sort cum liberal arts school for rich N.A. kids   with
the hugeness of the rocky terrain measuring their un-
flagging zeal. if i have learnt anything here its that
i dont need this kind of teaching gig   nor do i need
these incomparable mountains. i am beginning to feel that
the time is ripe for me to attend to those things i
still have to shape whc of course includes my own life:
it begins to seem like that time of my life, etc.

midway thru the 4th week i have been left behind by
my lovely daughters who have gone off to visit their grand
parents in Calgary and Edmonton. so it's Ratfink their
pet white rat, the teley, and i, staring at each other glumly.
i am impatient to get back to Vancouver and begin all
over again   like how the wheel keeps on turning and re-
turning over, and over, again and maybe– –there aint no place
to go(after remorselessly traversing Canada) but Up-
wards . . . . . .
                from peak onto peak leaving
                the bleak valley far below cumulus halos .
                "hullo is anyone up there?"

july '72
Banff Centre

dear Werner

    someone sd Banffs like Bennington or
Swarthmore one of them posh wimmen's colleges
in East America. like theres sure lots
of lovely-ladies abt   the ratio is abt 7 to 1.
George Ryga–over coffee–sayin'
the men in his playwriting group got no balls.
hes thinking of writing a play with all
the parts played by wimmen. he sez its their time
to assert themselves & it does seem so
Here: tho i aint askt the mountain abt it

anyhow this is to let you know im going to
want 1923-GRANVILLE ST. back by Sept. lst, latest
& send on any mail that comes there. the holy
book says theres time for fucken around & time
for planting & time for reaping & time for . . . ?
im hopin' when Fall comes i'll git down to biz
again– –clutter up me life   in the very act of
making t-h-i-n-g-s   & let it all overflow on
any street you wanta name

              – – –too bad you werent doing
                  the film thing here.   they could use
                  a good working man who
                  splices some keen-ideas together

'72

Dear Linney

    .... how many many times I have sat sat in
this red chair and re-read all yr wistful letters.
and how many many times I have listened to
the merest wisp of you on my cassette tape recorder.
S H I T my eyes my ears hang on to the bits
and pieces of you .... unable to make a *whole you*
ever. And the only time We talkt across these 4000
miles you told me how you got raped by a black
Guy (who served tea) when you went to enquire abt
a room for rent. I mean WHAT what cld I do do
for you?

    Then/ from Banff I continued to phone you.
On Sundays my funny Sundays when I always talkt
to your mother. She invariably sd you had just been
here and left or you were about to arrive at any
time and that they were expecting you. What what can
a man do with that that lack of recognition?
Whats any man to do with that absence? Meanwhile–
the gig goes on and on: We (the three girls and I) go
hiking we swim cruise and sit around We
watch television talk read sleep and draw
the mountain rising out of a mist .... (implacably
outside our Squirrel St. window.

3rd weekend in Banff: Paul Wong phones he sez
"why you dont fly out next Saturday .... Richard find
great place out in Matsqui." So I went to Calgary
caught the lst flight west on one of those perfect
ly clear days when you can see the ranges peaks
ravines slopes and valleys for miles around.
Paul and Richard met me at the airport We drove out
to Matsqui via Cloverdale w/ Richard at the wheel.
I dont/cant want to describe the site of that place:
Suffice to say its a 65 yrs old thick walled
three story high concrete tower–a former
power station w/ a hundred smasht windows.
Its more fucken space than we've ever dreamt abt its
Richard's place and our place Its where you
you can also also come to .... 'when' and 'if' you do?

2/

then w/ old friends Lionel and Maya I went down to
Frisco (without you. We could have gone down to Mexico
with them etc. I spent a lovely week in Bolinas w/
Jo Ann David and others. From the bus station I phoned
you in Halifax (as usual) I talkt to yr mother–
She sd you had gone to the Gaspe for a few days etc. We
had our usual conversation . . . . I am beginning to like
your mother. On the greyhound bus back to Vancouver I
dreamt I had a seat up front in the Peppermint Lounge– –
where this buxom girl w/ saucy eyes did her number.
it seemed that Im a habitue and always sit right up
front getting more and more drunk waiting for her flashing
rosy spotlight'd)Smile . . . . after which I get up
to stagger out into the night. I awoke–as the bus
hurled on thru the black northern California night with
the current playboy on my lap and I found myself laugh-
ing laughing outloud. Good Night Linney Good Night.

Labour Day: We Cheinchek Paul Richard and I planted a
4 yr old cherry tree at the very back of the property on
a true north/south axis. Cheinchek made the alignments
he dug the hole. Paul snippt the tin can holding the tree
he bent the cut pieces of tin outwards and lifted it
out roots and all and placed it in the hole. Richard then
grabbed up handfuls of the fresh dirt and patted it in
around the tree. Paul then watered it frm a bright plastic
water sprinkler as I danced abt in the tall grass taking
their pictures. Present to the occasion were all of those
mentioned plus Mariko Jennifer Dasa Lies and assorted
birds beasts and flowers. Then I lay in the tall grass–
stoned/I listen to Richard and Jennifer blowing on a flute
and trumpet as Paul and Cheinchek walk by in white shirts
creast trousers and tie. Hi Linney How are you?

Kozo our man-of-all-work and Shakuhachi player chips
chips chips away at the old plaster/ cement. He's removed
most of the stuff from the ceilings the walls even the
floor frm a dozen small rooms and theres still more to go.
Upstairs I've been smashing away at thick concrete foot-
ings (whc held the machinery) w/ a 16 lb sledge hammer– –
brute-work made tolerable by 'our' dream of rehabilitating
this old power-house. As for our unseen neighbours we've
had word back frm the municipality officials that they dont
want/like us us HIPPIES!   Imagine being thot that at 45!

early August '72
Banff Alberta

dear Victor

was in Vancouver last weekend long enough to
go out and look at then agree to purchase a long defunct
BC Hydro Bldg squat on 2 acres of woodland slope
overlooking the Fraser River Flatland just outside of
Abbotsford. its got abt 12000 sq. ft. on 3 floors
with over 100 (smasht) windows–no water, no electricity
or heat–just the awesome fortress-like hulk of
concrete abt 18 inches thick w/ enormous possibilities.
theres three of us in the deal Richard Turner/ sculptor
and Paul Wong our mutual friend and gallery-man.
after looking it over then agreeing to purchase it i sd
Im terrified of not being able to live up to what it
the bldg. seems to promise. three days later i still feel
that way abt it. next time yr in town Ill drive you
out there where we can get stoned then you can see it
for yrself   Ok

phoned Linda in Halifax to ask her if she was going to
join me . . . and a wee voice tells me the day before
she got raped by a blackman whom she went to see abt a
room advertised for 22 bucks a month. ". . . and you
you shoulda seen his face Roy the expression on it as
he rode me   trying it seem'd to utterly efface me . . .
O Roy I'll never forget that that wild expression . . ."
after which conversation im left dumb-founded and still
dont know if she will be coming

leavin on the 10th for Emma Lake & the Artist's Workshop–
till the end of the month then its back to Van again
where we can share grimaces if not a brimfill'd smile .

                        8/ 7/'72
                        (last letter frm)
                        332- Squirrel St.
                        Banff Alta.

Dear L i n d a

    since our wee talk 8 long days ago   across
these 3000 miles I've been as they say down in
the dumps even these words feel mired in-
side of my scatterings. Yesterday I phoned you
thru-out the day. – –When I finally got thru
 it was yr father on the other end who recognizing
my (now) familiar voice called yr mother to
the phone. "Hullo Roy, how are you, no Linda
is not at home, she's gone to the Gaspe for a short
holiday but I will tell her you called, again . . .
goodbye." She added (again) that she hoped
everything wld finally work out. SHIT! I've talkt
to your mother more times now than we ever got
together. And just a few minutes ago the phone I
have a phobia abt rings downstairs . . . and Im
holding my breath as it continues to ring fill'd
with the thought that IT could be you. Someone
is answering it and by their tone I know its some
body else . . . Its been 3 months since We trippt
through the Gaspe together and in 3 short days I
will be leaving for Emma Lake and the Artist's
Workshop. Linda, I've read and re-read all your
flighty letters. They keep telling me how spaced-
out you are. That your head soars in/amongst
the clouds while yr more dense body wobbles abt
on tip toes, mirthfully.
                        – –despite our pyro-technics
                        our science-future medicaments We
                        dont have a cure for love-sick
                        messes or feverish hearts

    in a room full of mirrors
    the light from a single small window

    gathers up the scatter'd dust
    to place particle by particle at her feet

    sez what phone calls cant

271

                    Fall '72
                    Vancouver BC

dear Chris/ Vivian

    just got me an old/new type-
    writer   an IMPERIAL calld The Good Companion
    made in Leicester, England, its a
    shiny black enamel job thats gotta be one of
    the verities of our adamant technology– –
    its least working part is   at least that. its
    the proper-alignment of these too too
    puny words their insistent proprieties. p/s
    we're fated, together .

    hows everything at the Cheese Factory? if
    i hold the three of you together–
    there   i get that luvly old-fashioned place
    we all find ourselves within:
    call it a family that sense of the familiar
    i also know but sometimes find
    Im standing on the edge of its hub-bub–looking
    in. Linda came 5 daze ago. theres Dallas
    Lies Dasa Mariko & Others as a sort of extended
    family. the familiar as inclusive   rather
    than the old exclusiveness which nonetheless
    persists, is, as they say, tenacious.

    bless your tender tenacities .

1972

Dear Richard

    Some Thots Concerning the Power Plant
    ----

you once sd yr line had no wit in it and
i agreed i remember saying   how i saw yr witless
line   long ago and it made me smile. *but* how
do any one of us 'draw' together the skeins of a
tangled life w/ wit, anyhow?   thats part of
our quest   even in Matsqui   O Easy Traveller !

you Paul Cheinchek and i make a linkt-circle.
i've never had that kind of compact w. others and
it feels good   nothing but good can come of it.
its the way i feel abt us and   its a new feeling a
rush of (whatever) i fumble to name: conjoined
with the rest of you   i stand A S T O N I S H T .

    Practical Concerns :
    ----

we shld try to get our hands on 'copies' of the
original plans and subsequent modifications   via B.C.
Hydro (archives) or thru the realtor. they cld be
most useful   viz our own plans for the place. like we
wld then know abt wiring/heating/plumbing/ etc.

we ought to begin at the beginning: that is fix-up
our living spaces. make them habitable as soon as possible.
then we can move in.   whc side East or West do you
and yrs want?   my own preference is West   just in case
you want the other. I'll abide by a tosst coin.

1st off we ought to shovel all the shit and debris out
off the windows then we can enclose them.   I'll get rolls
of heavy plastic to cover until such time as we can
afford to put glass in. did you know there are over a 100
smasht windows? and a dozen or more broken doors?

theres going to be tons of rubble/shit to haul away. or
we let it all accumulate and use it for fill. as for
the heavy timbers stored in the basement paul cld offer
them a price for it   or have it removed. *where* shld
the temporary shit-house be?   where will the children pee?

273

Im concerned abt our water-supply: have we a well or
some other source and where is it? whats its condition?
then, theres the other end of it all   the sewage its
disposal. have we got a septic tank somewhere?
here   the hydro-plans cld be most informative. *lets get 'em.*

like I sd   I'll be out there doing my bit when
I'm not teaching. abt 4 days out of 7. I wont be using
the plant to make things in til Spring at least
so I'll be able to focus all my attention on making
the plant habitable. re-habilitation. plus– –

Inside and Outside: holes/cracks/broken masonary etc.
ought to be filld   to prevent further seepage/ deterio-
ration, particularly the outside walls and roofs. then
the drainage-pipes those that take the water off   all
the roofs   have to be reamed out or replaced.

we ought to bring in competent tradesmen to advise us
abt the heating/ plumbing/ electricity/ etc.
all of the utilities have to be designed. We want
a single system for each   thru-out the entire building.
viz one huge propane tank for all heating thru-out.

all thots concerning the utilities shld include
our large communal bathroom the laundry room and dark
rooms for our photography. it shld include future
needs as well. I'm all for us getting our utilities in
right off. and how abt a telephone to help us?

– –is there a lumber company near by?   or better a
small mill. we've got enough tools between us to do most
of what needs to be done. what we do need is several
long and short ladders   including a steel scaffold to get
at the high places. yeah tools and a strong back.

I dont know how we're going to finance all this– –hope
Pauls got the bread. we shld get a contractor's license
whc will get us tools and materials for less as well
as extend our credibility. maybe we ought to incorporate–
I'm told thats useful for tax exemptions   permits etc.

Yes I do like the idea of a private arboretum over the
2 living areas. imagine having yr own enclosed garden to
wander abt in. and Yes a roof-deck to work and get
stoned upon. as the custodians of a power plant we shld

do all this and more for the sake of our dream/s.

does 46 Falls   make
a man an *easy traveller* ?

see you on the weekend
if not the day or night before

Sept. '72
Vancouver BC

dear Chris / Viv

    frm high above Point Grey's rooftops
    assorted ship lights dot/ dot/ dot the 2nd Narrows.
    moments ago these same ships floated upon a
    blue-green sheen of water–mirroring my varied thots.
    now, only their pin point lights dot the blue/
    black sea and sky. all the live long day I've waited
    waiting for a re-turn phone call frm Linda– –
    godamnit!–now i know she wont call again and
    all because Mariko answer'd our phone and holler'd
    "its Linda, long distance . . . ." by the time i got
    to it Dal our landlord (downstairs) grabbed it and sd
    ". . . . Roys not home, phone back later." . . . . I've
    been waiting a month for that queer'd phone call.
    so what else is NEWS ?

    (Im finding out (again!) if you wear yr heart on
    your sleeve its gonna get rippt for sure.)

Dear John (New?)love

    (right after yr phone-call

Yes yr right, one morning we'll all get up
to find there are no more Heroes. Nor Heroines.
All of them shredded into pulp in last night
's dream machinery. And standing in front of the
mirror we'll see as 'thru a glass darkly' the
utterly ordinary face of Mr. Everyman standing
on a heap of procrastinations, etcetera. How will
we re-enact a small glory (with or without the
usual ghastly consequences)– –to burn the accumu-
lated scum off our reptilian ids? How are you/
me/we goin' to do that, existentially?

viz a simple symposium for Art/Ed/Typicals
I in anger sd "if you dont stop meddling with Art–
it'll bugger you in the middle of the night."
And (again) I felt that way 'the waywardway' they
thought to coerce it with their dull methodol-
ogies their liberal/ arts/ pieties.
.

Yr pic on the jacket by Jeremy tells me again
 how we're all looped together. Like 'who' tosst
the lariat could be the 1st question. Nothing–
sustains but L-o-v-e, even its sheer impossibility
a lifelong sentence if not sustenance.

        Luv to MC and STEW and
        Irving Layton

late Fall /'72
Matsqui B/C/

Dear Chris/ Viv, John/ Rosemary

    well, here i squat in a splendid 3 story
former POWER-PLANT   2 miles north of Abbottsford BC
on the road to Mission: its a thick walled neo
Georgian facade building built abt 65 yrs ago as one
of a chain of power-plants thru out the lower
Mainland   all of 'em identical. its a misanthropic
utterly derelict Southern American Plantation w/
Richard and Jenny playing the part of a Rhett Butler
and a Scarlet O Hara   and i am their plantation
fore-man and score-keeper. its got abt 10.000 sq. ft.
on 3 floors with 4 flats each w/ 4 rooms off to
the sides. theres a lovely roof patio above them we
think of as our green house/arboretum. of course
the place has been thoroughly vandaliz'd   leaving only
this gorgeous georgian facade the concrete shell
intact. and because its built upon and into a slight
slope northwards theres a commanding view from
all of the hundred or so (smasht) windows. just the
other night Rhett took me up onto the roof. we
stood together facing north   the north star up above
the horizon level w/ our eyes   the massive
front door its broad approach directly below us. he sd
the power plant's alignment is on a true North axis
and thats a good enough omen for me   I of course
agreed with him, silently . thus Im a commuter once
more– –i usually spend 3 days in town and 4 days out
in Matsqui which means 'easy traveller'
the lady at the public library said. and
there have been those times while   chipping concrete
or shovelling out the debris i day-dreamt how this
this too too derelict grade 'b' hollywood movie-set house
might nonetheless become my permanent habitation. and
how splendid it is to work hard all day long then
utterly exhausted   fall into the depth of a dreamless
slumber. the manual labour has enabled me to re-
capture the sinews if not the whole prowess of my young
hard working manhood   i had begun to lament the
loss of. huh come to think of it its my Cheese Factory

Trip its abt the same distance into the big city and
of a comparable dereliction!   Fact/or/fiction– –
as long as breath lasts it all goes on, indivisibly . . . .

10/ 17/72
Vancouver BC

Dear Herb

– –rememberin the tone of your letter I'm
going to send on a handful of heedless words for
nothing. I mean how much are words worth after
a four thousand mile flight? Herb, aren't WE all
CARTOGRAPHERS the way we would compress infinity
into a few squared-off inches? Not to mention the
satellite images of weather's turbulences taken
from 100 miles up or the orb of earth from the moon.
And goddammit aint both cartographer and astro-
naut among the tribes of us humans who would measure
everything even the congeries of time. Ah Sack-
ville in the Fall the Marshland inn where the post
card on my dressing bureau sd 'Ah snow, how it
covers everything in blessed whiteness' or some such
homily. just yesterday I got round to cleaning out
my van. There under a heap of rejectamenta I found
my plastic water container with abt a gallon of stale
Atlantic water plus the hard heel of a fresh loaf
your friend gave me as I was leaving. Vestiges– –
of our lost commodities littering a vasty continental
shelf. The maple leaf forever, etcetera
 . . . its (believe it or not sez Ripley) taken over 3 hrs
to get this far. I have had to leave out the
stoned-conversation Im having with Linney who is
sitting right in front of me on the other side
of this desk. She's sitting there with a papier-mache
schnoz hooked on top of her own pert nose. And
I've just sd to her "Linney" I sd "for over 20 yrs
I've sat in front of my typewriter and whenever I
lookt up I stared at a blank wall–as if some long ago
dream had been inscribed upon it *but* now its your
saucer eyes that seem to ideogram me ."

        like How wash the stain-of-love frm
        the map of O Canada and callit
        anything but O Wilderness, O Herbert !

11/ 2/ '72
4533-West 2nd
Vancouver BC

Dear Michael

way down at the veritable bottom of a heap
of sundry papers I found an invoice for $150.oo
viz 2 of my screen prints. And, under separate
cover you shld receive the replacement for 1
dedicated to the Greenwoods, Ok? As for the so-
called extra one A/P No.8 why not add it to
your collection. I have 15 prints altogether
in 3 series each series comprising 5 distinct prints
which I could have the Bau-Xi send out to you if
York U. be interested.

– –back in the swarm if not
vortex again. Ah how the hunger of us humans
hooks us every time. All of which sez Im back at
it must be Home. From now on Toronto and even
Montreal will be a place to visit on long weekends.
Haven't begun to make things (yet) but will o yes
I will next Spring– –for the rest of my life's
etceteras.

11/ 13/ '72
Vancouver BC

Dear Adele Gillespie
(Public Relations Assistant)

. . . . to be wrappt, as it were, around your
annual report is more than I counted on considering
how I had completely forgotten abt O K I M .
I mean how could it have imagined itself
ending up on your board-room walls in mid Toronto
WOW! if you can send me a slide or colour
print– –to remind me what Okim looks like–I'll
say whether i think its useful to your pur-
poses as well as Okim's. Ok?

12/ 5/ '72
Vancouver BC

Dear Adele Gillespie
(Public Relations Assistant)

Y-E-S you can repro Okim for your annual
if :
    its repro'd as is
    in *full colour,* only . its repro'd
    whole not just any old
    portion to suit.
    that your titles, captions, et cetera
    be so placed as to keep
    Okim intact. that i see the
    colour-proofs before you go to press.
    (fidelity is important, otherwise
    why bother?) that the acknowledgements
    include the artist's name, title
    and medium. all this plus
    a $50.00 repro fee

(thankx for the polaroid snap of Okim)

2/ 15/ '73
Vancouver BC

Dear Adele

    the colour proofs are luvly– –run it
'as is'– –its afterall another 2D stage-prop to
exploit technos/ typology. nonetheless I
gladly own up to instrumentation if not pride of
ownership: All for the pleasure of an image
all images even the one to be wrappt around your
annual report known as Okim

it's 'acrylic' on canvas. it's your baby now.

                                        current addresses:
                                        4533-west 2nd avenue.
                                        3380-clayburn road, matsqui.
                                        2131-riverside drive, n.v.
                                        1923-granville st.
                                        fine arts dept. UBC c/o lasserre bldg.
                                        202-duke hall, ubc

dear Victor

    Thanksgiving s t e w w/ masht potatoes
at Gerry & Carole's w/   a splendid cast including
Linda & I plus the Robert's Creek Trio
alias the Katzenjammer Kids. A L L together we
thot of you your assorted conjugations.
yr side-kick that wordless wunder of the world of
type-faces & klassy-letters Bevington sat
beside us on preview night at the New Era watching
colour bars make rainbows in the landscape
plus other image Bank fool-the-eye pictures. Ah!
sweet labyrinth of imago/images   from across
those vasty N.A. d-i-s-t-a-n-c-e-s Olson wld
have us measure

              . . . whc i see as the pleasure in
                the (appallingly) human .

    Linda & I stand to each other like
double (profile) portraits on ancient coines.
but . . . see how the wrinkly corners of
his mouth begins to turn upwards as he turns
to see her yard-wide smile and huge mary
had a little lamb kind of saucy eyes. ah!–
the heart's derelictions   its unutterable pre-
dilections   its vise-grip Jack-the-Ripper
knew the solemnity of .

            send us some
            coach house books &

            love to all yr women all
            mothers of fate-full indiscretions.
            all of 'em awesome & comely.

            & love yourself.

11/ 14th/ '72
3380 Clayburn Road
Matsqui B/C

Dear P h y l l i s

    (. . . you aint a *webb* for nothing!)

Ah yes do come out to Matsqui (Easy Traveller)
when you can, particularly on Dec. 2nd.
tonight were all driving into Matsqui to sit in on
a council meeting. theyre going to hand down
a decision on whether to change our zoning regulations
from agricultural to light industrial. by the time
you arrive we should know if the power plant is to be
ours. we haven't got a telephone yet let alone water
heating even lights and all of our 100 windows
are smasht . . . but none of this turns out to be grim—
because we have our dream and convivialities to
keep us warm. yeah do come and bring yr sleeping bag
a heavy sweater, booze, and yr friend B .
+
re Maritime Poetry Readings you could try Liz Zimmer
at 1633-Walnut Street Halifax—she seems to know
her way around. no i dont know anyone at Dalhousie
or even any of the 5 other universities in town. it
ought to be possible to arrange some kind of reading at
each of them without exclusion—its worth a GO . I've
given a series of readings here: theres Monty Williams
director of the Confederation Centre Art Gallery
in P.E.I. who I am sure wld welcome you P/S he is a
former Victorian. theres Herb Burke in the Eng/Lit/Dept
at Mt. Allison U. in Sackville N.S. who wld be
interest'd in you. and Alden Nowlan poet-in-residence
at U.N.B. in Fredericton. Yeah—
you just gotta get over to P.E.I. w/ grey Atlantic surge
along entire length of eastern coast   but only after
coming out to Matsqui   Ok ?

                            now the pallid 70s are on us   will
                            Orwell's 1984 also be boring . . .?

11/ 20th/ '72
Fine Arts Dept. UBC

To Whom It May Concern :

    several women i know and respect   together
    with other women i havent met yet
    have askt me to write to you on their behalf–
    They want to publish a monthly magazine
    which would be a VOICE for Women all women particularly
    Those who cant speak out abt their malaise and
    are fearful of driving a wedge between themselves
    and everything they love .

    it is evident to me these women shld be support'd
    generously–for the sake of whatever clarity
    they can bring to bear on our mutual perplexities. they
    ought to be as well support'd as the local symphony
    or cancer fund– –like E v e r y o n e does live inside
    of a community and is equally responsible for
    the enactment-of-legislation thats useful and equitable
    to A l l.

          and i want to hear their voices added to
          the on-going soundings as much as any politicians
          academicians or professional do-gooders–

          how abt you . . . ?

               12/ 5th/ '72
              Halifax NovaScotia

dear S h e i l a

    heres the best of the stoned footwear photos They
    speak for themselves and the others I've kept back. i
    wish i had had the time to pair 'em with the stoned
    gloves–dont black and white images (even–) of what
    we encase our hands and feet in   deserve each other–
    as they slowly become the very dirt, imprint'd.

    cld there be   (at least)   a *foot-print* or a *fool's*
    imprimatura   for each and every thot–
    winding thru this our earthly/deathly Labyrinth ?

    Linda Vanasse arrived from Halifax wearing an incredibly
    scufft and tatterd pair of sneakers. now, gamin-like
    she holds em up   for me to acknowledge. she sez arent they
    beautiful   they talk abt my foot-loose trip
    across 4000 miles of O Canada.–arent we all fetish-
    istic the way we wld see significances

                    tell Norman Yates to lay em up as
                      he sees fit

12/ 5th/ '72
Vancouver BC

dear Frank D .

    . . . you aint no santaClause but some body
    his co-equal   or so it gleams this un tidy yule
    tide when assort'd members of my broodings
    keep yakkin' abt how much each of 'em shld get
    for family or fiendish friends & all that
    kindred gift-lip
                  as for contributing to O/Pen
    Let/Her its not likely as i dont write evaluations,
    criticisms, commentaries or poison-pen squibs.
    i am be it noted a 5c newspaper scribe who ab uses
    words when theres nothing else handy to make a
    shapley thot from   etc.

    m a r g i n a l i a :
    you shiT-Poets are gettin shoved into Can/ Lit –
    where you damned well deserve to p-e-e-r.
    i mean TIME MARCHES ON–& its your
    undone biz i speak of (w/ the sea stretching out
    frm under my feet. like its gotta be the
    merest beginnings & whats to come ought to be
    more torso . . . .
    .

                  anyhow   keep in thar til
                  all yr thwarts turn into homilies
                  .
                  &/ does me painting continue to
                  grab yr eye
                              now and then as
                        as good painting ought to?

4533 West 2nd Avenue
Vancouver BC /'72

Dear Phyllis

Yes i have read Peg's SURVIVAL tho not re-
read it yet. its got to be one of the deep probes
into Canuck-Psyche via mainline W.A.S.P. eyes.
I mean Peg does belong to the companions of Canadian
Shield Seers who via literature probe the litter
/compost of our i-denti-ties. But her is it thesis
is too too pat for yours truly who does not if
he has had thoughts abt it at all think of himself as
an anima/ victim despite the hazards of the 49th
Peril and Yankee mendacities. Its my belief that WE
who abide in the Westcoast do propose another take
which I wont go into here. (as complement to
Peg's tough-minded and occasionally ironic despair try
Ed Dahlberg's scathing indictment of Yankee Liter-
ature viz the anger at the fact of the utter lack of
memorable women in its entire oeuvres. O the flea of
Sodom! O Hiawatha! O Ernest Hemingway!

'not in ideas but in things' viz W.C.W. aint
become a syntactic relic yet.

                          Xmas gift to myself
Journey to Ixtlan the 3rd book of the teachings of
Don Juan and his side kick Don Genaro. Old D.J. must
be one of the great teachers 'cause he rigorously
proposes that HUGE LIFE is utterly a gift to be attuned
to. Nothing but that that awesome fact and the re-
sponsible telling. And it must be that 'shamanistic
spirit' we also live within that has something to do
with our take on Can/Lit: Survival.
                      totem/ fact/ polis

Nina Simone brushin the blues as
Linney accompanies her on a mouth organ while
Lily Lies's black cat meows to be let
out onto the snow-cover'd roof   as yr once
and future stoned friend makes it all
up H-I-G-H as a kite above the 2nd Narrows

      and/ the Indians bathed
      in the Ganges BC   you can do it too

4 F r a m e s / from Donna's Dream

for: all the men in her life/times

.

1st frame : Babel's Tower

>Sky-River
>torrent of wings
>
>beaks   feathers
>and claws
>
>faceless–
>in black space
>
>i am
>a throbbing ear drum

.

2nd frame : waste land doom

>englobed dawn:
>eggs
>
>strewn on a morning plain .
>then   the billion
>
>crackling bits
>as They peck through
>
>their shells to
>flutter damp folded wings
>
>and take-off– –
>only, to falter in mid air–
>
>their sleek bodies
>shrivelling

3rd frame : zoom / frame

    – –a feather mantled
    twilight plain

    through which passed a
    nameless (white?

    flickering-flame .
    I'm a rainbow tree w/

    flaring leaves,
    plugged into

    its circuitry   i stand
    in eternity

.

4th frame : touch: wood: gain

    standing at the edge of
    a forest clearing

    in northern Saskatchewan
    partridges drumming

    on a fallen tree call
    to the myriad voices of

    my bird soul . . . . though i
    have my feet grounded

    I'll never walk the same
    again . fated, i hummm

           Christmas Day '72
           Vancouver BC
Dear Chris / Viv

    its rainin' cats and dogs, etc.
    4pm Christmas Day
    high above dismal 2nd Narrows .
    Linda reading Carlos C.
    talking abt Don Juan. she quotes
    "there need be no enmity be-
    tween 'sanity' and 'ecstacy . . . ."
    which lead to our talkin' abt our
    old pal the Enemy .
    roast turkey smells comin' up frm
    downstairs: sez it

    a merry one to all of you
    at the cheese factory in glengarry county

In Gratitude/for Monica

"Lovers, O late-comers among the marbles and the
bronzes, in the lengthening fires of evening,

Lovers who kept silent in the midst of alien crowds,
You too will testify in honour of the Sea :"

                        (Seamarks /St.–John Perse

Let me be   nonetheless
Your Companion   unto Death . Let
The Heart-Break mend . Let
All the years We spent together be
Nonetheless among the best .
Let them be . Let our Children sing
Our Praises and Perversities.
Let them be our Witnesses . Let
The Broken-heart sing again .
Let it sing the Strife
Between a Man and a Woman . Let
Death part us 'who'   nonetheless
Pledged "til death do us part." Let
Our last gasp remember the first
Breath . Let all the nights we slept
Together the weather in the
Cities we laughed and cried in   be
Washt in our Dreams . Let the
Broken-heart the unfired Hearth the
Hatred and Hurt all mend . Let
the Flux the Fire and molten Metal
Shape and Temper all the rest
Of our lives . Let the toll of these
Words 'praise' you . Let Breath
Reign

        Jan. 18th '73
        my 47th birthday

H a i r : B i r d : S c a r   for Krisy

>"We might have given birth to
>a butterfly with the daily news printed
>in blood on its wings"
>
>   (Mina Loy

H e r E t c h i n g :

    after all the lovers have left–
    the great White Bird who swallowed the sun
    stands tall in the night surf
    a seahorse rocking on its shoulder

        mountains   lakes   rivers
        the skies   clouds and stars etched
        on its 'S' shaped body

        and my love lies curved against   its breast

        Seahorse   Seahorse   will she ride
        the wild winds of her desires
        to the white foam breaking on a distant
        shore   tomorrow?

.

her hair fine
light brown . mine black
streakt with grey .

half my age and twice as proud
her element is air .
mine the earth we slept around on .

we made out alright playing
clowns

thru long hot summer into late fall
her fair hair grew longer than Circe's . every time
she brusht it she said outloud–the longer

more silken you get the more I will have to cut-you-off .
the photograph shows November sun slanting in
across her bald dome . beyond white venetian blinds
the mounds of new fallen snow
seaweed and coral wreath her shorn hair.

.

        4 months later–
        I find the blue and white striped
        EDDY MATCH BOX with a hank of
        her hair coiled inside .
        touching it my hand . . . . wept

        .

        Love's
        – – – –
        Trance
        – – – –
        Canada
        – – – –
        Litter

        .

tugging the blue wool touque down to
hide the light brown fuzz she said "it was
the greatest movie I ever directed . . ."

.

        now that your hair has grown in
        and your life dont seem half-as-grim– – –

        do you go around tossing it for other men?
        have you told any one of them how

        you were once a bald-headed lover
        and I was your matchless middle-aged clown .

        .

        abt The Etching : the entangled-lines   high
        above the Great Bird's head: She said

        "Heaven's roots are thick/ entwined strands of
        human hair and thats how those lines got there ."

        .

netted
as I am I want nothing
more than that
small bird inside me
to sing a riff
of down-to-earth
b-l-u-e-s– – –
                once more

                             3/ 12/ '73
                              Vancouver BC
Dear Mariko

    got your letters   all of 'em–
    and got off on how you tell things with
    a liveliness that touches pulse   or
    thus it seems to Pa caught up as usual in
    the very thick-of-things   with no dim-
    inution of pleasure its awful twin pain.
    your grandpa phoned yesterday he askt
    what you and your sisters were all about
    and of course what I am about. he sd
    he looks forward to his 87th Spring so he
    can walk outdoors again. I am astonisht
    by his it must be virility and– –its
    a part of your psyche too. cant say we
    will make it to Castlegar for W.S.'s
    Tempest but will certainly try. otherwise
    each day utterly enfolds your Pa.

    say HULLO to Fred/ Pauline and Kenny

an open letter to the C. C.

To Whom It May Concern :

    The Issue is not dire need—certainly not for food
and shelter. My wages as a working artist have
always taken care of such needs entire. The issue is
to gain sufficient moneys to go on making sculpture
which the leavings of my salary dont enable. Theres
nothing else at stake viz my application—not even
the quantity/quality of whatever gets made.
the artifacts I have already caused made in the past
20 yrs ought to be adequate proof
of my seriousness—beyond mere good intentions.
These words wont accomplish more than words enable. What-
ever theyre abt they are not sculptures—its
afterall sculpture that I am talking abt.

                ————————————————
                SCULPTURE as
                tangible shapes in the air.
                ————————————————
                The Air (also) substance,
                as any other thing we put a name to. &
                Silence its awesome twin .
                ————————————————
                The itch participates
                in both   making a 3rd
                                      substantial thing
                ————————————————

dear D o r i s

    The itch to shape things coming back– –
    a quite insistent nudge .

        (yr Jack sez its momentum.
          Blake energy: myriad quantums
          of it. *the itch of it* .)

    Doris   its the s-i-l-e-n-c-e at the core of
    our hapless desires that gives us the itch to
    shape things. and its the whole biz of us
    artists to take with utmost seriousness both
    this silence and our assorted itches. i mean–
    arent we among the company of 'those' given to
    reveal the colourful shape of things and the
    immutable silence, their core. Heart's Comeliness
    i take it abides in such possibilities. etc.

most of the time when Im not shaping things i
stay stoned with little to say to anyone. you might
say that i am bereft of argument ideas or even
good old fashioned gossip hence our not seeing each
other as we used to do. recently spent a difficult
evening with John & Donna R. who couldnt abide Canada
& the West Coast and were impatient to return to
England, etc. and the difficulty was the fact that to
all intents and purposes they had already depart'd:
after a decade an ocean and a continent apart we had
nothing to say to each other that matterd–that sense of
utter speechlessness. then theres that mid-life morn-
ing–seeming like any other–when you get up and dis-
cover you dont afterall know a fucken thing not a
single fucken thimg and theres all that terrain you've got
to cover. 'like' i say mostly i stay stoned

        s c u l p t u r e:
        some thing shaped, placed
        out there. together
        with sky ground and air,
        plus silence their
        awesome partner. & The Itch

     is as substantial as any
     3D thing can be–its what
     makes it happen .

Gordon S's Show at the Bau-Xi sez
again) that the BC Landscape continues to
be persistent. Jack's recent work
or what i have seen of it sez the same in
its way-its almost as if the 'throes'
of the American 60s were no more than a low
hung cloud-embankment   thats finally
lift'd to reveal what has nonetheless been
going on all along. What ever happened
to the concept of an 'avant garde'– –did IT
also also blow away? And, why why should
'nt BC Landscape Painting persist   its
at least bed-rock Here where we perch on
the Pacific Rim its awesome 'demarcations'.
And the day B.Bros buy up huge chunks
of the Pacific floor–to subdivide into ocean
lots– –we'll all be lying, bottom'd .
Bert's small retro at UBC tells me how one
painter lost his rudder among the shoals the
back-eddies of modern art 'formalisms'–
its when he stuck close to the look of this
place the aforementioned BC Landscape He
had locus/focus and–its his work of the 50s
that are most distinctive. I mean Bert's
formalism aint got heft it lacks the 'outrage'
of SCALE his trad. cabinet/ easel paintings
dont get a handle on. Anyhow, there it
was and what a lovely whiff of boats bells
bark and buoys his drawings tell. Tell
yr Jack I sat in front of his OWL MURAL at
the Arts Centre in Ottawa and did feel their
lively numerical presences. I was re-minded
how an OWL even number'd ones are   birds-
of-poetry–feathery concatenations of a soul's
fanciful flights, etcetera. And I think i
now know that i shall have to make another
start–and accomplish what i am given to do–
like they say theres nothing new under

the Sunne but its constant re-new-all-s .
.

. . . I've been sittin to my typewriter almost
all of the time these past few years . . . I've been
putting word to word to give what shapeliness
a mere whiff of a life enables . . . Now, the words
dribble out heartlessly garbled and it seems
a propitious time to make something 'high' 'wide' and
'handsome' to utterly disappear into

                yours truly

Dear Ron

    I is flabbergasted by how few people
there are for me to turn to for a C.C. re-
commendation. And I'm pisst off at
having to substantiate the terms of my
seriousness after all these years. How much
credibility do any of us need!

    The U.A.T.A. Conference in Ottawa told me
again) how numb such gatherings are. Never again
is my pledge– –I dont need that kinda stir.
From here on in its time to tune in on
my own stirrings–give 'em a comeliness beyond
all such arguments, etcetera.

Now that Women's Lib is more than a quip–
I give you archaic-man–an old fashioned clan man
Who hangs on to his trophies as long as he can.
If the family den cant hold all of them the museums will.
Strung-up by even his entrails he would leave an
Excremental trail. Anthro/pologists say it all began
Once upon a time when Alley Oop dragged her off
To his pre-platonic lair by the scruff of her flaxen hair.
Glib ruminations frm Elysium Wastelands by a proto-
Typical Hermes (without a hernia) who sez Hurrah for the
Dames! p/s aint we all members of a lavender mob
viz witless homo sapiens .

    ––––––––––––––––
    Ron   will you tell the C.C. how
    it is with me?
    ––––––––––––––––

    – –my little trip East tells me
its high time I painted again–otherwise
I'm condemned to yearning for those
images I seem to be solely responsible for

    – –any day now the buds will open
the leaves unfurl   to cup the sun's warmth
this my 47th Spring   a stirring

Dear Hugh

    gotta hustle up some bread
    gotta scoop up emptiness to shove into a sculpture
    gotta lay another trip on you
    gotta rest from wrestling w/ words their shapeliness
    gotta give 3D substance to rotund ideas
    gotta change gears get a grease job
    gotta re-arrange my priorities
    gotta get on with it whatever it turns out to be
    gotta peak on new terrain
    gotta get going again
    .

    Hughie– –
    decline nothing or
    grab onto everything you can put hands to–
    feel the sap rising. the image:
    sapling and savant stoned on chlorophyll pills
    stand upright–as any decent tree will
    given, they say, half a chance.
    when all the snow goes and another diseased elm
    in the west-end comes down and all
    the birds return as the grass turns green
    when all this simultaneously occurs
    theres gonna be another serendipitous S-p-r-i-n-g
    her green obscenities
    sing
    .

    and when I am in Montreal and I'm seen
    standing at the corner of Sherbrooke and Guy its
    likely that I am heading your way. just as
    the corner of St. Laurent below Mt. Royal St. takes
    me to Milly and Henrys place. and it seems that
    all the corners I've ever stood on lead somewhere–
    if not exactly where I intended.
    .

    p/s dont mention to C.C. that I'm an amateur
    again–I mean let them find out for themselves when
    all the evidence is in

                              c/o Bau-Xi Gallery
                              3003-Granville St.
                              Vancouver 9 BC
                              5/ 5/ '73

Mr. Tadao Ogura
Chief Curator at the National Museum
of Modern Art, Kyoto Japan

Dear Ogura

    Yes, I accept your invitation to exhibit in
30 Japanese American/ Canadian/ Mexican/ Brazilian/
Artists, gladly .

                (I've been to Nihon several times:
the lst when I am abt 4/5 yrs of age. Memory has not
enabled me to retrieve that occasion tho my father sd
I got sea-sick coming and going. And an old photograph
shows me in Umagi with my cousin. 2nd in early 60s
when I spent a long summer in and abt Kyoto not more
than 10 minutes from the N.M.M.A. in Heianji Koan.
Kyoto Airs a small book of poems commemorates that lovely
summer. 3rd summer/ fall and part of the winter in
Kyoto and Osaka where I supervised the construction of
a tri-part steel and vinyl sculpture for Canada's Bldg.
at Expo '70. StonedGloves a book of poems and photos
commemorates that occasion. 40 yrs separates the lst and
last occasion. During that time my parents went back
and forth manymany times. Thus, I have always felt as tho
I lived as it were in the next village rather than on
the far side of the Pacific, etcetera.)

I speak a simple ofttimes garbled Japanese.

5/ '73
Vancouver BC

Dear Barry

– –if its got to be a choice of interviewing
Anne Murray or Busty R. I'd opt for the latter tho
her huge tits could be a mammoth problem. if
you buried the mike in between 'em her heart's
palpitations might tell meat's story as well as a
heart-throb, such as A.M.'s. Thats if the reso-
nance cld get thru all that ugh fat.
                                         In Nippon
they have a whole chorus line out in front of even
the proscenium – –all of 'em showing their powder'd
pussys (simultaneously! And the wretched men whc
includes yrs truly go MAD scrambling for front row
seats so they can put their sweaty heads up/in be-
tween her thighs etc. But its afterall a show and if
you happen to blow yr tool no one knows or cares
after the curtain comes down and you stagger outside.

Gawd Barry aint we a bunch of gorillas or some such
animammalian the way we spin bananas on the tips
of our noses while scratching a hairy armpit. And
aint the Piltdown Man our true blue forebear?
Wish I cld with a finger's snap turn into a dwarf w/
a shrunken if not utterly emptied head.

And now that Pablo Picasso is dead aint everyone
every last one of us a genuine kultur hero? p/s wld
like a duplicate of acetate outrage particularly
the mock the turtle bit in that pizza place after the
reading w/ Riggatoni and others.

                    thank gawd Im not a poet-modern
                    Frontiersman who has to abide a place
                    like Prince George. after Opal Alta
                    and the 2nd W.W. I feels I served my
                    penitences.

9/ 14/ '73
Richmond BC

Dear Syuzo

    old cliche: S-I-L-E-N-C-E is
gold, etc.
        but I still talk too much for
        my (as they say) own good, etc.

nonetheless

        C o n g r a t u l a t i o n s
        - - - - - - - - - - - - - -

on your marriage. mother told me yr
mother told her. sd yr busy build-
ing a home/studio between Osaka/ Kyoto
in Hirakata. etc.

mind awash in Kamogawa . . .
while fingers tip typewriter keyes

no other moment um (but) Now

anyhow, if Im lucky I shld be in Kyoto for
big show called Japanese Artists in the Americas
at the N.M.M.A. Tuesday Sept. 25th, 2 to 4PM
via Flt. No.401 C.P.A. Will phone you on arrival
YEAH   YEAH   YEAH

        S t o n e d G l o v e s are
        coming home to salute

                    9/ 14/ '73
                c/o Bau-Xi Gallery
                Vancouver BC

Dear Mr. Ogura

    Thank you for the handsome invitation and
    catalogue for J.A.I.T.A. Show.   Since
    then I have been at work on ways and means of
    getting there for the opening.   Needless
    to say my S t o n e d G l o v e s are equally
    anxious– –its going to be their 1st trip
    back to their homeland after travelling all a-
    cross Canada over to Paris and back. Even
    now I can hear their soft thuds inside
    thick plywood packing cases.

Wld you send an invitation to these:

Mr. Syuzo Fujimoto at
11-2 Miyakozima, Kitadori
2 Chome, Miyakozima-ku
Osaka City

Miss Masako Yoshimura at
446 Hachi ken machi
Furukawa-cho, Sanjo-kudaru
Higashiyama-ku
Kyoto City

Mr. Tetsuo Yamada at
Yamada Gallery
253 Umemoto-cho
Shimonzen St.
Higashiyama-ku
Kyoto City

Mr. and Mrs. Cid Corman at
c/o Yamada Gallery

    AND DONT BE SURPRISED IF I SHOW UP .

Dear Mr. Besant
    c/o Communications Centre at S.F.U.

re Barbara Schumiacher and Kenny Tallman: They
came by   Sunday afternoon to talk abt 'how'
to   carry on in the theatre on their own terms viz
put on Dante's Divine Comedy, next. As Kenny sd
"after the Tempest where can you go if you want to
make it tough for yrself?"

: a sense of their seriousness and capability.)

They workt together on As You Like It   together with
my daughter who designed all the costumes etc.

: precedent, therefore more than potential.)

(Kenny played Prospero as well as directing W.S.'s
last play The Tempest at Selkirk College/ Castlegar.
Barbara did more than the call of duty. Again my
daughter Mariko did the costumes.   Etcetera.)

: a 'collaboration' W.S. wld have approved.)

    They together with the rest of the cast
    average age 17) showed me T.T. as I've never been
    given to see it. Altogether, They re-created
    it with a freshness that totally permeated us
    e/g audience. There was none of that awful
    twitchy stardom biz. And I came away with the sense
    that its in their kind of collaborative-group
    ing that will be the REAL ENERGY in and thru what-
    ever possibilities Theatre will have in the 70s.

    Tony/ I cant remember what They were applying for–
    but if its got anything to do with gettin the ole
    show on the road then you ought to talk/take them
    seriously–without HA! further ado. And if hired–
    you should give 'em a context for putting on even
    a Divine Comedia – –I mean that much rope

    yours

                        Vancouver B/C
                        October '73

Dear Mother/ Father
    Brothers and Sisters

I've been back a week and I am listening to
cassette tapes i made in Nihon as i
write you this letter. *how are all of you ?*
Im listening to Masako who of course
lookt after me royally. needless to say i had
a lovely time and felt more at home than
ever. Syuzo Fujimoto and his new wife also took
good care of me. We 3 enjoyed each other's
company.   playing the tapes back enables me
to hear myself talking lousy japanese– –
dammit its sort of humiliating. Syuzo and i
together w/   Akira Dan and Mitsuro Akino spent
two and a half days in Kyoto's backcountry.
the first night out we slept at Akira's place–
i hardly slept as the crickets and frogs
together w/ other insects kept up a forest of
sounds it seemed all night long. then we
got into Syuzo's car w/ Mitsuro at the wheel
and drove thru farmlands forests and mountains
to Obama on the west coast then to Tsunegami
on the very edge of the Japan Sea. P/S I've got
a tray full of colour-slides of our trip whc
I'll show you when i come home. now Im listening
to the traffic sounds on Kawaramachi I've
walkt along both sides of the street   weaving
in and out off a thousand pedestrians w/ my
tape recorder. remember the canvas canopy up over
Furukawa-cho Market . . . theyve replaced it w/ a
sleek metal and plastic canopy that does a better
job of keeping the rain out. Masako is fine
she still drinks and perhaps smokes, too much–
but what a capable woman. needless to say
the whole week passed altogether too too quickly
and now that Im back Im wondering if my trip
wasnt just another day-dream.

1408-Westminster Highway
Richmond B.C.
October 19th 1973

Dear Deborah Turnbull

viz the exhibition EMMA LAKE YEARS 55/73 and
our conversation–I didnt get the impression that
(1) there wld be equal representation except
for the leaders. (2) that each artist wld be presented
with works frm the yrs 55/73 when possible.
(3) that the bulk of the show had already been chosen,
the wall space taken up. its understood that
all the details cannot be remember'd precisely viz
a phone call. However   I sent on the things I did in
good faith thinking that I could thus present
my self with the best there was to hand. There was
no other thought. I do remember insisting that
I would prefer not to show the 2 earlier works and
would send on other things etcetera. I dont
cant remember what was said viz packing and shipping– –

(remember the infamous rail strike and the
partial airstrike ?   we phoned all over town to get
someone to get them across the mountains to you
and the hurried packing job we had to do etcetera.)

and after getting them off I thought 2 things:
(1) you could hang all of it.
(2) or make a selection from them. either way
I simply assumed you would pay– –   as
the matter stands it seems that I am going to have to
cough up . . . Now what kinda deal is that?
I mean you get my works to put on show and I gets
the lousy goddamned bills! further: if your
not paying some kinda rental fee to each artist it
means your getting the whole show free!
you could at least pay for shipping and packing
charges. and who is going to have to pay for
getting the works back to me– –will we have a quarrel
about that too?

      meanwhile– –
      The Peking Art Treasures are coming to
      Nihon . . . think they've got the same

assortment of problems   or do the long
longdead always travel 1st class
collect?

10/ 16/ '73
Richmond BC

Dear Sheila

   – –if you want work for W.P. i cld send
callit a work-in-process: started a week ago
its hopefully the beginnings of a working
period I aint had for these many long months.
I wld just send on whatever comes each week
one page at a time tho theres no telling what
shitty biz might come of it etc. But I do mean
to be as they said diligent thus trust myself
to deliver the good etc. (apropo my lack of
spontaneity whc i've wanted for a long time etc.
right now i feel like a writing machine thats
abt to be re-tuned. Lets run a riff of words
shall We?

         (this if you want cld be the lst page . . .

    met a fine young man in Kyoto who
    pirates recordings and fine art ptgs.
    instance the enclosed poster is
    from his own colour slide. Like whats his
    level of Tantric-Consciousness?

   Hi to W.W.

                        10/ 21/ '73
                        frm the back of the lot
                        at 1408-Westminster
                        Highway in Richmond B.C.
Dear Claudia
    Francois and
    Susie

            Arctic Honey and Pesticide Free Money:
            -------   ------------

            met a Stoned-Professional-Pusher at a party
            who thinking (aloud) (and fast) abt a fast-buck
            said he's been working on a radical design
            for light-weight collapsible bee hives– –1000s of
            which would be air-freighted into the Arctic–i
            believe he sd 'tundra' (while– –) the pre-packaged
            drones buzzzzin around their queen would be on
            their way up frm California : the millions of them
            then would gather sweete arctic nectar thru the
            short but profusely flower'd summer, etcetera . my
            gawd he snorted (thru his coke)– –if a few of us
            got the number together We could prevail
            on the C.C. and pull it off– –for Ha Profit
            and and and We could grow good ole mari-juana on
            the side– –callit uh . . . ARCTIC GOLD and turn
            Eskimos on . And the Stoned-one talkt on
            jingling loose change

C: send us a cassette of Honey and
its as they say NICE TO hear you got a book out. like
theres nothin like a wee book as a gathering
place etcetera. all of the earth's multitudinous clans
have their wee books oral histories and/ or a
Story Teller. jeezus how substantive breath and its ah
complement words are– –i mean how (together) (they)
nonetheless, inform the necessary s-i-l-e-n-c-e-s. "pray
for me wont you" my friend sd as he turned and walkt
away .
            F: "aint Love fatal?" i mean 'how' the last time
            i saw you you hung on thar   when She was out
            of sight, qualified– –how dis-tracted you seemed.

aint Love fatal aint it a fitfull predilection
or is it (also) our malediction beneficence and be-
nign affliction– –certainly its got to be the co-
zee-est conundrum 2 humans ever devised. 'i' who
continue to be thus 'fated' say aint Love grand
aint it a aweful feverishness aint it fated ?

2/   (more of the same scenario :

– –if if i could hold all the women i've known
across this vasty dominion–this ouija board-in mind
simultaneously– –if i could just do this i might
get an overview of .'how' altogether we formed a dense
ly woven tapestry of which yours truly would simply
be a single (hopefully)(colourful) strand . if i
could and did then do this   without the image-of-a-nation
crowding my cranium i would be C.J.'s peer and D.J.
stoned adversary if not an absolute mad-man. "ho hum"
my oracle sez "yr wedded to Mistress Art once and
for all, forget it." and further, my oracle never sez
"dont kid yrself" knowing as his bones do   the
propensity of fools to do just that. Francois–aint We
thus fated–one way or another–til, as they say
DEATH PARTS US.   Keep in thar keep it up, Partner .

(and more :

C:F: and especially Susy– – yours truly will be
in Toronto come New Year for a reading– –do you want one
at Vehicule too? and if the Parti Quebecois get in
will i then need a 'passport' to travel from one strange
county to another? if its gonna be an image-war
instead of a battle of ideologies–I'll take Rene L.'s
rumpled looks over a pin striped Bourassa anyday.
then, thars that coyote named Tricky Dick– –wonder if
he'll end up in his own puke smiling thru the sticky
hysterics? i jus want say we oughta let Cannon work on
the WATERGAP CASE. aint 'politics' grand aint it but
the inside view of the hierarchy of a nuthouse e/g a
PENTAGONAL WHITE HOUSE

                                            these words come frm a

a five acre peat bog in the Fraser's
Deltaland–its so flat Here
I think more of the Prairies than
the Rocky Mountains

aint all this a mouthful ?

A SPACE
‾ ‾ ‾ ‾ ‾ ‾ ‾
        POETRY READINGS
        ‾ ‾ ‾ ‾ ‾ ‾ ‾ ‾ ‾ ‾ ‾ ‾ ‾ ‾ ‾ ‾

To Whom It May Concern : re
Kiyooka Reading at A-Space, Toronto. be advised
He is (most) willing to come – –
Providing the following matter is agreed upon.

    1. you will pay his way there & back via
       economy class air .
    2. you have the reading on a Friday/ Saturday/
       Sunday/ or Monday evening.
    3. that it take place on one of the above evenings in
       mid-December thru the 31st. or
       the appropriate days in mid-February.
    4. that if you cant afford an honorarium to cover ex-
       penses then (at least) provide room & board.
    5. that he be given sole right to do what he pleases .

        if the above is agreeable and the dates are
        satisfactory to both parties 'the poet' pro-
        poses to guarantee the following:

1. he will be thar as per agreement.
2. he will (as they say) deliver-the-goods.
3. he will waiver all rights to repro-
   duction. (fuck copyrights is his motto).
4. he will certainly smile and laugh.
5. he will be memorable.

– – –Ok. lets get it on. &
tell Victor theres more than one quiver left in
my quiver-sheath. yeah .

        yrs. sincerely,

october 22nd 1973 a.d.

dear Phyllis

    .... long time no see, no hear, no smell, no face,
no gossip, & no pomes. know not you dead or alive or
simply livid. &, aint Watergate enought to make
one more so? Gregory Corso with a huge bandaid a-
cross his nose where Bob Creeley belted him–Buffalo, N.Y.
circa 67. remember the Matsqui Power House –well We
traded it in for a 5 acre peat bog on Westminster & no. 6.
Who wld have thot 'ivory towers' are interchangeable?
it aint exactly Walden nor the Lake Country but then
I aint exactly your Thoreau or William Wordsworth. & – –
I'm wonderin' what his words are worth now. myself
aint read him for 20 yrs. do you think his side-kick
Samuel Taylor Coleridge is stoned out of his mind   HIGH
on the angelic ladder? opium vision/   ophelia floating.
Linney is down in Frisco. remember good ole San Francisco.
wonder whats cookin' down there now that the City
Lights & all the BEATS not to mention others have be-
come His/Story. . . . it all seems so remote.   someone sd
Phil Whalen is part of the furniture at the Zen Centre– –
it seems he finally found the way of licking his life–
long genteel poverty. & from all reports Robert C. is Bolinas's
laureate. & why not, he's among the few I can still
read and be haplessly held. yeah. 4 days less than 3 months
til my 48th yr. like they say Im pushin' 50 or half-a-cent-
ury– – –W O W ! am I dumb!!!!

                        wont you curtsy
                        or take a bow to show yr sittin'
                        across the way in another
                        pew ? in the dead of Night– –
                        rain gently falling rain
                        & a few wee thots (of) (for)
                        you.   take care

10/ 23rd/ '73

Dear Bob and Bobbie

    as they say, Times passes, etc.
    i am alternately fearful and then astonisht at
    its ceaseless passage. guess nothing
    assures us a passport to old age 'the wrinklies'
    my youngest daughter call'd it than this
    this awefull momentum .

    my Daughters are thriving: Mariko the oldest
    recently put on her 4th fashion show.
    she had her first one at 9 now shes almost a pro.
    at 17 she has almost left home. Jan our
    middle one hitch-hiked all the way across Canada
    to P.E.I. and back on 17 dollars. of course
    she stayed with our numerous friends along the way.
    now she is talking abt going to Japan to study
    dancing. she will be just 15 in May.
    Kiyo the youngest gave me a 60 page story she wrote
    for my 47th birthday. she is going thru the
    ganglies. 13 is her number. Now i can see the kick-
    backs the lovely astonishments of time etc.
    .

    Linda has left a carousel of 100 slides at
    The Quay for you. they purport to tell abt a long
    event-fill'd day in Berkeley, Bolinas and S.F.
    i like particularly the sequence taken at the Quay–
    theres some lovely shots of famili/air/faces .

    keep 'em as long as you like or get copies made.
    you cld return them
                       c/o Fine Arts Dept. U.B.C.

10/ 28th/ '73
Vancouver bc

Dear Chris & Viv (especially for
her summer letter .

: for   not having anything
to say all these several months.

litter/ letter
　　Lost – –
　　　　Love's Labour
　(nonetheless)
　　　　　l-a-s-t-s

& what does the forthcoming Quebec elections
look like frm the cheese factor?
is it goin' to be another bout of ideological pandemonium?
C.B.C. sez   the (beleaguered) WASPS are
solidly behind the LIBS. as one of 'em sd, 'theres
really no choice Im not abt to put my head
in the nooose for anyone . . .'

　　　　　mean/while: below
　　　　　tenuous demarcation 49th parallel
　　　　　R.M.N. usurpts prime-time:
　　　　　WATERGATEs gotta be the all time best
　　　　　GangBusters on any channel

2/

                    & have you notic'd how
                    the USSR and the USA (despite themselves
                    have become re-visionistic
                    as bedlam-fellows.   serves 'em right!–
                    as Mao's multitudes daily become
                    more visible .

i have a new Lady– –
she is half my age and twice as pretty.
i got as they say a **new lease**
on Life. wow didnt think it cld happen again
at almost fifty. wonder whatll be
in store for me when Im eighty?
my lovely young lady is scared of bees.
shall i tell her I've been stung
before . . . . thank gawd its never the same
sting, twice .

we live on 5 acres of benevolent peat
complete with large birch trees
in Richmond BC   half an hour frm Vancouver
and Blaine Washington. we go for days
without a glimpse of fabled mountains or our
old friend sea. Here, at the crossroads
of No. 6 highway and westminster its
at least as flat as my childhood Prairies
& it begins to feel like 'home'–if
home is where the heart feels ease

                    Viv: now that you have finisht
                    yr school-work its high time you did what
                    all of us sooner or later have to do.
                    which is to give our lives a shapeliness that
                    words/colours/   sounds/ etc enable. theres
                    nothing new under the sun but
                    i want hear your own utterly particular
                    voice tell it, like it is .

weeklaterNews :

just sent off a letter to Susy Lake abt my comin'
to Vehicule/ Dec. 19th/ '73   for a poetry reading plus
home-made movies galore. if it works out i shall be
able to see all of you, however separately: itll be my
mid-winter holiday.   viva la quebecois!
.

Chris   nothin' sticks better than bond-fast.
nothin' to see but immense sky/fields of iridescent colours–
a dazzlement of Nights and Days day onto day

3/

                anyHeyday   now
                Yankee super tankers gonna be ploughin'
                greasy wakes thru Juan de Fuca
                & we'll be ready for 'em–for the sake of
                oiling corporate palms. when– –
                it comes to year-end dividends its always
                hands-across-the-border, into each
                Other's pockets
                                ask ole sockeye abt it.

    fuck! it'll go on– –
    & on til the very last drops been siphon'd
    outa muthur earth's belly   &
    utterly burnt-up.
    Godard-like shot frm high-up   of vasty
    concrete highway   stretchin' a-
    way to pin-point horizon   strewn w/ millions of
    rusty burnt-out hulks of our
    tin dinosaurs. etc.   & Im
    diggin' my heels into soft sod. my hitherto
    soft white feet aren't abt to complain
    now theyre callus'd .

remember the infamous 'beef shortage' ? How
the affluent were grabbin' up huge slabs of meat to shove
into their installment plan freezers. do ya think

the same thing will happen viz fossil fuels?
already im working on a compact fuel siphoning kit–i
oughta make a fortune on it. then, theres the
huge pit in my backyard   ready for a 100.000 gallon tank.
i reckon it'll be large enough to keep me fuel'd
for the rest of my life.

                                              ectoplasmic fantasies frm
                                              under the birch tree
                                              at the back of the lot in
                                              richmond bc .

                11/ 11/ '73
                frm the back of the lot at
                1408-Westminster Hgwy
                Richmond BC

d(ear Pen 'pal' Chalmers

    O YES I AM coming on (winter) (solstice)
    December 21st '73ad with hoarfrost on my beard .

The thot of the thot of Xmas in Toronto be-
guiles my guileless soule . the thot of counting
all the stuffed and bewigged Santas fronting
Yonge Street stores is enuff to give me goose-
pimples . and the heavenly thot of whippt potatoes
and sliced turkey with gooey gravy at Harveys
cheers me hugely . then, the thot of the merest
thot of reading aloud to a number of friends
warms me cockles . Jeezus does that make me glut-
tonous or merely oleomargarine ?

and shall I entune my vocables to Xmas carols
write a wry winter/solstice epic and bring
a sprig of mistletoe along with the 3 wise guys
and the star over Bethlehem ? or/ or/ or/ or
you can take it as it comes come what may solstice
day .

        so send on my plain-fare– –
        I'll be there with tinkle-bells button'd
        on my green velvet pantaloons .
        –thats if me stoned ear dont get appalled
        at the ongoing clamour, etcetera

            (and I dont give a shit what
            the local denizens think abt the
            starlings–I miss their birch
            tree-top chatterings .

    n u a n c e s is what we're all abt aint
    it 'pen pal'?

                pox on
                politicians

                rheumatism
                and sugarplum pomes

Winter '73

pox on poetry's dolorous smile
- - - - - - - - - - - - - - -

a   bakers dozen for the poetry front

– –poems affront
those who cant say cunt or

tell an arsehole
from a hole in the ground

a leaky cess-pool
or Rosy Sweet Rosy O Grady

my fair Lady sez
its the gravy train   its

merest whiff works wonders
the rarities

include hermaphroditic
elegies

ball point pen
poem– –

a bird in hand
is worth two in a bull pen

O William
Carlos Williams!

how much is a mouth fill'd w/ words worth?
pox on poetry

its malevolent grimace
O the erased

s-i-l-e-n-c-e-s-!

.

advise to the canada council:
DONT TAMPER W/ WORDS   OR
(PAMPER) (PAUPER) POETS TO DEATH !

BLESS : BREATH : BREEDING : POEMS

        Nov.'73
        frm the back of the lot at
        Richmond BC

                11/ 13/ '73
                frm the back of the lot at
                1408-Westminster Hgwy
                Richmond BC

Oh Susy– – –

    A Space/ Toronto wants me to read on
    December 21st . How abt Wednesday the 19th
    at Vehicule ? it wld be a reading plus
    home movies (slides) and whatever else seems
    possible on the spur of the moment .

    We) will come a few days earlier and stay on
    til the day before the Toronto gig .
    –

    – –been (in)ACTive viz painting since Monreale .
    I've been more culpable/ gullible than say
    fallow . or, as Frankie sez "fools walk in where
    wise men fear to tread, etc" anyhow *the itch*
    is on me again and Im at least writing .
    paintings and/or sculptures cld follow . . . .

wish Godalmighty wld shove his om-
nipotent little finger into the WATERGATE to
stopper the torrents of judicial abuse .
wish He were a prosecutor or a magistrate .
I mean aint politics grand aint it a
Barnum and Bafley 3 Ring Circus of circum-
stantial mayhem .

        – – – – – – – – – – –
    an azure mandala
    for the Detroit whiz kid
    – – – – – – – – – –

    and aint we all
    both circumference and centre ?
    veracity remains a
    sublime capability– –
    worth reaching up/in/round for

  tell Hughie I'm coming wont you ?

                            frm the back of the lot at
                            1408-Westminster highway
                            Richmond BC / Nov. 16 '73
Dear Don
            re The Art Gallery of Victoria's
            modest proposal to establish a pension-scheme
            for its employees via donated works
            of Art–to be auctioned off, etcetera .

   – –to hell with pensionschemes of all sorts,
   particularly those to be paid for with works of art.
   like my hearts not in it no matter 'where' or
   'whom'. i have never thought to hedge my life by payments
   with such lousy odds)on my future–when it's the
   present the 'complete actual present' as Gertrude wld
   say thats important. and, so it is that i feel
   more or less the same viz 'others' even a Colin Graham
   or my old friend Richard Simmins. because i've
   moved abt so much i dont have a pension coming
   via any college or university–after 20 yrs
   and thats how i want it. what others do or want for
   themselves is their own biz more than any
   erstwhile pensionschemes etc. more importantly i've
   not made much saleable art since '69 and all
   i've got left is whats left of those. I've not made more
   than a labourer's wage from art and wouldnt think
   of asking for your or any one's assistance
   or rather i haven't the temerity to do so. no doubt
   that C. is lean viz money nonetheless i assume he's
   lookt after himself and will make out handsomely.
   i wld add that after all these yrs all-of-us shld have
   learnt to deal with basic economics adequately–if
   not with much grace. more importantly you ought
   to in your art gallery position push for
   Fed./Pro. moneys to support our Artifact-
   keepers viz their pensions etc. i strongly support
   the notion that each community has its own responsi-
   bilities viz such matters. And HOW how could good old
   Victoria that bastion of genteel old and young
   well-heeled folks forget that amongst themselves there
   are others who want nothing more or less than

BIG HI to BETSY and JOHN D
I've never met your children cause
theyre always asleep when I
came by . . . I suppose like mine theyre
almost young men and women

                              frm the back of the lot at
                              1408-westminster highway
                              richmond bc / nov 17th '73
dear Ernie

   just the other day i saw a ceramic portrait of you
   at the Vancouver art gallery. i almost passt it by– –
   thinking its just more of the same ceramic cuteness
   the room was fill'd with. some passing recognition made
   me stop and squint at it & my gawd! there you were big
   as life, however diminutive. then i thot i had better
   go around and look at some of 'em again to see what it is
   i might have missed. mr. fafard has got a lot going
   for him given the scale he works at. i wld like to see
   our friend Marsha portrayed at that scale! WOW!

   apropos yr letter: if the drawing of young/old entwined
   hands aint spoken for i wld (lst) like that: (cat. no. 94
   illustrated in the emma lake workshops catalogue). ernie– –
   if its going to be shown elsewhere i dont care–i want it
   despite such delays. if, you dont want to sell it or its
   already been bought etc. i will be most happy to settle
   for the one you mentioned. or another hand/s.

   (you might have heard abt my photo show called Stoned-
     Gloves . . . im sending you a copy of the catalogue/book.
     it will also add credence to why i wld want the draw-
     ing of the entwined hands.)

   – – –as for my part of *the exchange* you will have to wait
   til i get back to work 'cause i am not abt to give you
   something frm yrs ago. no sireee! Ernie, 'it' will have
   to be as fresh and lively as the day its done & slow-
   ly those days are coming back. Ernie – – –
   now that i am pushing 50 i think i can begin to do a few
   good things. count on me.

                              luv to Degen & Others
                              (Saskatoon is also some wee part of me)

11/ 29th/ '73
Richmond BC

d(ear Phyllis

    my gawd!
    yr stamina viz
    anima/ psyche
    is nonetheless
    Astonishing

               "into each life
                some rain mus' fall. . ."

                (tells abt gettin'
                one's finger/s burnt   or
                even cut off)
                                remember
                the I n k S p o t s ?

                i must have listened to to
                their 78s a thousand times
                in backcountry Opal Alta.
                circa mid-40s. they played
                huge part in my fantasies
                then and here i'm rememberin
                their sob songs 30 yrs
                later
                .

almost as if Linda sensed you had
been in touch with me she reads in the vanguard
how Bs wife has taken over M.Ps position
etc. despite the unwarranted little jealousies
which i am not the provocateur of we are
miraculously doing our version of the beauty
and the beastly bit. its Love Love Love
that makes the world go around–as long as theres
a bit of shit mixed in with it.
anthropomorphic lies . . . of course.

                        pox
                        on demoncracy

        hypocrites
        and sugarplum pomes

2/

looks like we shall be goin East for Christmas with
a reading (or whatever) at A-Space and Vehicule in Toronto
and Montreal respectively. were both glad to be leaving
this fucken sog behind for awhile even if it means sub zero
weather snowstorms and snarled traffic. anyhow, our trip
displaces an earlier intention of going to Saltspring to see
you. we'll be back abt the 27th and the New Year my 48th .

        Jeezus youve got lots of pomes
        and blushes in you   or Im using the
        wrong yardstick   the one named
        youthfilld seizures   or is it heart's
        bedlams . or else i am more
        the fool than you which hopefully aint
        altogether   true . . .

        may infanta paroxysms (if not true visions
        seize you and shake you, free .

        – –The Risen tell of making it
        even as they return humpbackt. like who
        goes such awful distances to return
        empty-handed ?

                . . . guess you cld say
                Im riding HIGH that is i feel less
                estranged frm myself more so
                than i have for a longlong time. or
                is it that which is familiar
                make things bearable   simply by
                its dailyness   whatever

                keep in touch
                sez tweedledum to tweedledee

Vancouver, B.C.
'73

Dear Father

    ... I took abt 350 slides while i was
in Japan. theyre mostly of the lovely green
countryside north and west of Kyoto   and
all the way across to Tsunegami on the Japan Sea
rocky promontories. ... I took them mostly
for you and will bring them home at Christmas time
so you and the family can 'see' them. Father
if for whatever reason you want me to bring them
even sooner ... just phone and I'll do that.
besides the slides i have a number of cassettes
w/ the varied sounds we moved thru, on them– –
I'll bring them along as an aural accompaniment.
theres one 90 minute tape fill'd w/ Night's
insect-sounds and another of the Japan Sea Surge
you'll want to hear.

    Father, do let me know

Dear Barry 'Mac' Kinnon

– –been watching our man
in China our PM in light colour'd suit
surround'd by multitudinous drab
the Ok uniformity. adding muscle to the whole
stately-faire none other than our own
vexatious Dr. Kildare alias Norman Bethune w/
tatterd red star on ragged sleeves. no
body can be more fervently RED than a Pres-
byterian WASP. i wonder if he met Ernie
Hemingway in Spain during the civil war before
the bells toll'd? just think of the multi-
million dollar epic the NFB cld produce with the
kind permission of Chairman Mao–like aint
all the ingredients there! i dont know a thing
abt his love-life the official story sez
his dedication to medicine and revolution left
no time for balling. NFB cld negotiate w/
Kirk Douglas to play N.B. and Anna May Wong or a
Shirley Yamaguchi to play his girl Friday –
the peasant girl whom B. trains as his assistant
but never makes a pass at. i can already see
that lovely sequence in a paddy field where side
by side theyre planting rice shoots as the
loudspeakers extoll the verities of his highness
holed up in his mountain lair. all this on B's
day off. getting back to the CBC teley– –
my favorite scene shows our PM chatting via inter-
preter with China's able chairman his thick
round shoulders backt to cubby-holes fill'd w/
official papers: Ah the homeliness the grandeur of
POWER! like how compelling the vista must be
from the top of the proletarian heap. the most
moving sequence showed peasants outdoors dancing
solemnly around the bed of the dead Bethune.–
WOW whata splendid way for one of our authentic
Heroes to go. Ah Barry dont the old fashioned
therefore infamous movies have their moving moments?
i like the thot that History is no more than
a few feet of acetate (acid) images. and/ Politics
of whatever stripe is a paradigm of all our

seeming contradictions   or a complex diagram
of a labyrinthian HELL .
p/s think the C.C. might give us a grant to read
our poetry in Peking?

dear V i c / D o r

    – –wonder if HughieHefner puts away copies of
Playboy   (like, the old Liberty and Little
Orphan Annie)– –to play-back in the yr. 2073 for
our great grandchildren's edification . wonder
if Malevolence and Automobiles will have gone the
way of nouveau Roman Gladiators and Chariots . O
Vic/dor who's gonna carry the torch when the
fuel runs out?

the Peat were squattin on averages 10ft
its breadth is most of the Fraser River Deltaland .
when it comes to the crunch even a Bog can be
a man's best friend .

                        see you all come
                        Dec. 21st

                        Nov. '73
                        frm: the sod at the back of the lot
                        Richmond B.C.

Dear S h e i l a

            whats up ?
            whats happened to my idea for W P ?
            _ _ _ _ _ _ _ _ _ _ _ _ _ _ _ _ _
            or has it ecologically speaking also
            been wiped out ?

balmy early November
day   the kind that makes one feel good to be
alive   if not in all ways lively .

not much difference between Richmond B C and
Opal Alberta – –as far as one man's
psyche knows . W H Y why do 'i' get stuck with
poor sod peat sand and muskeg instead of
rich red dirt, or loam . . . . unless its that the sum of
all the poor sod i have known   is meant to test   my
rootedness : My Mythologies : Kinship : Ties .

nonetheless– – " L I V E   I T   U P and   let the Devil
have the arsehole . " one wee voice sez .

            Wilfred   aint Anne of Green Gables just
            another garbl'd fairy-tale ?

            Wonder what Wyndams doin' in purgatory ?
            and will Hugh Kenner spend   his

            Sabbatical there ? And do you think Stern
            Tom Eliot has set up his pew   outside

            The Pearly Gates ?
            The Gates of Wrath A-gape .

over 20 articles/ notes/ quips/ and dire prognosis   not
to mention the car toons the jokes and bare-arsed lies in
the SUN abt foot-in-mouth tom fool pres-ident of the U.
S. A. etc.–aint We canucks got a ringside seat north of
the 49th Peril: Roman slaves watching the rise and fall of
the Gladiators . mean/while 'IF' the Venezuelans hike
up their oil prices and the rabid sheiks close down the taps
as the Yanks plunder our natural resources and P. Lockheed
carries on as if Albertans owned via legacy the tar sand pits
therefore deserved every last centavo of it and the day
after tomorrow we get up to find our houses cold and our cars
immobilized . . . . will We then and only then call upon our
Northern Brethren   to help us get into the seal fat biz– –
all for Grim Future's Sweep Stakes ?

        ball point pen poke :

        a bird in hand
        is worth two in the bull pen
        .

        H u r r a h !
        for B O U R A S S A !
        .

        — — — — — — — — — — — — —
        has the W P gone
        the way of all rare species ?
        — — — — — — — — — — — — —

        O Bird !

─────────────────────────
of Seasonal Pleasures
─────────────────────────
and Small Hindrances
─────────────────────────

─────────────────────────
marginalia:
writen at the back of
the lot at 1408-
westminster highway
for Linda Richard
Paul Xiza Fen Yee
Mariko and Eric
─────────────────────────

"say it again Sam
every lover knows that
I love you is
─ ─ ─ ─ ─ ─ ─ ─
a vocal variable to
be interpreted by
the vibrations"

Moon Dog– –
South of Westminster

Highway,
East of No. 6 Road
.

walking
behind my own breath

talking behind
these   words . . . .
.

if it gets any colder
I'll have to put on my longjohns

and toss another blanket
on my bed
.

one body
is

half as warm
as two
.

spiders in the bath tub
spiders in the sink

spiders in the marmalade
spiders in my dream
. .

one house
calls

to its neighbour– –
hullo is anyone at home?
.

echo
answers . . . .

echos always
at home
.

its nearly time for the last big jet
over my head . then a few more drunken drivers

before the early morning   birch

tree-top chatter of a hundred starlings

.

– –this flight is
dedicated to Mr. Luis Bunuel

listening to
the uproar in his cerebellum

.

though
I'm twice your age

you make me feel
half-arsed and

.

years ago . . . .
on a long week-end bender

one flat tire,
one bent fender and a   pukey suit

.

lets not hurt each other
further. lets kiss and make up

must be a script
written for other lovers

.

reading Jack Kerouac– –
I am no longer on the Road. neither

is Jack   he's tracking
Old Angel Midnight

.

what ever happened to
Kahoutek– – –

that burnt-out
metaphor?

.

his story

is this, this too
too sodden

peat. these empty
humpty-dumpty houses

.

Air's
heir . . . .
bearing
its weight

grace-
fully

.

intrepid
blue-notes:

all God's
children

are familiar
rarities

.

if you lose your familial pride– –
you might as well

throw the baby out with
the bath water

.

venerable
sages

like Fen Yee
are age–

lessly
three and a half

.

Tu Fu's
China

Whitman's
U.S.A.

.

link-
ages

link
ages

.

"nothing
ventured

nothing
gained"

.

Capricorns:

Richard Millhouse Nixon
Muhammid Ali
Henry Miller   Gladys Hindmarch
Charles Olson   and
yours truly

.

water-
gate

gold
wins

you
folly

.

in
Quo Vadis

Caligula
saved

his tears
in sequin vials

.

now that the BBC
together with the NBC and
the CBC re-play the
English Language edition of
the Allied Victories
may they all have mercy on
Poor Richard

.

fickle

star

glory

.

"once
scarred– –

twice
vigilant"

.

—if They open another karate/ kung fu parlour
I'm going to join The Terminal City Lawn Bowling Club

and buy a lifetime subscription to
The Watch Tower

.

. . . so everyone has a Buddha-nature but
heaven help us from another kick-in-the-balls

.

over-
population:

how many
many 0000000000000000s

can plausibly be
added on?

.

Mao's
China

Nixon's
U.S.A.

.

the case for anarchy:

revile those who play
high-power games

that leave some dead and
others maimed

.

how malevolence (if not kindness
can be anticipated— —

check-out your foreman's fortune
before heading off to the iron works

.

40s S–C–R–E–E–D:

"goddamned
yellow-bellied   son
of a bitch . . .!"

the japs
in Richmond and the lower
mainland keep to
a low-profile: like theres
no exultation without
paying on the installment plan
to sit in the same pews

.

"my country tis of thee"

true-blue Canucks
fondling their Union Jacks think
that the Maple Leaf is
just another post-biblical
cover-up job

.

for Mac and Bloedel

". . . its only a paper moon
out over a cardboard sea, etcetera"

.

foolishly fated to
crack– –

he would go
sunny-side-up

.

for A.B. and Co.

when the shit hits the fan– –DUCK
and then have another banana

.

– –Mirth my Agean half-brother sez
"despite all your goat-footed agilities
your curs't with an applepated-tongue
and a club-foot B u s t e r."

.

tic / toc
: : : : : : : :
thicktalk

.

for Gerry G. and Carole Itter
3)
yesterday

343

today
tomorrow

time)

past
present
future

3)
door
window
floor

and)

for ever more
ever more for
more for ever

3 more
in 3/4 time)

"I'm having the time of my life"
"my time is your time"
"time on my hands you on my mind"

.

"dope he sd
debilitates the pater nostrum"

.

"time
on my hand. you

in another's
sweet etceteras

.

Mother   O Mother   tell me
tell me the hoary old story   of love

wit and glory again– –
or put another record on the old victrola

.

nose-gay

no way to re-cover the curvature of
those sweete occasions. no way left but to make
my own home movies and caught up in each

flicker-frame   SHOOT my way out as the Bad Guy the
one who sd he's gonna wipe the slate clean
makes out with the addict'd Heroine.
no way out now but through a Hail Mary Sky
fill'd with bird-shit, bullets, billboards, dust
and poetry

.

for Daphne
Black   Winter   Water   North
Blue   Spring   Wood   East
Red   Summer   Fire   South
Yellow   4 Seasons   Earth   Center
White   Autumn   Metal   West

.

"– –will Wallace Beery and Miss Luise Rainer   PLEEZ
stand up and be counted or turn in their union cards"

.

fickle

star

holly

.

dancing round the granary floor with Miss Susy
i have a fearful heart-on. "I dont want to set the world
on fire . . . i just want to stop the flame in yr heart"
Ink Spots 3 for a dollar 78s via T. Eaton mail order – –
'D-Day' in Opal Alberta. now, minus its 3 elevators, pool
hall and blacksmith shop: the ghosts of Watanabe, the
McInnes brothers, Hawreluiks and Nishimotos gone under
scrub sand and burnt summer grass. the half-log 2 room
house i built collapsed pile of rotting logs wild oats
shoot up through. 30 years gone with the winnowed blue-
berries mother pickt each summer. nothing, nothing lasts – –
not even my anger: all the human beings incinerated
in Hamburg, Auschwitz and Hiroshima didnt prevent an-
other Vietnam.

.

"instead of
an erect tensile penis
dope dilates
the male hormonal glands
and induces

hallucinations"

.

egos
are fragile
film
too

.

from the back of the lot:

its taken most of my 47th summer
to re-build this once derelict farm hand's shack.
now that the small persistent rain falleth
i the stoned-king of a petit-palace wait   wait for
the fabled words to bring her to my door

.

fireweed, Heather sez
is great for bees my boy friend has
a hive in them. fingering
the silken fluff Sonia sez its too delicate
to weave but could be interwoven.
Richard likes the way they stand tall and upright
not giving an inch to the blackberries.
and on acid my eye-balls spun
their silken elements

.

Boxing Day December 24th '73
the 3rd anniversary of one lost middle-finger tip
and other sweete etceteras

.

for Muhammid Ali

Death– –
Brother,

Proposes
Another

More uniform
Colour

what the Master Magician said

"gear'd for even pain I am the original computer
an I.B.M. selectronic brain. I'm your Adam
your Eve   the Serpent   Apple   and the original

Mephistopheles— —

.

inside of the eye socket of a netsuke skull

    an uni-
    maginably

    tiny
    web its

    equally
    diminutive

    boss— —
    defining

    it must
    be— —

    my
    tenacities

    valorous vestments

        m a k e
    — — — — — — — — —

the best blue-chip
    investment

.

O the muffled
roar
    the coruscations—
the heft of my Pacific
    O Shaman !

        it
        .
        is
        .
        us

1/ 22nd/ '74
Richmond BC

Dear Mick

    this is for K i c k s / the K i d s or
    whatever such 'green stuff' is good enough for. had
    a lot of it pass as they say thru my fingers
    like the stream in back of yr place it's a swiftian
    green element passing thru the needle's eye.

    Here at the back of the lot in Richmond BC
    several of us are spuattin' intent upon gettin' some
    thing on–knowing, as we never did that the best of
    good intentions arent good enough. if we be makers whats
    this whiff of a life for? if not to go on making
    'a thing' that sings like Robert's Creek.
    .

    just the other day some guy sd
    he saw with his own two plain eyes a u.f.o whc
    turned out to be, he added just
    another pie-in-the-dky if not manna frm heaven
    or a kahoutek

                    imagine the day when we can really
                    screw stars

Early '74

Dear Linney

    when you went down to Frisco w/ Toby
    you wore a 'huge grin' under the purple felt hat
    I bought you in kyoto. you rode the trolley
    stood in front of your first Van Gogh posed
    beside Rodin's Burghers and drove across
    the Golden Gate Bridge. you sent a postcard home
    and returned in a many-coloured leather coat
    fast asleep now, you sd, "I walkt my arse off . . ."
    Welcome Home .

Dear Linney

    its been a fulsome year going into the 2nd
    – –I don't want 'more' or 'less'.
    Masako never let up abt my grey hairs–How
    she wld pull 'em out one by one.
    I had to tell her I want all of them, too.

    p/s where do you thing we'll go from here?

Dear Linney

    I am sick-to-death with our arguments:
    the murk of the substance of them. I keep asking
    myself How can I who shld know better *break*
    this vicious circle we turn more and more tightly
    within / without touching each other   except
    out of our desperation. I cant seem to deal w/ it
    without your cooperation. let me say that i
    wanted to give you everything including my years
    but havent been able to break new ground
    we could face each other in. and as I sit here
    at the back of the lot–my misadventures rise up
    in front of me even as my feet seem to be sinking
    further into the bog I thot to build a life on.

        from the back of the lot at
        1408–westminster highway
        richmond b.c.
                end of Feb. '75

dear   Linney

    with-or-without you is equally
    a pleasure and/or pain i cant seem to do without.
    all the live-long day ive thought tomorrow
    will be the first day of March and will i see her
    at least once more to tell   tell her
    how much i have misst her and want her to come back
    again. i sat at Richard's kitchen window
    sat there all night watching for his flashy blue mustang
    to bring you home. in the early morning– –
    before the birch tree-top chattering of a hundred starlings
    i walkt across to our empty house and fed Flint.
    then i walkt to the back of the lot and
    fell asleep in my derelict little writing room. tonight
    i drove across the Knight Street Bridge across
    town to the Crystal Pool where you said you always went
    swimming on thursday nights. i sat in the van
    before going in and toked up. high as a kite above
    the floating glistening splashing bodies
    i carefully noted each and every one but none of them
    were you. "whata bloody fool you are– – doin'
    the stupid things you do" i thought as i drove over to
    Gerry and Carole's place on Welwyn Street.
    "Carole" I sd "if i see her again and she is willing i
    intend to ask her to come back sink or swim."
    Carole thought that she thought it would be lovely.
    home again i know in my bones that you
    you wont be back, tonight. Linney   if you have any
    regard for me– –PLEEZ! DONT BRING YR YOUNG MEN
    HOME TO BAWL ON OUR FORLORN BED and PLEEZE LEAVE, LEAVE
    O QUICKLY. QUICKLY

dear   Linney

    even on this your last day in Richmond you had a
    so called visitor . . . thus preempting our getting together
    one last time. S-h-i-t. take whatever you need
    take even the fireweed honey and take good care care of
    yourself. (the year we spent more or less 'together'
    will nonetheless speak thru both of us). i feel heartless
    and divided . . . nonetheless, your good friend runs a-
    round and around on the palm of God's hand, daily

3 S l u g T a l e s

down on all fours he kisses a fat brown slug with
his camera. kissing it again he leaps up and
dances a jig in the tall wet grass. grinning he sez hey
hand me your camera i want to shoot the slimey
trail it left on my lens. down on all fours again Slim
shoots one lens with the other again and again.
the slug left without signing its name.

talking a blue streak abt a roadside S L U G S T A N D
Slim sez its a 1ST– –imagine charcoal-brazed slugs
on a skewer dippt in a special slime sauce i've just concocted.
later when askt abt their edibility he retorted– –
compared to what Krafty Foods are packaging a roast slug couldn't
be all that bad. its all meat theres no fat no bones
nothing but sheer meat. trick or treat .

and the last guy who saw Slim was the Chinese sage who
invented firecrackers. Slim he sd gravely– –
turned into a flawless match six feet tall with a glowing
 phosphorescent head. as he turned to walk away he
added with what i thot was a touch of envy– –that Slim's
glow could be felt a hundred yards away. if you're
worried abt Slim get in touch with the Chinese sage.
i've heard he is trying to get Mao to make Slim
a mandarin .

                        for Ralph and Betty Gilbert

the aurora borealis
　" shadows, and skeins of light
　" enflamed body
　" fire the flames the sunkist orange
　" curtains the valences
　" waves 'the laps of' a cradle
　" conifers the lichen
　" moss th rocks the 'hide and go seek'
　" haircut its diamond wave
　" fun-limn'd peyote
　" fart the holy fart the howl
　" heave the early morning
　" lake I psst into
　" wind the high wheeling gulls
　" trout the catfish
　" hair the scars the million pores of
　" eyes the ears th nose
　" hand the touch the absolute emptiness
　" cave the lair
　" the lyre the entuned hear the ache
　" door the floor
　" abominable appetite

_ _

"Heaven's roots" she sd
"are thick entwined stands of human hair"
_ _

　　　　　　O Art !
　　　　　　O Lorelie !

　　　　　　c/o
　　　　　　Lac la Ronge, Saskatchewan
　　　　　　August 1960

　　　　　　dates the H o l y V i s i o n
　　　　　　　　　　_ _ _ _ _ _ _ _

Dear Angela

– –among a heap of papers the confused litter
of 49 yrs these bits and pie-eyed pieces of that
lovely summer afternoon in Glengarry County . . . .
before any one of us thot 'I'm not young any more
etcetera." Bob's *Pieces* echo thru these leavings–
w-o-r-d-s at least, for you

E N T R A N C ' D – – – – – – – –

each mimic motion its ecstacy): you sat on a high stool
watching them dance. from knot to knot They turned– –
serpent-wise each movement a firey affirmation . H D's
ember'd Helen   re-appearing) . later when you danced
along the roadside   lifting arms and legs in slow motion
we watching you through the trees could see their move-
ments in your every gesture . it was after all   our bodies
caresst by the sun and waving grass that moved
in their fashion   it's the way of all things under the sun.
now the charred/warpt board   heaven's ouiji board re-
enters its mother Night   and the dancers fall   in a heap
of sleep in the shadows . one by one by one the lights go out–
taking the shadows the dancers the painted hoardings
the wind the laughter the nervous giggle the children the toad the
dog the slough the flames the embers the ashes the inflammable
gestures   all with them . o holy holy funeral pyres!
o blessed conflagrations! o night!

> – –like Who is doing it to whom?
> is it the grass tickling my toes   or
> my toes doing it to the grass?   ah– –
>
> its Mr. Toad the Sunne God's dwarf
> that's doing it to both. toucht even
> the white discs on my red blouse   laughed

tongue-
tied

you— —
spoke

thru
yr eyes

      July 6th '69
      and other sweete etceteras
      — — — — — — — — — — — — —
      winter '74 Vancouver BC

      Winter '74

Edited Inches
— — — — — — — —

the 1st word
on the front cover
'edited' (and

the last word
on the back cover
is 'inches'

'edited inches'
a measure-of-soundings
found on a Sunday

afternoon for
George and Angela
Bowering

11/ 29/74/ 5.35PM

Dear Correspondent /s
_ _ _ _ _ _ _ _ _ _ _ _

     – –thinking to 'collect'
     all my Letters to you I have without your
     permission/s   re-read/   alter'd/ a–
     mended/ and re-written them . if I tell you
     its all for the sake of the 'I'/'ME'/'WE'
     revealed in and thru the litter– –
     will you believe in my good intentions ?

11/ 30/'74/ 1PM

When   I asked *"How abt Dear Heart/s ?"*
She sd "Yuk its so senti mental." Then "How abt
transcanadaletters?" (pause) "Its fitting
but not all that telling." "Its, I suppose OK tho."
long pause) *"How abt yrs./yrs.?* meaning
years/ yours." She asks. And I say "its like one
of your own brief titles viz leaf/leafs."
Then (pause) "How abt a *A Packet of Letters?*
"Ez" I sd "used it but its definitely a contender."
n even longer pause) "How abt this– –
*In / Quest A Book of Letters/ Sources/ Scourings/
and Friendships?"* "Ok but Talon has already
advertised it as the TransCanadaLetters."
"Shit its harder to name a book than a baby or
Canada's No.1 Poet" I mutter. She agreed.

    "The Letter! The Litter!
    and the soother the bitther!"

           (J.J./F.W.

Dear Susan

    Mus(k)grave: Permit *the mushroom*
    in me to say to the woman you are   that
    your gift of the magical elixir is
    is ISIS the Egyptian goddess and patron
    aint of the movie house by that name
    on lst Street West between 11th and 12th
    avenue in Calgary Alta I attended as
    a 30s lad. Even today I can see I S I S
    pronounced 'I'-siz   flashing frm
    the marquee. And if for whatever reason
    you dont or wont let this Egyptian
    bird speak in and thru you you nonetheless
    deserve Her. Dear mushroom-giver its
    hightime you also took some of whatever
    the Queen Charlottes (AWESOMELY) gives to
    even a mushroom/ sez the rain forest
    Dwarf who tends them w/ love.

            wonder how Gulliver wld have
            dealt w/ it after eating a bushel?

February 18th '75
1455-Cypress Street
Vancouver B.C.

Dear Chris

    Heres a long list of names and places
promist you a while back. It covers everything
that I cld remember during the 4 days spent
writing and remembering. Theres no doubt
in my mind that some things have been forgotten
and perhaps we shld be grateful.
Nonetheless I've
tried real hard to retrieve everything that
presented itself. And as I lookt into the inter-
stices of my life I came upon things I
take no pride in acknowledging. Use it as you can
and to hell with the rest of it–whatever it
is. And YES do keep coming back at me Now
 the unravellings begun .

After youve been East a-hunting we will have to
get together to look at the slides and talk abt
the show, its parts, with attention to all
the small details. there is the matter of
coordinating the LETTERS with the CATALOGUE also.

.

. . . wonder what F. H. Varley wld think of
our working together?

RESUME OF THE SHOW

1950/'55: call em the formative years
the years of initiation. *locus* Calgary
Edmonton, Toronto, Nelson B.C.
and Mexico. I'm 29 when I begin teaching
at Regina College. As a painter I'm
groping.

1956/'60: the Regina College/Emma Lake years
the transitional years.
includes the Mexican works, the Emma Lake W/Cs
the ducco drawings, and the all-white
'Hoarfrost Series'.
lst attempts to write pomes.

1960/.65: the Vancouver years/ the Break-thru
the relief ptgs., the enamel-on-paper collages
the lst large scale acrylic hard-edge ptgs.,
including the beginnings of the 'Ellipse Series'
Kyoto Airs and Vancouver's poetry scene.
the Vancouver School of Art.

1956/'69: Montreal Mainstream.
Sir George Williams U. and the Galerie
du Siècle. the 'Barometer', 'Court'
and 'Ellipse Series'. the last 'all-blue' works.
the fiberglas sculptures. 2nd book of pomes
Nevertheless These Eyes. and the 4 part 16 ft. high
steel and vinyl sculpture for Expo '70 in
Osaka Japan. the San Paolo Biennial
and a silver medal.

1970/'75: Vancouver (again.
with teaching gigs in Calgary, Banff, Emma Lake
and Halifax. the cedar-laminates, silk-screens,
all of the photography including Stonedgloves plus
the writing the incessant writing. U.B.C.
Japan again. The Book-of-Letters and
yours, 25 years at the V.A.G.

.

(- -that gives us 5 phases with

        any number of divisions within them: each division
        corresponding to the kinds of things I am
        then into. (not incidentally) these divisions form
        a series of related works which is the mode
        I started to work with in the late-50s all-white ptgs.
        even my pomes tend to work serially. all
        of whc is a clue to hanging, re chronology.)

  apropos: my Book-of-Letters
        theyre almost finisht-i've got another 25 pages
        that need editing whc I shall attend to when
        I get the wind up for them. anyhow, Talon Press
        hopes to do them in April or May.

Heres all I can grab up to fill in *the gaps*
with the names as they occur, underlined. Think it
as an extended 'footnote' prompt'd by the above
too too brief a RESUME, Ok .

                      y o u r s, 2 5 y e a r s
                      _ _ _ _ _ _ _ _ _ _ _ _ _ _ _ _

1950/'55:
- - - - - -

its the time of learnin *How* thus an *initiation.*
These so-called Early Works date frm the time I left art
school in my 3rd year to go to Toronto where I painted
The House I Live In. Monica K. has this work and its the lst
piece of evidence re chronology. All the way over to the
ugh) the green landscapes (after Cezanne) I painted in Nelson
B.C. before leaving via Regina for San Miguel de
Allende in Mexico. In between I am in Calgary working as
a show-card artist and ad man. *The leavings* of my early
works are all in the *Calgary area* with the exception of the
N.G's large oil titled City My City. The Glenbow Foundation
presumably has a blue (cubist influenced) still-life and
a large oil on masonite titled **City Pastoral**: both important
works of the period. **John Boyd** then a young lawyer has an
important **bldg. ptg.** plus a **lovely young girl's head.** (Weve
got to try hard to get a hold of him). Then, theres one

Peter Moore an oil company executive/maverick (well known as such in around Calgary) who has the **w/c sketch** for C.M.C. and other works including an ugh self-portrait. **Stanford Perrott** head of **Alberta College of Art** (a former teacher) and a **Marnie Hess** then a local collector and patron might be useful. See brother Harry abt all these possibilities. My mentors then were **Mr. Luke Lindoe** and more importantly **Maxwell Bates** and **Ron Spickett** a fellow student/artist. (Ron and I shared rooms in Toronto at 272-Parliament St. Later we were in Mexico, together.) **Art McKay** and **Tod Greenaway** were important. Tho most of the work of this period is to say the least AWFUL and even as I finisht them I thot as much– they quite properly belong in the show. Afterall, we all begin somewhere, etc. My beginnings in art are rootd in Calgary, Alberta and further back it must be in Shikoku, Japan.

1956/'60:

I brought back 2 dozen ptgs. a folder full
of drawings, together with household utensils and a
sick dachschund in a '47 Pontiac coupe. I dont know
where the bulk of it got to–if its not in/around Regina
or Saskatoon. We know that **Cliff and Pat Weins,**
Bob Howard the photographer and **Norah MacCullough** have
some to them. As do **George Bowering** and **Monica Kiyooka.**
the former are or used to be in Regina. the latter
are friends who live in Vancouver. Again I wld insist
that its this work plus the Calgary work we need to
re-cover and it'll take some doing. **Lee Collins** formerly
the head of the **Saskatoon Arts Centre, Ernie Lindner**
even the **Mendel Collection** might have or know of some of
these works. Theres also **Moris Schumiacher** Lawyer
and erstwhile collector in Regina.
The series of Emma Lake W/Cs belong to this period. Again
theyre scatterd and I dont know who has them. Some
if not most of them got sold thru the old New Design on
Pender St. in the early 60s. I know that **Otto Gerson**
now dead) of the former **Marlborough/Gerson Gallery** in New York
bought the best one when he came up for the Lipchitz Show
at the Norman MacKenzie Gallery in Regina. You cld ask
old friend **Ron Bloore** who organized the show abt them he
exhibited them and *owns one*. Yeah, ask him for it. then

Ken Lochhead might have one   he was there.
so might Art McKay tho I aint sure abt it. I think my brothers
Harry and Frank   have something frm this period.
(Now I see that 'ledgers' were made for people with crummy
memories like me   but I never did learn how to use one.)
Then there's the all-white ptgs. the 'Hoarfrost' Series
whc are really my first sustaind (abstract) field
ptgs. (Bloore and I were into titanium white concurrently.
The Agnes Etherington in Kingston, Gladys Hindmarch,
John Keith-King and Monica Kiyooka have a few as does the
Bau-Xi Gallery. (p/s We dont have to worry them.)
There are also a number of black and white (ducco on paper)
drawings of trees/roots in Emma Lake but to hell
with them . . . unless they show up. The **Norman MacKenzie's large
ducco on masonite** work plus the **Non Still-life Monica** has
culminated (in so far as my work cld be sd to do so) the
previous decade's work beginning in '46.
for the record I want to say that tho I helped to organize and
attended several of the Emma Lake Artist's Workshops I
didn't do any ptgs. of consequence at them. All the works
painted there (the W/Cs etc.) were done during the summer.
And last but not least   2 large commissions:
The mosaic mural for the **lst Presbyterian Church on Albert St.**
and the mosaic mural panels for the **Biology Bldg. at U. of
Saskatoon.**

1960/'65
------

lst the **large square ptgs**. that come out of the
all white works i was doing in Regina. theyre more colourful
and more structured viz a square canvas with square
on square on square, etc. plus the seemingly random 'criss-
crosst brushstrokes. The Bau-Xi has several of these
which were never very saleable.
ptgs. and collages that followed these are *the last of* the
abstract-expressionist influenced works. I did the **illustrations
for George Bowerings book The Man in Yellow Boots** at this time.
it's also the last time I painted w/c's using
bands or stripes of pure colours with merging edges.
In '63 I went to Japan and returned–to the UBC Poetry Conference
where I met Robt. Creeley, Charles Olson, Philip Whalen,

Margaret Avison and others. **My lst book of pomes titled Kyoto Airs** got printed then by Tak Tanabe's Periwinkle Press.
I got into acrylic paints abt this time and it was decisive in changing the colour/form of my work. The lst **elliptical ptgs**. followed on a number of large canvases which are the beginnings of my so called 'hard-edge ptgs'. I am teaching at the Vancouver School of Art where I organized noon-hour poetry readings. Among those who read were a number of the poets who have subsequently made Vancouver one of the poetry centres in N.A. In the beginning I showed with the **New Design Gallery run by Alvin Balkind and Abe Rogatnick.** Later I showed there with **Betty Marshall**, and **Doug Christmas** who bought the gallery. He started the **Ace Gallery** and I showed with him once, before going over to the **Bau-Xi** which is now my only gallery. The bulk of the work of this period is in the Vancouver area. We shld have no trouble getting a hold of what we need for it. for what it's worth: my work had very little to do with what the locals were doing or what the geography proposed–it's only later   1970 onwards   that the lower mainland takes place in my images,
particularly in my photographs. The **4th Avenue Pomes in G.B.s Imago** tell something of the despair in which I left.
summer of '65   Montreal and Sir George Williams University .

1965/'69

Where Im the head of the painting section. But, its mostly painting   painting variations on the ellipse. These were the cumulative yrs of exhibiting–I showed in the **San Paolo Biennial**, the **N.G's Biennials**, at **Grippi and Waddell in N.Y.** and at the **Edinborough Festival**, etc. Continued to write. Using **Stanley Spencer** as a mouthpiece I wrote **Nevertheless These Eyes** which I illustrated. For what it's worth it's a homage to all the women in my life tho at the time Im not sure of what I was writing abt.
I'm exhibiting with the **Galerie du Siècle** whc was the best gallery in Montreal. Remember the big 'computer bust?' Stokeley Carmichael and Mirian Makeba at McGill that awful chill they sent thru the audience? Abt '67/'68 I'm into all **blue ptgs**. the last works. Then, it's the **fiberglas sculptures.** Both (together) got shown at the **Laing Gallery**

and **Doug Christmas's Ace Gallery** and elsewhere. Tho the all
blue ptgs. were saleable the sculpture never sold at all.
in between all this there was Expo and the Sir George W. poetry
readings whc I helped to organize. Thru these readings I met
a number of extraordinary Canadian and American poets.
There was the S.G.W.U. Fine Arts Dept. Festival
an opus of mixt-media light/sound/ image/
movement/ drama bacchanalia. Tho I had no intention of
returning to Sir George, I got a half-sabbatical and left for Japan
to make a **large sculpture for Canada's Pavilion at Expo '70.**
It's also the beginnings of a mania for **photography viz Stoned-
gloves** and subsequent images. The sculpture I made
called '**Abu Ben Adam's Dream**' no longer exists except in
slides and photos. It got dismantled and salvaged
after the big show closed. On Dec. 24th returned
to Vancouver and several hundred photos and a pocketful of
money and dreams. It was the end of a phase and the beginnings
of an awful new one.

1970/'75
------

includes 1/ the **cedar-laminates** 2/ the **silk-screens** of
whc there are 3 suites of 5 prints total 15 distinct prints.
3/ **Stonedgloves** a large photo-show together with a book
of pomes w/ the same title. 4/ a **40 page photo-book** one of
the B.C. Almanac Books edited by Jack Dale and Michael
de Courcy. 5/ **artscanada afloat** a 16 page newspaper with Gerry
Gilbert, Carole Itter and Krisy Van Eyck. 6/ the **trans-
canadaletters** publisht by Talonbooks. 7 / 100s of other
photos, slides, and asst. writings. 8/ readings in Vancouver,
Edmonton, Calgary, Toronto, Montreal, Halifax, Sackville,
Charlottetown. 9/ the **NEW WORKS?**

> I'll be in Toronto and Montreal in
> early March. Intend to do some leg-work for
> the show. Shall we get together again
> before you also head east?

2/

viz: *The Show* I definitely dont want it
even referred to as 'a retrospective' even in letters.
Sheila Watson wise old bird, writer and dear
friend sd "why Roy yr too young for a . . . ."
Others say the same thing w/ mischievous smiles
and you know that I
agree with them–we already talkt abt it. There
are the imperatives of good scholarship and the
imperatives of a painter–
and I wld suppose 'our' problem consists in
designating the show to satisfy both.
Let's keep the matter open til it discloses
itself, all by itself, etc. Meanwhile

    y o u r s ,   2 5   y e a r s

    (not incidentally the above title   also
    suits the book-of-letters, the catalogue's twin.
    think abt it and let me know.)

to hammer– –
tho it will inevitably be 'retrospective'
I want   more than anything
for it to be *prospective* (forward-looking.
I have the sense that the next
DECADE will be crucial to whatever
I become .

    Spring '74
    Richmond B.C.

                                      Cabin 8
                                      "Glen" Cottage by the sea
                                      Qualicum Beach
                                      Monday April 14 4pm

Dear Daphne

    – –W/ the middle-aged couple who have just now
    come down to the beach: She watching as he sets up
    a tripod to take a picture   of the calm blue
    mid-day sea/sky-ah technicolor'd VISTA. i want to
    say that I have nothing to say   nothing thats
    quote worth repeating. . . tho that wont stop me frm
    saying it 'over' and over again etc.

        the GARBAGE
        Daphne   the litter
        the refuse of
        a life   the heapt plastic
        waste-catcher   with
        two banana peels the quarter'd
        orange skins   tea bags
        the mother hubbard chocolate roll
        spat out in disgust   the
        bits of hair the leavings
        vegetable scrapings
        the strawberry pips and bruised
        tomato   the
        absolutely lovely stream of sunlight
        coming thru the window
        blesses each and every tiny
        left-over bit   even as
        a too too early summer fly buzzes
        over

                Nothing to tell   but
                how what i have eaten becomes
                blood meat words   or

                my 9am turd   etc.

   . . . We who be in
   McLure's sense MEAT must then be

even the pain of all we
have had to kill to sustain us

. . . i mean how the meat
the meat i am the carnivore must then be
the threshold of that pain   an
actual 'crying out'

. . . . seeing . . . . seeing
my hands roll the thousand and one cigarette. . . .
now its stuck in my mouth with a
small fire on the end of it . . . . THERE, I've
said it– –for the first time– –even as
it sits (how did it get there?) in the half-shell
ashtray . . . . ember'd . as . . . . the Sea
the sea stretcht out in front of me will
extinguish it . ashes ashes and dust . . . .
sifting down into her illimitable depths .

Qualicum Beach: The Reaches of
for the love of a THRUSH

Dearest Daphne

    . . . . the birds the assorted birds   how how
they occur and re-occur   occulted in and thru
these few days these late monday afternoon
words   the circling the eddying the aqueous
move ments of them their   it must be pleasure in
the fullness of the tide the sheen gleam calm
of their floating their follow-the-leader move-
ments their weightless buoyancies i wld if
if i could take a dip into . and and in and be-
hind what my ear wants to be attentative to the crow
caws the coal black crow now high on a branch
of the tree the unleaved tree right in front of
me my window–the pleasure of the absolute gift
of sight-ings. if i could i would use words to
to make make parabolas such traceless demarcations
as these ducks yes they are canvasbacks make on
your mind's retina the acuity of which i sense
even as these ducks sense their lovely ambiences
 etc. and and that that pair of ducks on the ledge
as we enter'd into their domain at Ward Island
and all the lovely arcs and flights and movements
of their kin and that one seemingly singular one who
engaged us on our own ground at the very edge of
his element he with whom we conversed and and
let be and all the rest of them how they dippt in
and out of the green leaves etc. then as we left
left them to their domain and walkt back along the
board walk–there they were sitting there on   that
same rocky ledge 'guardians' of our exit. etc.
then there was the bird the woodland bird at the very
edge of the ocean at La Push   the bird you heard
which i named (improbably, a thrush) and and and
all the other nameless birds i have been attending
to in and thru my words my gropings these Letters
which thank god are are are at an ending

                        – – –6pm
                        Cabin 8
                        Glen Cottage by the sea
                        Qualicum

B/C

Sept. 1 1971
Halifax NovaScotia

April 15 1975
Qualicum Beach B.C.

AFTERWORD

"Now the unravellings begun": Re:reading *Transcanada Letters*

                                                Pleeze return my dossier
    intact as its all I have between me and anonymity .
    H A ! (Dear Ian Baxter, 1/16/.67)

    . . . And as I lookt into the inter-
    stices of my life I came across things I
    take no pride in acknowledging. Use it as you can
    and to hell with the rest of it—whatever it
    is. And YES do keep coming back at me Now
    the unravellings begun . (Dear Chris, Feb 18, '75)

I first came across Roy Kiyooka's *Transcanada Letters* in the early 1990s in the window of R2B2, a bookstore in Vancouver's Kitsilano owned by Rene Rodin, a writer and long-time friend of Kiyooka's. I remember standing in R2B2 bewildered by the physical and material aspects of the text—its *Maximus*-like proportions, quotidian focus, and remarkably unconventional design—and slightly bemused by its price—$25 used, a lot on a TA's budget. At the time, I had only a vague notion of Kiyooka. Having read *Pear Tree Pomes* and *Fontainebleau Dream Machine*, I knew he was a poet but knew nothing of his role in the development of a Canadian vanguard—nothing of his international renown as painter or sculptor or of his influence on an emerging cohort of Canadian writers. For me, Kiyooka was an enigmatic presence. I'd heard him play his shakuhachi as often as I'd heard him read his poetry, and I was used to him wafting into R2B2 or the Western Front, disrupting, or better re-syncopating, readings by the likes of George Bowering, Daphne Marlatt, Michael Ondaatje, Fred Wah, Phyllis Webb, or a number of his other friends. Handling *Transcanada Letters* for the first time, taking up this massive text, puzzling over the names referred to in the "letters," flipping through the photos, I remember feeling overwhelmed by the depth of the history it proposes and excited by the aesthetic possibilities it provides. After some deliberation, I decided to follow Rene's advice—I bought the text.

    At the time, I had little idea how important *Transcanada Letters* might be. In the years since, I have spent countless hours pouring over its "letters" and images trying to piece together Kiyooka's life and thoughts, while gleaning details about the specific spaces and times he moves through. And I have written countless pages attempting to work through some of the varied questions it raises. Now, after years of cherishing a nearly thirty-year-old copy of *Transcanada Letters*, it is wonderful to have this new edition in hand, at last. "Now the unravellings begun."

    To put it in slightly more objective and critical terms, I might say that Kiyooka's *Transcanada*

Letters is a rare work of literary and cultural prescience, an "anomalous" publication that has become—and will no doubt continue to be—increasingly vital with time. Both the physical heft and intellectual scope of Kiyooka's original publication, which foregoes many of the usual means of textual organization including pagination, indexing, or authorial gloss, presents readers with a somewhat overwhelming challenge vis-à-vis questions of legibility, tradition, or even perhaps intention. In terms of classification or categorization, *Transcanada Letters* self-consciously flouts generic expectations and literary conventions: Is it a book of poetry? Or prose? Art history? An artist's book? Idiosyncratic criticism? Letters or collected correspondence? Yes and no. *Transcanada Letters* is all of these things—and more. To settle on any one such designation is to risk flattening the complex layering of the various registers and interests Kiyooka's writing brings to bear. Kiyooka's project of gathering his letters places this text at the crux of a number of discussions relevant to thinking about contemporary culture. In this way, *Transcanada Letters* proposes one of the single most important sites in the field of contemporary Canadian poetics and cultural theory.

In an earlier attempt at rationalizing the lack of critical response generated by *Transcanada Letters*, I argued that the singularity of Kiyooka's magnum opus has in effect placed the work beyond the purview of mainstream literary criticism. Kiyooka's virtuosic poetics—autobiography as cultural critique, aesthetics as social history, the prosaic as poetry, family album as masterpiece—prefigures the critical and cultural debates of CanLit's heady decades, the 1980s and 1990s. That he mounts a critique of the dominant nationalist discourse at a time when most critics were preoccupied with articulating, if not celebrating, a cohesive national identity, certainly kept Kiyooka on the periphery of the literary tradition. This, along with his formal experimentation, kept readers at bay. As a proto-typical "example" of Canadian multiculturalism, Kiyooka's work confronts the nation as a key aspect of his own identity formation; at the same time, however, the refusal to accept a marginal position within an emergent nationalist project makes his writing difficult to reconcile with a dominant literary discourse. Kiyooka's thoroughgoing attack on the longstanding privileging of Eurocentric, colonial values, particularly as they inform prevailing notions of Canadian culture and official multiculturalism, put *Transcanada Letters* beyond the pale of Canadian literary criticism, particularly at the time it was published.

Similarly, even though *Transcanada Letters* reflects directly on Kiyooka's work as a painter and on the relationship between his visual art and writing, it has attracted very little attention from art historians or cultural critics. Again, we might speculate that the reason for this has had to do with the formal—writerly—elements of the text. Inasmuch as the "letters" raise vital questions about the interdisciplinary nature of Kiyooka's art, they do so in a manner extrinsic to the discursive practices of such disciplines as literary criticism, art history, and cultural studies. Clearly, *Transcanada Letters* is the work of a visual artist. It deals explicitly with Kiyooka's exhibitions, collaborations, and aesthetic ideas, and the centrepiece of the text is the massive collage *Long Beach to Peggy's Cove*, an important visual counterpoint to the "letters" that is now part of the Vancouver Art Gallery's permanent collection. However, despite their obvious artistic and cultural relevance, Kiyooka's "letters" articulate a new poetics that is akin to the work of Charles Olson or the New American poets. In so doing, he situates his discourse on modern art in the space of postmodern literature, effectively placing *Transcanada Letters* outside the purview of

Canadian art history *per se* and away from the strictly defined concerns of more ardent Canadianists. Thus, the text is not only formally innovative, but it is also ideologically troubling to certain cultural nationalists.

Transcanada Letters seems to have been waiting for the rest of us to catch up, or should we say catch on. Even though one is still unlikely to find "a sign for the writer-Kiyooka," as his friend and editor Roy Miki puts it, "on the road map of designated sites along the transCanada canonical way" (*Broken Entries* 54), it is clear that many writers, thinkers, and artists—old friends and new—have begun to see Kiyooka as an important influence. For those working across the uneven topography of literary and cultural studies, Kiyooka's work exists as a valuable guide or map. His "letters," both those reprinted here and those forthcoming in *Pacific Rim Letters*, one of his unfinished manuscripts, serve as particular reminders of the struggles and triumphs of a truly critical, creative spirit.

As a Nisei, or second-generation, Japanese Canadian artist on the vanguards of modern art and postmodern literature, Kiyooka's life and work testify to the problematic existence of a racialized subject within the restricted realms of Canadian arts and letters. In this sense, *Transcanada Letters* documents Kiyooka's commitment to interrogating the limits of creative being—as social act and cultural location. In a letter to his parents, in which he attempts to explain "*the mess*" of his life (his divorce and move across the country to Halifax), Kiyooka writes:

> . . . As you both know I have always
> been (crazily) obedient to my own (foolish) promptings.
> For what my life has been worth such promptings have
> brought me this far and—they'll carry me into whatever
> future I also also have. everything I have done since 20 stinks w /
> my promptings viz Art and thus my innermost feelings
> are hinged to such predilections. some say 'addiction'
> no mater I know you know what is meant. I wld add
> for what its worth that Art is not separable from the I
> that wld be a family man a husband father and brother.
> How shall I accomplish—thru Art the very shapeliness I
> can sometimes 'see' as my life, etc. remains the most
> insistent and compelling need. . . . (12/ 12th / '71)

Kiyooka's "letters" then speak to the complex and often contradictory labour of eking a living out of a prolonged investigation of his own history and being—i.e., within the context of a social space dominated by the hegemonic drives of a white culture. In "We Asian North Americanos," a statement about "growing up yellow in a white world," Kiyooka describes this experience in terms of a life-long struggle with English: he concludes that "whatever my true colours, I am to all intents and purposes, a white anglo saxon protestant, with a cleft tongue" (182).

Ironically, however, and with time, the duality of Kiyooka's work—his speaking and writing—seems to have become a central element of his legacy. Far from continuing to render his writing inaccessible, the complex machinations of his own struggles with the English (Canadian) language and culture seem to speak to a new generation of readers. To use one of Kiyooka's favourite terms, we might say that his writing remains a midden—fertile ground in which to track the passing of predecessors or find the impetus for new work. Kiyooka's "cleft tongue"—one side peeled to "high" cultural concerns, the other to exigencies of everyday life—provides a model through which to think the contradiction of creating art and literature in an increasingly global culture.

The challenge of Kiyooka's example lives on as a crucial element of his influence. Henry Tsang, a visual artist and one of Kiyooka's students in Fine Arts at UBC, writes that "Roy spoke about the nitty-grits, like buying groceries, making meals, washing the dishes, and the challenge of finding the balance between the incidentals of living in this world, of having to sustain oneself financially for instance, with that of being an artist." To this end, Tsang suggests, family is a "recurring topic" in Kiyooka's work and "a major source of inspiration in his writing and photography" (85). Tsang remembers: "to hear an art professor speak about the importance of family was, at that time and place, surprising. To make art from who you are, where you come from, what you know was, well, intimidating" (85-86). In *All Amazed: For Roy Kiyooka*, a publication marking the 1999 symposium in honour of Kiyooka and his work, Michael Ondaatje, one of the organizers and another long-time friend, comments further on the power of Kiyooka's "creative voice." In a characterization that might be helpful in locating some of the many Kiyookas that come through *Transcanada Letters*, Ondaatje notes that "Roy was like the eye of the fly, he was a musician, he was a painter, a writer, a photographer, a teacher." But, "Most of all, for a lot of us," Ondaatje continues,

> we remember him as a talker, a great talker, who was tremendously articulate with a lineage of language that was utterly perverse. Somewhere within him was Wallace Stevens and Stanley Spencer, Jiminy Cricket and the art of Fontainebleau. He was the only person I knew who could use the word "demarcation" regularly. He was the only man who could stretch out the words "phenomenal" and "amazing" to an excessive length. (64)

Before this gathering of friends—musicians, artists, painters, writers, photographers, and teachers—in Vancouver, Ondaatje recalls Kiyooka's immense capacity for friendship and dedication to an ethics of self-scrutiny and class awareness. Confessing "to a moment of embarrassment" in which Kiyooka catches him having his shoes shined in the Toronto airport, Ondaatje speaks of Kiyooka as a mentor who corrected "our foibles . . . with his laughter." He tells us that Kiyooka "was stunned to see me in the midst of such a bourgeois act. There was much judgement and laughter . . . you can imagine . . ." (64). Even though this anecdote is celebratory, it is also indicative—symptomatic almost—of the haunting effect of Kiyooka's work on contemporary discussion of Canadian culture.

Kiyooka's presence, the ethical drive behind his work, exists as a reminder of an avant-garde's commitment to questions of social justice. After his death, Kiyooka's sense of history, the moral outrage at what he calls "Capitalism 's veracities" ("Dear Michael and Louise"), exists as an ethical force. Moving to the heart of his importance as a literary figure, Ondaatje's story evokes the carnivalesque aspect of Kiyooka's work: the unsettling memory of class struggle and mirth that haunt literature's serious intentions. Kiyooka's "letters" remain a playful or "laughing truth" that lives on as a reminder of the limitations of bourgeois culture. Distilling Kiyooka's language to his use of these three terms—"demarcation," "phenomenal," and "amazing"—Ondaatje isolates Kiyooka's uncanny ability to draw together the political (demarcation), the material (phenomenal), and the spiritual (amazing). Ondaatje's choice of words is entirely apropos the critical issues Kiyooka's work raises for contemporary readers. Recognizing the importance of Kiyooka's idiosyncrasies, the "utterly perverse" range of discourses they feed on, Ondaatje suggests the importance of the specific, often contradictory, historical engagements underlying Kiyooka's texts. Kiyooka's "laughing truth" reverberates with a deep knowledge of nineteenth- and twentieth-century cultural traditions, "high" and "low," as well as a complex engagement with the travesties of justice they bear witness to, particularly postwar. Encapsulating Kiyooka's importance to present cultural and critical contexts, Ondaatje echoes recent essays by Roy Miki and Scott Toguri McFarlane: two important readers of Kiyooka's writing.

Seeing Kiyooka's work in terms of "being stoned," or an ontology of astonishment, McFarlane locates the excessive nature of Kiyooka's language or voice in a complex matrix of historical and material relations that explicitly shift the parameters of the twentieth-century avant-garde poetics with which Kiyooka works. Situating Kiyooka's writing in relation to globalization and the problems of thinking through a political economy of post-humanist aesthetics, McFarlane writes that "anyone who has heard Kiyooka read knows a 'g' is not merely a letter but also a syllable, or perhaps what he would call a syllibant.' The 'g' is a gritty 'guh' that scratches its marks on the *global* return of the 'round.' The exhalation of Kiyooka's poetics are thus more gritty and more grinding than Olson's trochee's heave. Kiyooka's breath is marked by the gravely trace of being stoned." Linking this pun to the materiality of Kiyooka's language itself, McFarlane argues that Kiyooka's work "attempts to preserve a trembling 'inglish,' a broken syntax and slant vernacular that escalates the haunting force of being stoned" (144). The gritty particularities of his writing, Kiyooka's "trembling 'inglish' . . . broken syntax and slant vernacular"—evident in *Transcanada Letters* as much as in *StoneDGloves*—speak to us of an absent or exilic presence, a "being stoned," that ridicules the rational juridical subject of transnational global culture. As Miki argues, Kiyooka's writing performs "insider disruptions of a 'nation' whose 'self' had been identified through (a) its ethnocentric origins in British and French colonial histories, and (b) through the externalization of the 'others' in its midst" ("Unravelling" 71). To put it another way, we might say that Kiyooka's text draws readers into the *trans* or zone in which the lines of demarcation separating insider and outsider continue to be crossed and re-crossed. *Transcanada Letters* might then be seen as a material manifestation of an important historical struggle with or resistance to the normalization of cultural production: a troubling remainder that is vital to current discussions of dominant ideologies and the institutionalized divisions of labour they promote.

While *Transcanada Letters*, its chronological structure and geographic focus, suggests a kind of epic narrative, reading it as such risks asserting a coherent social order over it and reifying one view of Canadian geography or history. It risks normalizing the fragmentary, contradictory nature of the subjectivity it performs. Throughout *Transcanada Letters*, Kiyooka inhabits a plurality of positions that shift in response to the situations and individuals invoked in the "letters." Kiyooka the father, lover, brother, child, friend is also Kiyooka the poet, painter, or photographer. Imposing a cohesive narrative on the text, epic or nationalist, would essentialize Kiyooka's subject position by presenting the poet-narrator as a unified figure. *Transcanada Letters* resists this kind of reading by positing a complicated web of identity relations that draws attention to the specificity of Kiyooka's own variable experiences with the nation and its identity formations. Like that other wanderer, the green-eyed Odysseus, Kiyooka longs for home. However, in this case, "home" is triangulated across a system of spatial and temporal differences in which Vancouver, the Coast, the prairies appear and disappear on the horizons of Canadian history relative to the poet's drive to find a place to live and work.

Chronicling Kiyooka's movements through various Canadian cities—Montreal, Halifax, Calgary, Vancouver—and his travels to Japan, *Transcanada Letters* provides unique glimpses of post-war Canadian culture as it is developing. Marked by the traces of censored letters, expropriated lands, and forced displacements, *Transcanada Letters* performs a re-appropriation of the artist's own writing and so becomes a counter-archive, recording—not quite completely, not quite historically—the formation of a racialized national subject. In contrast to the idealized discourses of an emergent multiculturalism, *Transcanada Letters* presents cultural difference in terms of unsettled debts or proprietary relationships that keep the present open to the (unfulfilled) promises of the past.

For Kiyooka, cultural memory is a matter of form and substance. The everyday elements of his life, detailed in the "letters," provide a critical aspect of what drives his work. In his verse essay "Notes Toward a Book of Photoglyphs," Kiyooka returns to the theme of "the mundane" at the heart of *Transcanada Letters*. He writes:

> odd to have come to that time in one's life
> when all the things one puts their hands and mind to
> goes on and on within the parameters of one's
> daily dalliances and in that ambient attention turns
> indelibly into grist. the mundane, grounds us. (79)

Here, the slippage between the individual and communal draws out a central aspect of his work, particularly *Transcanada Letters*. For Kiyooka, the mundane provides a matrix the shared practice of making meaning—writing and reading. It "grounds us."

Mirroring the so-called westward expansion of the nation—from fragmentation to integration—the textual structure of *Transcanada Letters* re-cycles a dominant trope of Canadian history. Kiyooka's allusion to the backbone of contemporary nationalism, the Trans Canada Highway, brings readers into a journey that reaches from "coast to coast": "Halifax, Nova Scotia" to "Qualicum Beach B.C." However, the lackadaisical quality of this quest, the often intensely specific concerns to which the "letters" speak, resists the grand themes of arrival or self-realization upon which nationalism feeds. Finding a coherent path across the ten years accounted for in the "letters"—or for that matter, the four years of its composition "Sept 1 1971" to "April 15 1975"—is challenged by the specificities of Kiyooka's journeys and returns, as well as by the particularities of his various interpersonal relationships spanning Canada spatially and temporally. The model of correspondence upon which Kiyooka structures the text ultimately defies a linear historical logic. Describing a state of constant movement or social being in *trans*it, the text confounds a stable, unified sense of the here (and now). The second-person address in each letter imagines at least two places at the same time. In so doing, the text places readers in the liminal space of a mutual being. Ultimately, the conspiratorial tone of the "letters" becomes central to the text's critique of a discourse of nationalist development.

While depicting Kiyooka's relative alienation from people and places dear to him, *Transcanada Letters* does so from various positions within a network of friendships or correspondents. Contrary to the colonial model, which hinges on the reification of a singular metropolis from which the writer/explorer set out across space and time, Kiyooka's writing moves in relation to the movements of family and friends and a shifting set of needs or desires. Focusing on the interrelationships between individuals and communities, Kiyooka's text proposes an entirely different view of identity formation than that formulated in the thematic criticism of his well-known contemporaries Margaret Atwood and Northrop Frye. Countering the contention that Canadian culture is preoccupied with an unforgiving geography, *Transcanada Letters* critiques the Eurocentric notion that Canada begins as an obstacle blocking westward passage to the wealth of the Orient. For Kiyooka, coming as he does from west to east, travelling as a Nisei, carrying with him the memory of his parents and grandparents, Frye's "alien continent" is the imaginary construct of a dominant (white) culture. The hegemonic powers of European colonialism and Canadian nationalism are the alienating forces with which Kiyooka grapples. For this reason, *Transcanada Letters* proposes an entirely different sense of national history or its social traditions—a corresponding change in the way "we" reads.

Discussing the 25-year "retrospective" of his work at the Vancouver Art Gallery, for which *Transcanada Letters* is to be "the catalogue's twin," Kiyooka makes an important statement about the future of his work. While "*The Show* . . . will inevitably be 'retrospective'," Kiyooka says, "I want more than anything for it to be *prospective* (forward-looking." And, from his place on "the back of the lot at 1408 westminster highway richmond, b.c.," he writes, "I have the sense that the next DECADE will be crucial to whatever I become . " One might be tempted to argue that Kiyooka's timing was off by a decade or so; however, it is important to remember that the decade in question marks his transition into writing and photography, and thereby into new areas of critical and cultural interest, including those stemming from his travels to Japan. Furthermore, for Kiyooka, *becoming* did not so much have to do with public recognition or maintaining an elite position in the art world. The ephemeral, small run publications that he moved to at the end of his life seem to suggest that "whatever I become" was an issue that would depend on the circle of friends and students around him—on those for whom his work would continue to matter. Thus, this republication of *Transcanada Letters* takes place amongst a growing number of posthumous publications devoted to Kiyooka and his work: a special cd publication in *Collapse*'s "The Verbal and the Visual" (1996), *Mothertalk: Life Stories of Mary Kiyoshi Kiyooka* (Ed. Daphne Marlatt, NeWest 1997), *Pacific Windows: Collected Poems* (Ed. Roy Miki, Talonbooks 1997), *All Amazed For Roy Kiyooka* (Eds. John O'Brian, Naomi Sawada, and Scott Watson, Arsenal Pulp/Belkin Gallery/Collapse 2002), and a special issue of *dANDelion* (2003). With (that I know of) the companion volume of letters, *Pacific Rim Letters* (edited by Smaro Kamboureli for NeWest), and the forthcoming collection of critical essays (edited by Joanne Saul for

Guernica)—this recent flurry of publications testifies to the growing appreciation of the importance of Kiyooka's writing across a range of locations and communities.

Now the unravellings have begun.

Glen Lowry, Vancouver 2003

References throughout this afterword are from the following: Roy Kiyooka's "We Asian North Americanos" (*West Coast Line*. 24.3, Winter 1990) and "Notes Toward a Book of Photoglyphs" (*Capilano Review* 2.2, Spring 1990). Roy Miki's *Broken Entries: Race Writing and Subjectivity* (Mercury, 1996). Miki's "Unravelling Roy Kiyooka: A Re-assessment Amidst Shifting Boundaries," Henry Tsang's "Art Calling Fool Scold: The Discursive Pedagogy of Roy Kiyooka," a transcription of Michael Ondaatje's statement for the 1999 conference, and Scott Toguri McFarlane's "Un-ravelling *StoneDGloves* and the Haunt of the Hibakusha," all of which are included in *All Amazed For Roy Kiyooka* (Eds. John O'Brian, Naomi Sawada, and Scott Watson: Vancouver, Arsenal Pulp/Belkin Gallery/Collapse, 2002).

Glen Lowry lives and works in Vancouver, BC where he edits *West Coast Line*—a literary and cultural journal out of SFU.

ACKNOWLEDGEMENTS

This edition of *Transcanada Letters* is identical to the original publication that Talonbooks published in 1975. Only a few obvious typos have been corrected, and an Afterword, by Glen Lowry, added. I would like to thank the Estate of Roy Kiyooka for permission to reproduce *Transcanada Letters*. It was while I was editing its companion volume, *Pacific Rim Letters*, left unfinished at the time of Kiyooka's death, that Roy Miki and I thought it would be important, in fact necessary, to make *Transcanada Letters*, long out of print, available again. I would like to thank Diana Rutherford and Marika Strobl for their assistance with scanning the original book. Scanning is not always faithful to the original; proofreading at the final stage was a cumbersome and laborious process, and I take responsibility for any errors that I may have missed. I would also like to thank Glen Lowy who helped me track the photographs included in the original edition. Roy Miki and Phyllis Webb have been "there" – as always – offering me much welcomed support.

The founder and Editor of NeWest's 'The Writer as Critic' series, Smaro Kamboureli taught Canadian literature at the University of Victoria for many years. She joined the School of English and Theatre Studies at the University of Guelph as University Research Chair in 2004. Her most recent book is *Scandalous Bodies: Diasporic Literature in English Canada* (2000).